DAILY LIFE THROUGH

TRADE

DAILY LIFE THROUGH

TRADE
Buying and Selling in World History

JAMES M. ANDERSON

The Greenwood Press Daily Life Through History Series

 GREENWOOD

AN IMPRINT OF ABC-CLIO, LLC
Santa Barbara, California • Denver, Colorado • Oxford, England

Library of Congress Cataloging-in-Publication Data

Anderson, James.
 Daily life through trade : buying and selling in world history / James M. Anderson.
   p. cm. — (The Greenwood Press daily life through history series)
   Includes bibliographical references and index.
   ISBN 978–0–313–36324–5 (hardback) — ISBN 978–0–313–36325–2 (ebook) 1. Commerce—History. 2. Commerce—Social aspects. I. Title.
HF352.A533   2013
381.09—dc23   2012044705

ISBN: 978–0–313–36324–5
EISBN: 978–0–313–36325–2

17 16 15 14 13   1 2 3 4 5

This book is also available on the World Wide Web as an eBook.
Visit www.abc-clio.com for details.

Greenwood
An Imprint of ABC-CLIO, LLC

ABC-CLIO, LLC
130 Cremona Drive, P.O. Box 1911
Santa Barbara, California 93116-1911

This book is printed on acid-free paper ∞

Manufactured in the United States of America

I gratefully and affectionately dedicate this book to Sherry

CONTENTS

PREFACE

Trade is one of the distinctive characteristics that set humans apart from the animal world. This facet of behavior, and its effect on the lives and interaction of people is the focus of this book. Each period of technological and social advancement from the Old Stone Age to modern times brought forth new products and new trade routes.

The quest for trade has engendered exploration, exploitation, scientific achievements (especially in navigation), and the spread of cultures and religious doctrines. At the same time, commercial rivalries have begotten destructive wars, colonial empires, mass slavery, piracy, plunder, and even genocide.

The role of Muslims, Jews, Christians, Hindus and others in the formation of trade diasporas, and their often bellicose attitudes toward one another, as well as peaceful coexistence and co-operation in the pursuit of commerce, are part of the story. Mastery of the great oceans made long-distance global trade possible, linking the once remote regions of the earth.

This story embraces the major influences that shaped commerce, the problems that beset it and the countless benefits it bestowed on humanity. Trade developed according to people's needs and was often based on their geography. For instance, those living in high country needed wheat, barley, and warm garments to wear. In return, they could trade timber, stone, gold, silver, and copper to the lowlanders.

Exchange and possession of objects with only social value such as trinkets, pendants, bracelets, and beads are also in evidence from the remote past. A desire for jewelry and cosmetics appears to be as old as the earliest humans. Like many animals, for instance the peacock, decoration is a form of sexual attraction. How important were such items as a polished stone necklace? Or ochre to paint stripes on the face? Or a headband of bright feathers for prestige and power? If not in the local environment, such items could be obtained through barter further afield. Beads, that are not only pleasing, but are easily transportable, appear to have had a role in every culture from the Stone Age down to the present day, consistently appearing in grave sites. They come in many different shapes, sizes, and materials and because of their durability and beauty, beads have always had an important role in trade the world over.

A community's view of the world is shaped by language, culture, and environment and different languages and social development are prone to cause misunderstanding when cultures come face to face. Fragmented by social and religious strife, Europe imposed its will piecemeal on other regions of the world during the period of early modern history. From 1415 onward, European traders, soldiers, sailors, priests, and colonists set out in the thousands across the oceans to establish new trade routes, bring Christianity to so-called heathens, and conquer or construct cities and towns in remote and often hostile territory. Few of these endeavors were to remain free from the antagonism of the local populations whose lands and resources the Europeans coveted. Frequently ignorant and arrogant, and carrying with them their own prejudices and traditions, many Europeans treated with contempt the rituals and customs of native people, provoking hatred and retaliation rather than mutual cultural enrichment. In not a few cases, entire cultures disappeared forever as a consequence of ethnocentric and Christocentric Europeanization. The Chinese and Japanese, too, were disdainful and felt superior to foreigners, and their trade with the "barbarian" West was sometimes erratic and confrontational.

Trust, that is, one party having confidence that the other will fulfill its obligations, is a large component of trade that has always been a deciding factor in close-knit communities such as the Jews and Armenians, although trading partners might be separated by great distances. Failure to make good on a debt could ruin traders and their families, who would be ostracized by the business world.[1] The same principle applied to all traders, whatever their background, but problems arose when one group distrusted the other, often for political and religious reasons, that sometimes inhibited and even ceased commercial activity. Merchants often cooperated with one another in a peaceful atmosphere, however, as was the case with centuries of harmonious trade across the Indian Ocean where Jews, Muslims, and Hindus found mutual benefit in collaboration.

Today, trade is usually carried out with money changing hands for goods and services. Such was not always the case. It was once exclusively a matter of barter: a beautiful robe for a few ounces of spice, a chicken for a pound of wheat. Some items took the place and role of money and were used as such, for example, Roman soldiers were once paid in salt (their salary). Cowrie shells (and sometimes other shells) were used in Africa, China, India, the Pacific islands, among American Indians, and by Australian aborigines. They had value as body ornaments. The shell was known as *porcella* in Latin, that is, "little pig," and Chinese pottery that arrived in Europe was often so much like the shell it was called "porcelain." The classical Chinese character for money originated in the shape of a cowrie shell. About 1850, Heinrich Barth a German explorer in Africa, frequently found cowry shells in the region of Timbuktu. One of the kings in the area was worth 30 million shells collected from his subjects for various taxes.

The ancient Mayans, Aztecs, and others of Mesoamerica used cocoa beans for currency in commercial transactions. Beans were of different sizes and quality, hence also of different values. How many beans were paid for an egg or a simple cloak depended on the condition of the beans that were also used to pay fines, for services (such as a porter), or for a woman or a slave.

The first known coins appear to have been minted in Lydia (Asia Minor) from gold and silver in 687 BCE. They were soon copied by the Greeks, who gave up their use of iron nails as money. Coins among the Romans were minted in gold, silver, bronze, and brass. Paper money made an appearance in China in the ninth century CE and became, along with coins, a form of state currency. Europe learned of the use of paper money from Marco Polo. With the expansion of the Muslim world in the Middle Ages, the silver *dirham* became a common coin of exchange and has been found even well beyond Muslim lands, for example, in Scandinavia and Russia. The gold coin or *dinar* was also circulated throughout Muslim lands and beyond, and was much in demand.

This book of 21 chapters is designed to present the reader with geographically designated trade regions arranged in chronological order. It relies heavily on the work of others whose contributions to an understanding of the history of trade and its effects are documented in endnotes and a bibliography.

NOTE

1. See Francois.

ACKNOWLEDGMENTS

I would like to acknowledge the following colleagues, friends, and family—all of whom had input into the process of producing this book in various, invaluable ways: Corri Anderson, Dr. Siwan Anderson, Anja Brandenberger, Adrienne Burton, Richard and M. J. Dalon, David Dunn, Dr. Patrick Francois, Dr. and Mrs. Stanley Goldstein, Howard and Winsome Greaves, Dr. and Mrs. Risto Härma, Barbara Hodgins, Dr. Diana Hodson, Jill and Paul Killinger, Dr. and Mrs. Jean Larroque, Cameron McEwen, Dr. Bernard Mohan, John and Lucrezia Paxson, Drs. Carol and Joel Prager, Drs. Bernard and Anne Rochet, and Dr. Bob Ware. Special thanks go to Denver Compton and Bridget Austiguy-Preschel of ABC-CLIO and to Suba Ramya Nambiaruran and Sarah Wales-McGrath.

1

EARLY TRADE BEFORE
1000 BCE

In 1982, a Bronze Age ship was discovered off the coast of southeast Turkey lying in about 50 meters of water near the town of Kans. This ship was estimated to date back to sometime in the fourteenth century BCE. It seems to have been en route to the Aegean Islands from the Levant or Cyprus. Carrying a vast amount of cargo, it had been driven onto the rocky shoreline, perhaps by a storm. Little of the wooden vessel had survived the ravages of the sea, but it appears to have been about 20 meters long and carried a single mast and square sail. Its cargo bears witness to the international nature of commerce at this early date for found aboard, or spilled from it, were large amounts of basic materials such as 10 tons of copper ingots and a ton of tin for producing bronze. These were probably for trade and were accompanied by what appeared to be gifts such as many jars of Canaanite origin that were once filled with various items such as glass beads, olives, and resin destined for royalty or for other persons of high rank. Colored glass ingots stowed in the ship were perhaps of Egyptian provenance, as was some jewelry made of both gold and silver. In addition, there were ebony logs, ivory from both elephants and hippopotamus teeth, Cypriote lamps, seashell rings (maybe from the Red Sea), amber beads (possibly from the Baltic coasts), and Canaanite jewelry. A gold scarab engraved with the name of the Egyptian Queen Nefertiti, who lived in the fourteenth century, was found, along with some foodstuffs such as pine nuts, almonds, and spices as well as a host of other articles. Since some measuring devices, such as weights and measures, were found, it is assumed that accompanying the crew were merchants travelling with their cargo. As well, the tiny mandible of a stowaway house mouse yielded the earliest evidence of the dispersal of rodents by sea. It is unknown if anyone made it to shore.[1]

Civilization began long before the ill-fated ship plied the waters off Asia Minor. Not far away, in the southeastern corner of present-day Turkey, near the border with Syria at a place called Göbekli Tepe, the so-far first glimmer of a sophisticated society has been uncovered under the accumulations of some 11,600 years of sand and debris. The Neolithic hilltop site of colossal limestone pillars, arranged in circular patterns with depictions of wild animals set out in bas-relief, seemingly a place of worship, was abandoned about 1,000 years later and covered over. The many people engaged in the construction of Göbekli Tepe had to be supplied with food, and the bones of gazelles and aurochs found at the site suggest workers ate wild game brought from some distance. Nearby, at Nevali Çori, some of the earliest signs of agriculture have been found. Ancient sites in eastern Asia Minor and in the Fertile Crescent, dating back to between 11,000 and 8,000 years ago underwent the changes from hunter-gatherer societies to the Neolithic or farming communities at different periods.

From very early times through to the present day, ideas, commodities, languages, religions, cultures, and social values were dispersed through the means of trade that also provided employment for many. Wars were generated as empires were created and destroyed.

Ancient Mesopotamia, the Levant, and Egypt form part of the Fertile Crescent where civilization prospered. Nourished by the alluvial soils of the rivers Tigris and Euphrates in Mesopotamia, and the Nile in Egypt, agriculture flourished, and cultivation of plants for food allowed people to settle and accumulate surpluses that accorded some of them time to engage in tasks other than farming, such as artisanal activities, construction of buildings, religious practices, and the development of trade networks both locally and far-reaching for items they could not produce themselves.

SUMER (AROUND 2900–2330 BCE)

In the southern part of Mesopotamia, the Sumerians, a farming people, formed one of the world's earliest societies. They arrived

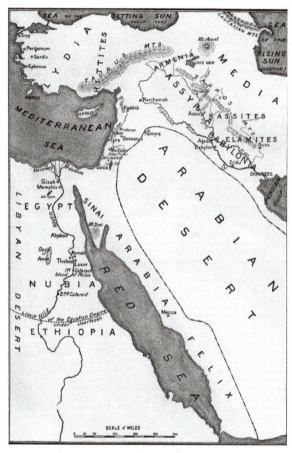

Map of the ancient Near East, birthplace of civilization. (North Wind Picture Archives.)

there in the fourth millennium, replacing little known older farming communities—Ubaidians—who had domesticated both plants and animals. The Sumerians promoted technical innovations and trade, and became the dominant people of the region by establishing a number of city-states including the cities of Ur, Uruk, Kish, and Lagash.

Prompted by the need to keep commercial records, the Sumerians invented a writing system called cuneiform from the wedge-shaped indentations on clay tablets.[2] Writing began in Sumer about 3000, and scribes became essential members of society by recording business contracts and transactions, and keeping systematic lists of important data about the economy. The Sumerians are also credited with inventing the wheel, the plow, and sail-propelled boats.

City-State of Ur

After Ur, at the head of the Persian Gulf, became the capital in about 2100, considerable trading took place whereby the Sumerians exported textiles and oils to Makkan a city or state of unknown location but recorded in the Sumerian texts, receiving in exchange copper, ivory, and beads. They also carried out trade with India.

Within the city-state, a temple to the gods was located in a holy enclosure along with the royal palace. Outside this precinct, the ordinary houses, constructed of mud-dried bricks, lined the narrow dirt streets. Some would be two stories with kitchen, servants' quarters, and a storage room below, and a living room and sleeping chambers above. A house like this would belong to someone wealthy, such as a merchant,[3] and entertainment came in the form of festivals and music, and perhaps opium since the poppy was cultivated in Sumer and was referred to as the "joy plant." It was probably a trade item as the use of opium spread to Egypt and throughout the eastern Mediterranean.[4] Ancient Greek ceramic pots from Mycenae containing traces of opium have been uncovered in the Near East in tombs and settlements dating back to about 1400. Turned upside down, the pots themselves resemble the poppy pods, and enough of them, similar in shape and about 12 centimeters long, have been unearthed to suggest a thriving Middle Eastern trade in drugs during the Bronze Age. They appear to have been used for medicinal purposes; Egyptian writings from the third millennium BCE suggest that both opium and hashish were used to relieve pain, as well as employed during surgery. Hashish was also offered to women during childbirth and to ease menstrual pain. How lucrative this extensive trade in drugs was, is unknown.

That trade was an ongoing business in the remote past is evident from Ur, where many imported items were found in gravesites, especially the rich foreign objects in sixteen royal tombs that contained lapis lazuli from Afghanistan; gold from Egypt, Persia, Western Anatolia, and India; along with red limestone and shells from elsewhere. Ur engaged in trade with regions many hundreds of kilometers away and became a major trade center by 2500. Most likely, the majority of commerce was carried out by the sea that linked the Persian Gulf with the Indus Valley River. By the eighteenth century, Ur was on its way to becoming an uninhabited ghost town in part, it would seem, due to the loss of trade routes with the Indus Valley (now in Pakistan).

The last of the Sumerian civilization occurred under the third dynasty of Ur when Semitic peoples, the Amorites and Akkadians, invaded the region.

Long distance sea trade between Mesopotamia and India no doubt skirted the coastlines. Merchant seamen became middlemen and profited from the shipments of commodities between these regions. Inhabitants of Magan, a city and transit point en route, probably located in present-day Oman, also served as middlemen and as a source for copper. Other commercial stations were developed along the way such as Dilmun, which seems to have been situated on what is currently the island of Bahrain. Archaeological excavations there have uncovered burials of very wealthy citizens. Around 1800, the trade that enriched Dilmun decreased along with a decline in Mesopotamian markets and troubles in the Indus Valley. Also about this time, an alternate trade route developed along the Red Sea through the Gulf of Aden and across the Arabian Sea that in effect connected the Mediterranean with India.

Surviving contractual documents from Ur indicate that commerce was generally in the hands of private individuals who may or may not have traveled with their goods. Loans for a voyage were possible, and several merchants might cooperate to finance a shipment. The government had a hand in the food trade, and perhaps textiles— some to Bahrain in exchange for copper that was lacking in Mesopotamia. The government taxed all trade.[5] Mesopotamian men of commerce also reached northern Syria and the Mediterranean in search of business, and other routes went on to Anatolia (Asia Minor, now Turkey), the Iranian plateau, and the Caucasus.

One of the earliest trade items, nonexistent in Mesopotamia, found at volcanic sites, was obsidian, a glass-like material easily chipped to make cutting edges for weapons or tools. Quantities of this vulcanized glass whose origin was some 600 kilometers distant in Anatolia have been found in the upper Tigris region. Other non-local items, for instance, shells from the Indian Ocean 1,500 kilometers away, were found in Syria, dating to the fifth millennium BCE. From Iranian sources came alabaster, carnelian, marble, mother-of-pearl, and chlorite.[6]

ASSYRIA

Documentary evidence from Kultepe (ancient Kanesh) in Anatolia affirms the presence of Semitic Assyrian merchants who appeared in Mesopotamia about 2000 and were well known as traders who plied the route between Ashur, a city on the Tigris, with their donkey caravans, trading cloth and tin—the latter acquired from the Iranian plateau but lacking in Anatolia—for gold, silver, and copper. The Assyrian settlement at Kultepe, long before the Assyrian Empire, was perhaps the first trade diaspora. As long ago as the eighteenth century, the Assyrian merchants formed a kind of guild to protect their interests in Anatolia that made loans to merchants, arranged transport, held merchandise and money on account, and from Kanesh, the headquarters, operated a trade network to many other cities in the region. The various princely authorities in a fragmented Asia Minor collected taxes and protection money from the traders but realized the danger in excess, as the merchants could simply depart if profits were not up to expectations.

An ancient Sumerian and Amorite city, Mari is considered to have been inhabited from around 2900 to 1759. Archaeological finds there include some 13,000 cuneiform tablets as well as remains of a 4,000-year-old palace situated on some six acres and containing about 300 rooms with walls standing in places up to 16 feet. It included kitchens, baths, and pantries, and murals on some walls. As a center of administration, it also had warehouses where traders could store their goods as well as army barracks and all the paraphernalia that was needed by a contingent of troops permanently stationed there. Court was held on a daily basis and included, besides local affairs, matters of trade and dealing with foreign rulers. When relations were good with other heads of state, the court was mostly concerned with trade and merchants, who were important members of society.

At feasts, the court menu was mainly vegetarian. Vegetables and fruits included cucumbers, peas, beans, truffles (a great delicacy), dates, grapes, and figs. Breads were normally unleavened, and beer and wine were drunk—often copiously—the former made locally, the latter imported.

Some of the officials at court were eunuchs, but if this were not the case, then they would undergo an arranged marriage and continue living with their parents until they could afford to live in their own house. If an official were to find an attractive woman among captives, he could take her home to be a slave for his wife, as well as a concubine for himself. For entertainment, slave girls provided music, and stories and fables were related by poets or minstrels.

Besides merchants, occupations included boatbuilding and repair, carpentry, tool-making, leather-working, and weaving.

Artisans cut gemstones, painted jewelry, and made perfume; payment for their work was sometimes in the form of oil for cooking and lamps.

OLD BABYLONIAN EMPIRE

Begun as a city-state, Babylon was able to reap the benefits of its location on the Euphrates River and soon swallowed up the old cities of Sumeria. Its rising power reduced Assyria to a vassal state, and prosperous Assyrian trade with Anatolia ceased as Assyrian goods were now being sent south and traded at Babylon.

Temples seem to have owned much of the land and exercised control over a great part of the economy, including commerce. The agents of the temples traveled extensively in this capacity, including to Syria to purchase olive oil that was taken by pack mules to the Euphrates River and then sent downstream to Babylon. From Asia Minor also came alum and metal ores. Cedar was obtained in Lebanon. These goods were paid for with wool or barley. The rich and powerful temples owned or hired ships to bring the cargo down the rivers. All transactions were recorded on clay tablets.

Free men were occupied in a variety of professions, including making mats, weaving, stonemasonry, goldsmithing, fishing, boating, making shoes, carpentry, and shearing sheep. Houses seem to have been three or four stories with flat mud roofs and ceramic drains fixed in the walls. There was only one outer door that led on to the street; inside rooms and an inner courtyard were for privacy.

Meat, fish, and poultry formed an important part of the diet of the wealthy, whereas the poor ate vegetables and fruit such as onions, garlic, peas, beans, salad, figs, pomegranates, apricots, and grapes. Unleavened bread and porridge were made from barley. Dates provided sweetening. Beer, water, and wine were available. And slaves poured water on the hands of diners, who used napkins to clean their mouths and hands. Although farming was the mainstay of the economy, Babylonians engaged in extensive trade; poor farmers were in no position to support the monarchy in the style it aspired to, nor could they pay for the wars that were always just around the corner. The nobles and kings were well aware that trade was the way to wealth and good living, hence merchants were often subsidized to increase the flow of goods.

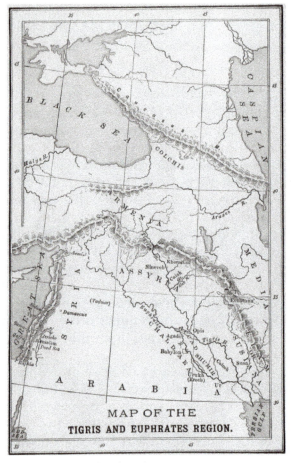

Map of the ancient Tigris and Euphrates region.
(North Wind Picture Archives.)

Governments could also bring money into state coffers by taxing
the traders. To encourage trade and increase their own profits, officials often tried to make the roads safe from bandits, keep them in
good condition for quicker delivery, and supply soldiers to guard
them. It was beneficial for men of commerce and the government
if one empire commanded the trade routes, but wars arose over
which empire that should be. The rule of Hammurabi (1792–
1750), who came to control most of the land between the Tigris
and Euphrates Rivers, employing the cuneiform writing from
Sumer, set out a code of 282 laws for the society. The laws included
aspects of trade concerning duties and obligations. A merchant's
money, for example, entrusted to an agent, had to be replaced if

the agent suffered a loss through being robbed. The merchant also had to give a receipt for money given to him by the agent. There were, in addition, certain financial penalties if one party attempted to cheat the other.

PRECIOUS AND BASE METALS

Gold, easily malleable and noncorrosive, was a perfect substance for decoration. Trade in gold dates back at least to the end of the Neolithic period. The nearly 5,000-year-old cemetery at Varna (Bulgaria)[7] near the shores of the Black Sea, for example, has yielded over 3,000 gold artifacts since its discovery in 1972. Gold decorations existed alongside stone implements in many areas of Sumeria and ancient Egypt. Goldsmiths on Minoan Crete produced the finest filigree work; hence traders from all parts of the Mediterranean were attracted to the island. Coins and pins to dagger handles, belt hooks to bowls, as well as every sort of ornament—all could be made of gold.

In the fourth millennium, from Cappadocia in Eastern Anatolia, appeared the first silver in large enough amounts to supply silversmiths throughout much of the eastern Mediterranean. In the second millennium, silver mines in Armenia supplied silversmiths in the Aegean, Minoan, and Mycenaean spheres. As a trade product, silver was much in demand.

The discovery of copper ore appears to have been sometime after 6000. Smelting the ore to produce pure copper seems to have transpired a little later, but its appearance and use occurred at different times in different places: copper smelting, according to some experts, may have begun at Çatal Hüyük on the Konya Plain in southeastern Anatolia, once an important trade center for timber, flint, obsidian, shells (imported from as far away as the Red Sea), trinkets, textiles, and a host of other items that included copper beads. The cemetery at Varna contained copper tools in some graves. Copper metallurgy had spread to India by 3500 and to Europe and China by about 3000. Copper tubing in ancient Egypt has been found in tombs and temples. The Sumerians obtained it from Armenia around Lake Van, and imported it from the Red Sea hills and later from Cyprus. Copper became highly valued, and the seafaring Phoenicians living along the Levant began searching for it around the Mediterranean and finding vast quantities on the Iberian Peninsula about 1200. Ancient Greeks employed copper to protect the bows of their ships when they engaged in ramming enemy vessels, and many ships' hulls were later coated with the metal to protect the wooden hulls from barnacles. It was learned that adding a little tin to copper while heating it caused it to become harder and more durable. The result was bronze. The Bronze Age began about 3500 in Sumeria and spread between 3000 and 1800. Weapons and farming implements were soon cast in the harder metal.

From about 3000 BCE, an increase in sea trade in the eastern Mediterranean is evident from archaeological finds. Various factors influenced trade and trade routes in the early days of sail, and increasing knowledge of weather and winds dictated the times and routes of commerce. Progress in the construction of ships built for the open sea and increasing navigational knowledge all added to longer and safer journeys.

The first people to extract iron ore then smelt and shape it are unknown. Ore is found in many places; some attribute the earliest iron working for tools, decorations, and weapons to the Hittites of Anatolia, others to ancient Egyptians, some to the regions of the Caucasus, all during the second millennium. Like copper and bronze, the Iron Age began in different regions at different times depending on the period when the technology for its production first reached a given community.

POTTERY AND GLASS

Utensils such as bowls, jugs, and cups, fashioned from hardened clay, had been around for centuries; and by around 2500, more elaborately shaped and decorated pottery became an item of extensive trade. The distinctive, bell-shaped Beaker pottery, for example, was polished or burnished and traded throughout Europe in the Bronze Age.

Glass was first found only in nature in the vicinity of volcanoes, where it was created in tremendous heat. An early form of glass manufacture, *faience*, was made up of ground-up quartz mixed with other ingredients such as calcium, sodium, or potassium. Shaped into beads, rings, or bracelets and heated, it resulted in a hard glazed surface of various colors according to the mixture. The product was a trade item as far back as the Bronze Age. Glass similar to what we know today made by combining silica (ground quartz, flint, or sand with potash for strength) was first produced about 3000 in northern Syria and Iraq.

A caravan approaching Sidon, a seaport of ancient Phoenicia. (North Wind Picture Archives.)

Near the final decades of the second millennium, numerous kingdoms arose, including the Phoenician trading cities of Byblos, Sidon, and Tyre along the Mediterranean coasts of the Levant. The Phoenicians of the Levant also became experts in glassmaking using the rich coastal deposits of silica-based sand mixed with lime. Phoenician glass was exported throughout the ancient Mediterranean world. Such items were at first expensive and traded as luxury objects until glass blowing spread and became common.

CRETE AND THE MINOAN AGE (AROUND 2000–1450 BCE)

Sometime in the Neolithic period, the Minoans settled on the island of Crete and took up grain production and raising sheep. By the third millennium, settlements had grown into small towns and trade was evident from artifacts from other islands. Elephant tusks and stone bowls from Egypt were found at the Cretan palace at Knossos. Incised Ware pottery from the central Aegean and marble figurines imported from the Cyclades islands were also encountered by archaeologist. Ivory and Egyptian scarabs appeared in tombs dating from the end of the third millennium. By the beginning of the second millennium, imported pottery from the coast of western Anatolia was common. Cretan pottery has also been identified throughout the eastern Mediterranean from about this time.[8]

Beginning about 2000 BCE, Crete evolved from an island of small villages into a group of centralized states whose kings constructed magnificent palaces—the most famous being Knossos—in a style reminiscent of the Middle East, where they had long been in existence. About 1900, potters' wheels were introduced and Cretans became excellent craftsmen, with their pottery in great demand.

EASTERN MEDITERRANEAN

After the rise of the palace states, imports and exports of trade goods rose considerably along with a writing system for recordkeeping, now called Linear A, impressed on clay tablets. Minoans began to sail the Mediterranean Sea before 2000, making contact and trading with Asia Minor, Greece, the Levant, Syria, Mesopotamia, and Egypt as well as with the settlements around the Aegean Sea. They were in regular contact with Egyptians, as certain plants on Crete were important ingredients needed for the mummification process.[9] Written documents indicate a high standard of living and a good deal of commerce. Crete was well positioned for maritime commercial ventures between Africa and Europe, and especially between Egypt and Greece.

Greeks and the Mycenaean Age

Before 2000, an Indo-European people, sometimes called Achaeans, settled in Greece and absorbed the indigenous inhabitants.[10] They ruled from fortified strongholds such as Mycenae and Pylos. By about 1600, the Mycenaeans had developed a civilization, in part borrowed from the Minoans with whom they traded. The Mycenaeans too became seafarers, both pirates and traders, and planted colonies in the Eastern Mediterranean in areas such as the coasts of Anatolia. The capital city, Mycenae, was situated in a strategic position on a well-used trade route across the northeast of the Peloponnese. Other fortified sites with palaces and tholos throughout Greece were the residences of kings.

Mycenaeans conquered Crete shortly after 1450 and devised a local script, Linear B (a form of ancient Greek) to keep records that show that grain and wine were used as payment of wages, and taxes were collected in kind.[11] Mycenaean Greeks took over the old Minoan trade routes and expanded their own by establishing colonies outside Greece: the two earliest were Rhodes and Cyprus. Greeks became the primary long distance traders in the region and reached the apex of the Mycenaean Age between 1300 and 1200.

A commercial rival for eastern Mediterranean trade, the City of Troy, stood in a favorable position on the Hellespont, able to monitor traffic, both land and sea, between Europe and Asia. The Mycenaeans destroyed Troy after a long epic siege for its audacity in having abducted Helen, Queen of Sparta, or so relates Homer in *The Illiad*. It is not known exactly when Troy was destroyed (sometime in the late second millennium) or how much, if any, of the war was based on trade competition with Helen, perhaps, as the pretext.

Mycenaean civilization fell to another wave of Greek invaders, the Dorians from the north, about 1200. The Dorians also drove the Ionian Greeks on the mainland to settle along the western coasts of Asia Minor. Greece was well populated about 1300 but by 1100, the numbers had dwindled considerably.[12] (There is some doubt as to the role of the Dorians in the destruction of Mycenaean Greek cities.) Wide-ranging commerce stagnated for centuries under the Dorians while warring groups dominated Greece, and a dark age beginning about 1200 overtook the eastern Mediterranean with the invasions of the so-called Sea Peoples. Roads fell into disrepair, writing disappeared, pottery degenerated into coarse ware, grand stone buildings ceased to be built, kings and bureaucracies faded away, villages were abandoned, and trade and even contact with foreign nations declined dramatically.

Egypt

The climate of North Africa was once very different than it is today. A lush, green environment supported abundant animal life, some of which is found today only in the tropics. Desiccation of the region began about 6,000 or 7,000 years ago, resulting in the vast Sahara Desert. Small villages developed along the Nile River about this time whose inhabitants engaged in farming. The river people who occupied the upper and lower Nile were consolidated around 3000 under Menes, the first pharaoh. The predictable behavior of the river in the rise and fall of the water level that annually covered the land with fertile silt was harnessed with irrigation canals and sluice gates. Agricultural advancements led to surpluses in food products. With resources in excess, the government turned its attention to exploitation of minerals in the surrounding countryside, trade with neighboring states, and maintenance of a large army. Under the ensuing royal dynasties, commercial activity seems to have been under government control. Besides Egyptian traders, foreigners came to the region to trade for needed items. The people of Lebanon, for example—interested in Egyptian-made objects such as cosmetics, painted vases, jewelry made from ivory, lapis lazuli, and gold, or *faience*—would bring their famous cedar wood to Egypt to exchange.

Around 2500, government trading expeditions were sent to the south up the Nile or down the Red Sea, reaching Yemen and Ethiopia to trade homemade products for gold, ebony, and frankincense. Commerce could flourish or stagnate for decades, depending on the whims of the royal court.[13]

Some 640 kilometers south of Cairo, among scattered villages along the Nile River, a small trading post began under the Old Kingdom around 2700. By the time of the New Kingdom (1550), this trading post had grown into the rich city of Thebes, famous for the wealth of its palaces, temples, and shrines. During the time of Hatshetsup, Queen of Egypt (1508–1458), a fleet of five ships was assembled at the Red Sea port of Elam on the gulf of Aquaba for purposes of trade with the land of Punt to the south. Punt's exact location has not been identified, but it was probably somewhere on the African coast of the Red Sea.[14] Trade from the south to Thebes included frankincense, juniper oil, myrrh (sometimes in the form of trees to be transplanted in Egypt), and natron that was not only a necessary ingredient in the mummification process, but was used also for cleaning the home and the body as a kind of soap, as well as a preservative for meat. Everyone, including merchants, was controlled by the pharaoh, who was considered to be a god and who made all important decisions. Thebes declined as a center of trade as the lower Nile took on more importance.[15]

Egypt itself had in its Nubian mines the preeminent source of gold for the oriental world, and the letters of the eastern kings to the Pharaohs are often requests for gifts of the precious metal for which they sent in return lapis lazuli, enamel, horses and chariots, slaves, costly furniture, and works of art.

Hittites

An Indo-European people, the Hittites began to move to the Anatolian Peninsula from the northeast in about 2000. They established a capital at Hattusa and soon began to expand their territory. In the sixteenth century, they moved south to seize trade routes in Syria and the Levant, contested by Egypt and the Mitanni, the latter a kingdom in upper Mesopotamia whose influence extended from the coasts of Syria to the Zagros Mountains. The Mitanni fell prey to the Hittites, who in the fifteenth century took Aleppo. Not only were lucrative trade routes falling into Hittite hands through control of trade between Greece, Egypt, and the Levant, but natural resources were also at stake. Egyptian interest in Syria and the Levant was threatened.[16] The Hittites had a certain advantage in the use of iron and an abundance of iron ore for the production of better weapons. Commerce flourished throughout the Hittite Empire protected by the authorities and army whereby traveling merchants, for a fee, were safe on the roads. The medium of exchange was silver measured by weight; and the unit of weight was the *shekel* (60 *shekels* made up one *mina*). These Babylonian names indicate Hittite and Babylonian trade connections. According to the law code discovered at Hattusa, the price of a fine garment might be 30 shekels, while one of sheepskin might be one *shekel*.[17]

Battle of Empires

Egypt's expansion northeastward along the Levant while the Hittite Empire of Anatolia spread southward led to a clash of interests. The result was a great chariot battle at Kadesh (Qadesh) around 1275. Rameses II of Egypt engaged the Hittites. The stakes were the Levant, and especially Syria, where trade with India was a source of wealth. The result was a costly stalemate that brought on a peace treaty, perhaps the first, in 1258.[18] The fall of the Hittite Empire about 1193 was sudden and has been attributed to the appearance of the Sea Peoples.

When the Hittite Empire fell, trade declined, and in the ensuing chaos migrating peoples from the northeast overran the empire that split up into small kingdoms.

WESTERN EUROPE

Rudimentary farming, animal husbandry, and the construction of crude shelters—activities that had begun in the East several millennia earlier—reached grotto and cave dwellers of Europe during the Neolithic period. Settlements acquired the making of pottery and the use of metal. While there is no direct evidence of European and Near East trade at this early time, there are significant cultural similarities that imply contact. At Los Millares in southern Spain (dated to about 2340) and at Vila Nova de São Pedro in Portugal (about the same time or a little earlier), close affinities with the Aegean region can be seen in the construction of walls, decorative styles, pottery types, and chambered tombs.

Metal industries in Europe were common by the end of the third millennium.[19] Long-distance trade in metal after 2000 is evident between merchants in Syria and the peoples of south-central Europe who mined copper ore and received, according to grave finds, axes and daggers, and metal pins for garments.[20] The second millennium was the formative period of early Europe and saw the migrations of Indo-Europeans into the area north of the Alps (Celts, Germans, and Slavs) and trade with the more advanced cities of the Near East.[21] Early trade appears to have taken the form of raw material from the West and finished products from the East. Major European trade routes at the time followed more or less defined paths: a route from central Asia ended in Hungary, another linked Transylvania to Denmark, at the head of the Adriatic ships unloaded cargo that was transported to Bavaria and the Rhineland. Britain and Brittany were within reach of Mediterranean seaports such as Narbonne on the south coast of France, from where goods could be taken overland to the Loire for river transport.[22] Archaeological artifacts found in rich European graves—including gold, amber, and imported beads—presuppose trade routes crisscrossing Europe. Contact with the Mycenaean world is evident as early as the sixteenth century BCE in European grave goods with objects of similar if not identical design of Aegean craftsmen.[23] Trade routes also occurred through the Alpine passes between Celtic tribes and Greek and Etruscan cities as demonstrated by archaeological finds. The 5,300-year-old ice-covered mummified body, the so-called Iceman, discovered in the Alps in 1991, may have been that of a trader moving between Italy and Austria. An arrow shot by someone in the vicinity killed him; if he was a trader with goods, these were no doubt stolen.

CENTRAL ASIA

Early records show items consisting of precious stones like lapis lazuli, rubies, and jade, crossing Central Asia before 1000. Lapis lazuli was mined in the third millennium in what is now Afghanistan, and sent to Egypt and Mesopotamia. Jade was known to come from only a few locations in the ancient world but was greatly valued. It, too, has a long history of being traded, dating back to about 4000 BCE. Green jade from Central Asia has been found in China, Egypt, Mesopotamia, and Europe, indicating ample long-distance trade in the semi-precious stone.

THE INDUS VALLEY

Not unlike the Tigris, Euphrates, the Nile, and the Yellow River in China, the Indus River that drains the western Himalayan Mountains and flows into the Arabian Sea near Karachi was also a cradle of a civilization. The Indus Valley Civilization, dating to the fourth millennium, was the first major urban culture of South Asia and reached its peak between 2600 to 1900 BCE. Sophisticated craftsmanship and extensive trade networks developed.[24] Many settlements are known, the largest being Harappa and Mohenjo-Daro.

The region was a network of farming and trade settlements surrounded by mud brick walls. Luxury goods such as seashells, lapis lazuli, and turquoise were imported from as far away as Persia.

Harappa, on the Chenab River, a tributary of the Indus, was one of the larger cities of the Indus Valley civilization and existed for about 500 years (2750–2250). Priest-kings ruled over the cities, and local standards appear to have been uniform in the size of the building bricks and standard set of weights and measures. Wheat and barley were the staple diet of the people, who also cultivated peas, dates, and melons. Cattle supplied milk, meat, and fertilizer and were also used as work animals. There is evidence of sheep, buffalo, and elephants along with pigs and dogs.

The short texts in pictographic signs remain undeciphered. Town planning with ordered network streets is still apparent in the ruins. The lower town in most places contained dwellings and workshops, while in a raised part, a walled citadel housed public buildings, religious structures, and warehouses.

The Indus cities and towns produced high quality pottery, fine jewelry, metal and flint tools, and other objects. These commodities were distributed far and wide throughout the Indus region in exchange for food from farmers, fishermen and pastoralists. Rivers were used as major highways. Indus traders traveled as far as Mesopotamia exporting timber, ivory, gold, and jewelry.

Mohenjo-Daro was located at the crossroads of the Indus Valley Civilization with the river providing the highway from the highlands to the northeast and the sea to the southwest. The city was a center of trade and manufacture with workshops of bead-makers, potters, metal-smiths, dyers, and shell-workers.[25] Other cities also show similar high quality workshops. A substantial commerce linked the city with the Persian Gulf.

Merchants' houses ranged from many rooms around spacious courtyards to single room tenements. Items exchanged with Mesopotamia were gold, precious stones, ivory and spices for oil, figs, cloth, pottery, and beads.[26]

The remains of houses in the lower town, built around courtyards, show a high standard of living with stairs to upper floors, brick floored bathrooms with drains connected to the city's drainage network. Many had toilets and private wells while public wells supplied the less affluent. Mohenjo-Daro and Harappa declined about 1900 for unknown reasons. One view attributes the decline of the culture to destructive invading Indo-Europeans from the north. Another view attributes it to disease that rampaged through the region. The city's decline is evident by squalid housing and the random disposal of bodies in abandoned buildings. The bodies show signs of serous disease.

Trade meant contact with other people, and from the very beginning of the first cities where inhabitants massed in close-knit numbers, contagious diseases were always a problem, and traders could spread them from city to city. A particularly virulent microbe might decimate entire villages or cities.

There is some evidence of the catastrophic spread of killer diseases in the remote past. Besides disease in the Indus valley, Egyptian pharaohs were not immune; it seems that Ramses IV died of smallpox in 1156. This virus apparently dates back to the very inception of village life and those who were stricken with it had a good chance of dying from it. The pack animals of traders could also carry deadly pathogens from place to place, and ships harbored diseased, seafaring rats and fleas that might wander ashore at any convenient port. Sometimes wheat or vegetables carried infectious microbes that could also strike down a community.[27]

In the Indus Valley international trade ceased, towns with their well-structured brick-built sanitation systems and even the writing system, disappeared. Some communities continued to exist and even prosper, but on a much smaller scale.[28]

The world's earliest dockyards, built in the port city of Lothal in Gujarat around 2400, may be the oldest known. The dockyards connected to an ancient course of the Sabarmati River on the trade route between Harappan cities in Sindh and the Peninsula of Saurashtra when the surrounding Kutch desert was a part of the Arabian Sea. The city gave high priority to the construction of the dockyard and a warehouse to serve the purposes of sea trade.

The site of an Indus trading colony situated on the Amu Darya River about 1000 kilometers north of Harappa may have facilitated overland trade to Persia and Afghanistan. Land transport was carried out by wagons pulled by oxen according to figurines from the area, while other goods went by river and sea. After the destruction of the Indus Valley civilization new settlements arose further east along the Ganges River beginning about 1000.

THE FAR EAST

As in other parts of the world, the first inhabitants of the Far East were hunter-gatherer clans. The remains of occupants of a cave in the limestone hill of Zhoukoudian near Beijing have been identified as modern humans (Homo Sapiens) of about 30,000 years ago,[29] not unlike the inhabitants of caves in southwestern France and northern Spain of about the same time. Also like other early civilizations, settlements and agriculture developed along a major river; here, it began with mud, wood, or bamboo dwellings along the Yellow River in the seventh millennium BCE. Villages grew into towns and cities sustained by the river that irrigated their fields of crops. Throughout its turbulent history, all-powerful emperors, both domestic and foreign, ruled China.

Of the shadowy first dynasty, the Xia (about 2000–1520), there is scant evidence, but for the second, the Bronze Age Shang (around 1520–1050) and their capital at Anyang in the province of Henan, there are significant archeological remains. By then, society had become rigidly hierarchical, and while there is little evidence of the common people, excavations of rich tombs and artifacts display great wealth for the highborn such as two-wheeled chariots that have been found in some graves along with jade imported from Central Asia. The basics of later Chinese culture were laid down during the Shang dynasty.[30] Cities were walled with cemeteries situated outside. Both humans and animals were sacrificed when the kings and queens died. The vast majority of the people were farmers who, in northern regions of the country, grew wheat and millet and in the south, rice.

As a food and trade item, rice has a long history. It grew wild long before cultivation. Chinese documents mention it as far back as 2800. It soon spread throughout Asia.[31] Some scholars believe cultivation of rice began first in India. The various peoples of China were subjects of landowners to whom they supplied agricultural products and labor. In wartime, when tribes from the north and west raided and pillaged Chinese villages, these subjects served as soldiers. Ancestor worship appears to have begun about this time; it was believed that ancestors were of utmost importance since their celestial presence allowed them to influence the gods for the benefit of the family.[32]

Pictographic writing displayed on oracle bones and used in divination between about 1400 and 1200 was the forerunner of the current Chinese writing system. Information on commerce at the time is nearly nonexistent.

On the islands of Japan, the early people, surrounded by sea, relied perhaps more on fishing and seafood from the shores and less on agriculture than many other early communities.[33] Semi-sedentary, the Jomon, related to people in Korea and Manchuria, lived generally in pit houses arranged around a central open area. Similarities between pottery produced in Kyushu and Korea suggest that trade relations existed between the Japanese islands and the Korean peninsula. The Jomon were replaced by the Yayoi from Southeast Asia, probably via Korea, who brought metal implements and coins of Chinese and Korean origin.[34]

NOTES

1. http://archaeology.about.com/od/qt
2. Hansen, 82–122.
3. *Past Worlds*, 126.
4. Opium Timeline, opioids.com/timeline.
5. *Past Worlds*, 126–27.
6. Curtin, 64–68; Bernstein, 26.
7. For the aforementioned findings at Varna, see Aston and Taylor, 33.
8. Around 1450, Crete suffered a devastating earthquake and perhaps a tsunami that destroyed Minoan cities, but various reasons for the collapse have been given.
9. http://www.phoenician.org/minoans_phoenicians_ppe r.htm.
10. Polomé, 64, for the view that Mycenaean Greeks may have replaced the Pelasgians; see also Lockwood, 12.

11. Chadwick (1958), 14.

12. Trump, 191.

13. Curtin, 73.

14. Herrmann, 51 ff.

15. Wallbank et al., 21–23.

16. For details see Gurney, 31–37.

17. Gurney, 84–86 for these and other prices.

18. Ceram, 186 for the view that the Hittites were victorious.

19. Piggott, 76–78.

20. See Piggott, 102, for details.

21. Piggott, 107.

22. Piggott, 120.

23. Piggott, 134–138.

24. *Past Worlds*, 130.

25. Aston and Taylor, 54.

26. Bahn, 338.

27. For more detail see, Diamond, 205–214.

28. Bahn, 194.

29. *Past Worlds*, 60.

30. *Past Worlds* 146–47 for more detail.

31. Some scholars believe cultivation of rice began first in India.

32. For a detailed survey of Chinese religions, see, Larousse, 271ff.

33. The Jomon period (about 10,000–300) constitutes Japan's Neolithic period. The name derives from the characteristic pottery made during this long period of time. Varley, 2.

34. Perez, 9–10; http://www.metmuseum.org/toah/hd_jomo.htm.

2

THE FIRST MILLENNIUM BCE: THE EAST

By about the year 1000 BCE, some of the old trade empires, cities, and routes in the East had disappeared. In the first millennium, commerce was more widespread across the world, new trade depots and empires arose, and trade routes altered, while shipping by sea became more common.

NEW ASSYRIAN EMPIRE (934–612 BCE)

From an earlier kingdom, the Semitic Assyrian Empire arose in the tenth century and faded away in the early seventh century. Assyrian domination from the eastern Mediterranean to the Persian Gulf encompassed the trade routes of Mesopotamia, the Levant, and westward to Egypt. Assyrians traded base metal, especially tin and lead, along with textiles and surplus grain, for precious metals and building stone. They developed the most powerful empire in history up to that time, controlling vast amounts of commerce. Each year, the ruler Ashurnasirpal II (883–859) led his army on expeditions to maintain his power over the great trade routes of the Near East. By a rule of terror, taxes, and tribute from subjugated peoples, the Assyrian elite became wealthy and a capital city was built at Nimrud a little north of Ashur.

Under Sargon II (721–705), a network of roads and rest posts were constructed to facilitate royal couriers and traders. Upon

Sargon II's death, his son established the capital city at Ninevah. Local feuds, civil war, and constant battles with neighboring states eventually sapped Assyrian strength and an alliance of Medes and Persians on the Iranian plateau, along with Scythians and Babylonians, finished off the Assyrian Empire, conquering Ashur and then Ninevah in 612.[1]

MEDIAN EMPIRE (728–550 bce)

Sometime during or before their migrations from the Indo-European homeland, Iranians broke up into tribal groupings linked by common ancestry and consisting of Medes, Persians, Parthians, and Sogdians in the east, and Tajiks in the northeast (Tajikistan), and Bactrians (Afghanistan) The Medes unified Iran in 625 and took charge of the east-west trade route, reaping a vast income trading valuable metals and other products, some of which were produced locally, others that included gemstones, dye, and cloth brought from lands in the east. The beneficiaries of the wealth were, as usual, nobility who could capitalize on the flow of trade. Median society was made up of several levels: priests, military, artisans, merchants, and an agricultural class. With the capital established at Ecbatana, the Medes ruled over an area from Afghanistan to Asia Minor.

NEW BABYLONIAN EMPIRE (612–539 bce)

From the time of the old and prosperous empire, Babylon was beset by invaders and conquerors intent on its riches. Hittites, Assyrians, Kasites and others had controlled the region for nearly 1,000 years until independence was achieved in 625 under the imperially ambitious leader Nabopolassar, who established the New Babylonian Empire and sought relations with the Medes and Persians.

Centrally located in Mesopotamia, Babylon was a thriving trade center. The Euphrates River provided the nourishment for agriculture as well as for herds of cattle and sheep. Bountiful fruit, vegetables, and meat allowed surpluses to be traded for raw materials such as gold, copper, and wood from which jewelry, weapons, and other objects were made and again traded.[2] The wealth of New Babylon derived from controlling the east-west and north-south trade. This wealth attracted merchants from Anatolia, Egypt, and Europe and from the east, Persia and India. Control over the port cities of the Levant only increased its wealth. The strongest state in

the old world after the fall of Assyria, Babylon succumbed to the
Persian armies of Cyrus the Great in 539.

PERSIAN (ACHAEMENID) EMPIRE (558–330 BCE)

After Cyrus deposed the Median king Astyages, he became king
of Persia and founded the first Persian Empire. He extended his
rule west to Lydia after defeating Croesus, the wealthy Lydian
king—the first to use coin in trade. After securing control of Asia
Minor, and seizing Babylon, Cyrus released the Jews from captivity. He built his capital at Pasargadae in Fars province. Mortally
wounded in battle, Cyrus' son and successor, Cambyses, conquered Egypt in 525. The Achaemenid prince Darius came to the
throne next, and peace prevailed throughout the empire. At its
height, about 500, Persians had conquered the Near East from
the Mediterranean to the Indus River, along with Egypt and
Libya. Tariffs on trade were one of the empire's main sources of
revenue.

For traders across the Persian Empire, travel was facilitated by
the Royal Road from Sardis in Lydia to Susa and on to Persepolis
in southern Iran, a distance of about 2,500 kilometers, and a three-
month journey. Along the route were over 100 stages, or rest stops,
guard posts to pass, and rivers to navigate. Merchandise and royal
messengers in relays traveled this route, as did Alexander the Great
later in the conquest of Persia. During the Achaemenid period,
Darius I (522–486) instituted several trade reforms: he invented a
system of weights and measures, and encouraged the use of the
new Lydian custom—coinage—for trading. The Persians not only
traded across their empire, but also along sea routes in the Persian
Gulf. They introduced several new trade routes to India focused
on Fars province in the south of Iran. They traded linen, wool, cotton, perfumes, brocades, carpets, exotic jewels, incense, silk, frankincense, myrrh, gold, and much more. Excavated palaces of
the Achaemenid Empire show Susa as the administrative center
and Persepolis as an important residence of the kings. The empire
included Egyptians, Turks, Armenians, Medes, Parthians,
Caspians, Babylonians, and Assyrians among other ethnic groups.
Tribute trade is well demonstrated in writing on clay tablets and
extant friezes on palace walls such as those of the main audience
hall of Darius I in the palace at Persepolis, where the ceremonial
stairway shows carved reliefs depicting delegations bearing
presents to the king. Some of the gifts included lions from Elam,

Arabian camels, gold from India, and horses from Scythia. Other gifts were clothing, metal vessels, ivory, and various exotic animals such as antelope and okapi.[3]

GREECE AND THE BLACK SEA TRADE

By the seventh century, the growing population of Greece and the diminishing fertile land forced the populace to seek other sources of grain supplies beyond their watery frontiers. The rich soil around the Black Sea, especially along the north shore, was a treasure trove for the Greeks, and colonies were established there and in the fertile valleys of the Dnieper and Bug Rivers. Here, bountiful timberlands supplied lumber for shipbuilding. Pottery, wine, oil, and textiles were offered by the home cities in exchange with the Black Sea colonies. The Greek city-states fought for control of the narrow waterways leading from the Mediterranean into the Black Sea. In response to this crucial situation, Athens developed a strong navy to protect the trade route through the Dardanelles and the Bosphorus. The navy then patrolled the Black Sea during the months when trade was feasible and protected the cargo carriers. Athens also benefited from the importation of Black Sea cattle, wool, and fish.

GREEK CLASSICAL AGE (AROUND 510–323 bce)

A time of decline and anarchy in Greece ended with the emergence of the classical Greek civilization throughout the western end of the Mediterranean. For the Greek states, in particular Athens, seaborne commerce became the most important factor to maintain their economy. The Greek states began founding colonies first in the Aegean, then gradually all over the Mediterranean basin. It remains unknown in a divided Greece exactly what each city-state traded and what were their commercial ports although in Athens, along with its primary port of Piraeus, such products as grain, timber, iron, copper, salted fish, hides, slaves, wines, drugs, paints, dyes, papyrus, and linen passed through its warehouses.

The centers of the classical Greek period were the city-states that acted autonomously, ruling over the surrounding region. With a population of around 300,000 by the fifth century, Athens became the leading city. It was the first semi-democracy where men of the city voted for city officials; women and slaves were excluded. Militant Sparta, on the other hand, Athens's primary rival, instituted laws that totally mobilized society, forcing male children as young as six to live in military barracks and train for the day that they would join the army. Spartan men were obliged to serve in the military between the ages of 20 and 60.

THE PELOPONNESIAN WAR (431–404 BCE)

The Greek city-states were not immune to forming alliances and fighting among themselves as in the Peloponnesian War. There were various reasons for the war such as the growing power of Athens and the ambitions of the Spartans, but pursuit of commerce played the major role. Tension between Sparta and Athens was at an all time high in 431. The Spartans invaded Athenian land and burned the fields of crops, yet Athens felt secure with its great walls extending to the port town of Piraeus by which supplies from the sea trade could be brought into the city. For the Peloponnesian League led by Sparta and its allies against Athens, this war was essentially over who would dominate trade, especially in grain. Athens had maritime supremacy and controlled seaborne trade; Sparta, an agricultural economy, was more powerful militarily. There were several phases of the war spread throughout Greece and even the colonies, but the initial spark was set off by Sparta to deprive Athens of its hegemony on commerce. Athens' navy was in a position to sever the supply of Egyptian, Libyan, and Sicilian grain to Sparta's allied cities in the Peloponnese. Corinth, particularly concerned, urged its powerful neighbor, Sparta, to initiate hostilities. In the end, Athens lost not only the war, but also its navy, and was reduced to subjection under the Spartans. Greece would never be the same. Its golden age in art, philosophy, and science that flourished even during the war was over.

ALEXANDER THE GREAT (336–323 BCE)

By the end of the fifth century, Macedon, to the north of Greece, emerged as a military power under Philip II, who seized control of all of Greece. With Philip's assassination in 336, his son, Alexander, secured the throne and began a series of further conquests. Asia Minor was wrested from Persian hegemony in 331, followed by Syria, the Levant, Egypt, and then Persia as far as India. Alexander founded numerous new towns, including Alexandria Eschate in 329 in the Fergana Valley (Tajikistan) that would become a point of departure for the northern Silk Route. The Macedonian Greek conquests and consolidation of territories not only Hellenized the way of life, but gave fresh impetus to old trade routes, opened new ones, built ports and harbors, and brought new people into an expanding trade diaspora. Several of the new cities contain his name, the most famous being Alexandria at the mouth of the Nile.

MAURYAN EMPIRE (322–185 BCE)

India became a nearly consolidated country around 324. Included within its confines at the time were present-day Bangladesh, Afghanistan, and Pakistan. The unified state, except in the far south, was under the Mauryan Empire. The ruler, Maurya Chandragupta and later Ashoka the Great, extended the empire by military conquest. To facilitate merchants and the movement of merchandise across the northern section of the country, the Mauryans constructed the Grand Trunk Road from Patna in Bihar (eastern India), to Taxila near Islamabad (now in Pakistan). For many centuries, the Grand Trunk Road served as the primary route across northern India from the mouth of the Ganges River to Peshawar in the northwest (now in Pakistan), connecting many cities along the way. It traversed the Khyber Pass into the interior of Afghanistan and the city of Kabul. Beyond the Hindu Kush lay the Silk Road to China. India's fabled wealth in pearls, gemstones, minerals, metals, and spices brought invaders and traders from the east and west to the Road.

Land-bound merchants who needed to access India had to come over the northwest mountain passes from inner Asia. The high and nearly impassible Himalayas impeded passage from the north, and the thick jungles of the east inhibited trade routes to Burma and China. The road to Central Asia was far from safe; not only did raiders sometimes lie in wait to ambush if the caravan looked vulnerable, but wolves lurked about waiting to attack pack animals. Local village residents on the north Indian plain were often hired to both help guard the caravans and to guide them to shelters for the night. The road was marked with stones that also marked distances to the next village.

SELEUCID (312–150) AND PARTHIAN EMPIRES (240 BCE–224 CE)

Upon the death of Alexander in 323, his empire disintegrated as his generals fought to stake out their territories. Seleucus Nicatore emerged victorious in the eastern half and over the next half-century the Seleucids expanded their control from the eastern Mediterranean to India and from the Caspian to the Arabian Sea. They established their capital city at Seleucia on the Tigris River a little south of Baghdad, about the year 300 BCE, that grew into a great trading city. With a canal connecting to the Euphrates River, it prospered from the traffic on both rivers.

Another capital was founded at Antioch on the Mediterranean about the same time. The Seleucid dynasty was in a favorable position to greatly benefit from the east-west trade along the Silk Route and merchandise heading west to the Roman Republic and other Mediterranean ports. The Seleucids also created many new towns as trading settlements. The Roman army thwarted further expansion into Greece, a country the Romans subjugated in 133.

The Seleucids minted coins that were used as exchange along the Silk Route and the Levant. Neighboring kingdoms were also interested in the east-west trade, including Armenia, Greece, the kingdom of Parthia to the northwest, and Egypt. To prevent serious encroachment on their valuable trade, the Seleucids made whatever treaties or arrangements they could. Weakened by wars and rebellions, the Seleucid Empire was taken over by the Parthians, also known as Scythians, almost in its entirety. After this conquest, Parthia controlled the richest trade routes and confronted the Roman Republic in the west. Their capital at Ctesiphon was across the Tigris River from Seleucia. The wealth of the Parthians was greatly enhanced through the silk trade.

Archaeological remains at Seleucia show three clear levels of occupation: the lowest, Seleucid, 307 to 141 BCE; the next level was an autonomous city of Hellenistic culture but under Parthian rule 141 BCE to 43 CE; and closest to the surface of the desert sands, Parthian occupation from 43 CE to 116.

Like their Seleucid predecessors, Parthians controlled the western approaches to the Hindu Kush passes that led to the East and the Khyber Pass, a major trade route, connecting India to the East and West. Chinese merchants' goods travelled the long distance as far as Parthia, where they were taken over by local merchants whose government allowed no foreign goods to pass the frontier unless transported across the empire by their own people. Such arrangements raised the price of merchandise and did not please Rome. Numerous indecisive wars were fought over control of Mesopotamia and the trade routes. Weakened Parthia, the major obstacle to direct Roman trade with China, finally succumbed to an uprising in Fars province led by Ardashir, a rebellious subject who defeated the Parthians in 224 CE and established the Sasanid Empire, a new deterrent and obsession for Rome and its eastern trade that outlasted the Western Roman Empire.

PTOLEMAIC DYNASTY (EGYPT) (323–30 BCE) AND ALEXANDRIA

Ptolemy I, one of Alexander's generals, ruled Egypt from the capital of newly created Alexandria at the mouth of the Nile. Trade flowed steadily through the city as the Ptolemys, who styled themselves as the last pharaohs, encouraged commerce.

Alexandria, became the most important of the Mediterranean commercial cities, reshaping the trade patterns of the eastern Mediterranean. Here, with a population of around a million, merchants dealt in essential wheat, glass luxury products, jewelry, linen made from flax, papyrus, and other items. Its eminent library and museum made the city a focus of learning, and their destruction was one of the great tragedies of history. Many and sundry nationalities mingled on the bustling streets of Alexandria, and trade was the primary occupation, causing the city to grow in size with an affluence not seen before. Alexandria remained the capital of Egypt for nearly a millennium.

Warehouses overflowed with textiles, cosmetics, perfumes, ointments, gems, spices, and incense brought down the Nile from Ethiopia; cedar oil from Lebanon; and local agricultural produce all destined for shipment. Textiles were also made from goat hair, wool, reeds, and palm fibers, and the city was a trading point for textiles and silk from the East.

Cargo vessels from Egypt, the granary of Rome, regularly crossed the Mediterranean to ensure the flow of vital grain to feed the Roman masses. Grain was of such importance that Rome made Egypt a province in 30 BCE, and shortly thereafter, the Emperor Augustus employed the Roman army to clean out silted irrigation ditches from the Nile River to the fields. Also destined for Rome on the approximately 20-day sea voyage from Alexandria to Ostia were African ivory, tortoise shells, palm oil, and slaves. Much of Alexandria's wealth came from the spice trade from which the city collected taxes and duties. Arab middlemen controlled commerce from India, Africa, and southern Arabia. Valuable trade items also included metals, for instance gold, silver, and copper, as well as minerals available from nearby desert mines. Raw materials were frequently traded and worked abroad.

INDIA AND ROME

Rome made its appearance in the East about 200 and by 64, Syria had become a Roman province. But Roman trade contacts extended beyond its frontiers. Trade with India increased due to the Roman penchant for Indian luxury goods that included wool, cotton, timber, ivory, spices, incense, glass, pearls, dyes, and slaves.

The Romans offered gold and silver, various types of food, and cloth. Land routes connected Rome with India, but the Roman traders with their able Greek seamen preferred sea lanes for a variety of reasons: overland routes were subject to fall under the control of rulers that were not friendly to Rome, and they would sometimes exact heavy taxes on traders who crossed their land. They often did little to protect the traders or maintain the roads. To bring large amounts of goods overland required many pack animals that needed constant attention. Even though traveling by sea could be treacherous, traders could carry more goods at a faster pace, and more cheaply, than they could overland.

JEWS

Ancient Hebrews, occupying the land of the Levant, were in a favorable geographical position to conduct commerce between Asia Minor, Syria, Egypt, and Arabia over land and by sea to Mediterranean ports. Exports to Egypt and elsewhere included spices, myrrh, honey, and almonds, wheat and oil in exchange for horses, chariots, and linen.[4]

Marched off to Babylon in 587 BCE by a Babylonian army, the Jewish people were held in captivity until 538, when they were allowed to return to Palestine, which was then under the Persian Empire until it was conquered by Alexander the Great in 332. By this time, the Jews were well dispersed. Because they no longer had a homeland under their own trade rules, as had been the case earlier in Palestine, Jewish trade became a matter of family affairs, or with colleagues scattered throughout Mesopotamia, the Levant, and the Mediterranean. Alexandria attracted many Jews, who settled there in large numbers. Some settled in India and entered the silk trade, much of it done through Jewish associates in other countries. Jews who remained in Palestine lived in rural areas and sold agricultural products such as oil, wine, figs, and dates along with barley and wheat. With the Roman conquest in 63, subsequent rebellions by the Jews ensued. Merciless killing and destruction by the Roman legions forced many remaining Jews who were not sold into slavery to join the ranks of those already in exile. Those who settled within the Roman Empire were increasingly persecuted as the Christian communities grew stronger and more antagonistic toward them.

NOTES

1. Caubet, 105ff.
2. *EWT*, 94.
3. For these gifts and others, see *Past Worlds*, 158–59.
4. *EWT*, 550.

3

THE FIRST MILLENNIUM
BCE: THE WEST

THE MEDITERRANEAN SEA

Stretching well over 3,000 kilometers from end to end, the Mediterranean has a surface current running counterclockwise along the coast of North Africa before it turns northward along the Levant.[1] Knowledge of this was invaluable to the ancient mariners who plied their trade under sail or by oars. The western Mediterranean includes the section from Italy to the Strait of Gibraltar, an area little known to the civilizations of the eastern part at the beginning of the first millennium. Throughout the following 10 centuries, the western reaches of the sea were explored and exploited by eastern states, and especially by Phoenicia and Greece seeking iron, copper, silver, and tin.

PHOENICIANS IN THE WEST

After the collapse of Cretan-Mycenaean power in the Aegean about 1200, Phoenicia, an aggregate of maritime trading cities on the coast of present-day Lebanon, assumed much of the Mediterranean trade. The Phoenicians were a Semitic seafaring people whose exports included glassware and purple dyed cloth, the latter a major export item made from a shellfish extract found along the coasts and in demand among royal houses. Other manufactured items included fine jewelry and wooden furniture from the cedar forests in the nearby hills.

In their quest for needed materials, the Phoenicians ranged the western Mediterranean and even beyond the Straits of Gibraltar. To maintain records of their trade, they developed a syllabic writing system of 22 consonants in which vowels were inferred. From the cumbrous cuneiform and hieroglyphic writing, this new system was a great benefit to commercial recordkeeping and was taken over by the Greeks, who added vowels from redundant consonant signs not needed in Greek. Such beginnings would eventually serve as the basis for alphabets the world over.

The Phoenician city of Tyre, a leader in trade but short on metals, was instrumental in exploration of the western Mediterranean, where these commodities were known to exist. Food supply was also a consideration that the Phoenicians hoped to enhance through western sources.[2] They developed settlements in the west at several places along the North African shore in the eighth century, the most important being Carthage (Tunisia). Others included Gadir (now Cádiz) on the Atlantic coast of Iberia (Spain), and trading posts and settlements on the Iberian Mediterranean coast where now stand the present cities of Málaga, Almuñécar, and Adra. From these and other sites, they exploited the natural wealth of the Iberian Peninsula, followed in the sixth century by Greeks from their colonies in southern France.[3]

FOUNDING OF CARTHAGE

Now a residential suburb of the city of Tunis, Carthage was built on an easily defensible peninsula of low hills and a safe anchorage. The entire settlement was oriented toward seaborne trade. Known for their massive commercial vessels capable of carrying large quantities of goods, Carthaginians traded not only purple dye, whose secrets of manufacture they retained from the home country of Phoenicia, but also salt from the Sahara, amber that had come over trade routes from the Baltic, and an immense number of items of African origin among which were skins, cinnamon, spices, ebony, ivory, and metals, as well as food products, ceramics, and glass. The rise of Carthage coincided with the fall of the cities in the Levant to Assyrian authority. By 586, Tyre and other Levantine cities were ruled by a foreign empire and Carthage, along with other commercial outposts of the Phoenician homeland, were on their own. Carthage assumed the mandate for western Mediterranean trade to become a prodigiously wealthy city.

Carthaginian merchants were found in every major port in the Mediterranean and beyond, buying and selling. They set up ware-houses where possible, or conducted their bargaining in open-air markets after disembarking their ships. The rapidly growing city maintained a strong grip on the entire coast, from present-day Libya to the Atlantic coast of Morocco, and engaged in trade with Greeks and Etruscans while developing a powerful fleet, the most formidable in the Mediterranean.

Tin was in short supply in the East and was treated as a precious commodity. Trade disputes between Carthaginians and the Greeks centered on Iberian precious ores such as silver, copper, lead, and gold with which the land of the Iberians was well endowed. From the African interior, the Carthaginians obtained valuable ivory and salt.[4] They also traded eastern spices, made glass in rainbow colors that was highly valued throughout the ancient world, and their high quality furniture was in great demand. Carthage was dependent on trade for its survival and became the center of commerce for the western Mediterranean region by the fifth century BCE. It controlled the Mediterranean southern littoral with colonies in Sardinia, Malta, the Balearic Islands, the western half of Sicily and the southern coasts of the Iberian Peninsula. The Iberian trading partners were significant sources of silver and, more importantly, tin. Carthaginian trade fleets sailed north, founding colonies along the Atlantic coast of Iberia, as did their Phoenician predecessors, and it is thought they even reached as far as Cornwall in the British Isles, seeking precious tin. Their ships reputedly explored the African coast as far as Senegal.[5] Carthaginian traders purchased Baltic amber and other gems to trade in Mediterranean ports along with wine, grain, fruits, nuts, and dried fish from the Atlantic.

Greek trading ventures in the western Mediterranean alarmed the Carthaginians, who considered the western seas their private sphere of influence. When Greek colonies began to appear on the Iberian Peninsula around 600, Carthage became more aggressive toward the Greeks. The Phocaean Greeks not only were a menace to Carthaginian trade, but also to Etruscan commerce from Corsica to Italy, and the two powers formed an alliance against the Greeks about 540.

ETRUSCANS

Around 800, the Etruscans (of unknown origin) established the first civilization known in Italy in the modern-day region of Tuscany. They also played a role in early trade.[6] During the seventh century, they developed a powerful state, establishing a number of towns as far south as present-day Rome and as far north as the Po River. As a trading nation, they held both the important trade routes of the Brenner Pass and the Adige Valley.[7] Through trade, both by land and by sea, they reached a high level of development. Significant items imported into Etruria from the east included bronze items in the form of horse bits, stands for cauldrons, helmets, and silver bowls—much of which began to be copied by the Etruscans themselves.[8] They soon produced ceramics, gold, bronze, iron objects such as hammers and saws, furniture, leather harnesses and shoes, and woven cloth.

The Etruscans traded with (and engaged in rivalry with) Greeks and Phoenicians exporting furs, wood, and slaves, and were well known for excellent work with tin (probably from England), and other metals as well as marble. Their bronze mirrors and candelabra were prized objects. Imports consisted of spices, jewelry, Greek vases, and first Phoenician and later Carthaginian goods, all of which have been found in large numbers in Etruscan graves. Archaeological excavations of Etruscan cities show that their civilization traded over several centuries with Carthage, long before the rise of Rome. The Etruscan city-states were, at times, both commercial partners of Carthage as well as military allies. Overland, the Etruscans sent manufactured items, especially bronzes, to Celtic people beyond the Alps.

The vast mineral resources exploited in Etruria brought yet more riches to its inhabitants as trade increased with their neighbors.[9] Wealthy families built magnificent mausolea, and foreign cultures began to change the tastes of the Etruscan people.[10] Many goods, especially vases from Attica, entered the country, and during the seventh century, luxury items were imported. Jewelry, carved ivory, shells from the Red Sea, and decorated ostrich eggs are among items that have been found in tombs.

By the sixth century, Greek influence on fashion is apparent, the men wearing beards, long hair, and togas over which was a short cloak. Women had long, short sleeved tunics covered by a cloak. Their hair was long in ringlets. Leather sandals with turned-up toes were worn by both men and women. Roman influence is apparent in the attire of the orator, who wore a toga along with high leather boots tied with fur thongs—one of the special pieces of clothing worn by a Roman senator.[11]

Many roads, constructed by the Etruscans, cut through solid, living rock, with drainage ditches at the sides. Packhorses, donkeys, and mules were used by merchants to traverse these highways, and chariots were employed to transport citizens. In this case, land transport may have been safer than sea shipments since Etruscan pirates often terrorized foreign merchant sailors in the Tyrrhenian Sea.

Colonization in southern Italy and Sicily, beginning in the eighth century, allowed Greek control of the trade routes through the Strait of Messina, bringing on conflict with the Etruscans and Carthaginians. Subsequently, the Etruscans fell prey to both the ambitions of the tribe of the Latini whose most influential settlement on the Tiber was Rome, and to Celtic incursions in the northern Po Valley. Rome expelled the last Etruscan kings about 500 and the Celtic invasions from the north, in the fifth century (even sacking Rome in 390), sounded the death knell for the Etruscan civilization.[12]

Southern Italy and Sicily

Due to their persistent need for grain, the Greeks sought trade in the Black Sea regions but, at the same time, they looked for markets in the West and established colonies. Until the mid-sixth century, trade in Greater Greece (*Magna Graecia*) that included southern Italy and parts of Sicily, was under the sway of Corinth, that exported Corinthian amphora containing olive oil in exchange for grain. Syracuse, a colony in Sicily, became a major trading partner. That city and others like it in both Italy and Sicily became politically independent and even minted their own coins. However, with a powerful navy, Athens was foremost in sea trade, exporting Athenian pottery to southern Italy and to Sicily, and it increasingly exerted its influence over trade to the western colonies. Syracuse dominated much of Sicily and rivaled any other in the Greek sphere of influence with major temples, majestic civic buildings, monuments, and a theater, one of the largest ever built in antiquity.

GREEK MARITIME TRADE

Wheat was obtained from Egypt, Italy, Sicily, and regions around the Black Sea. Other imported products included spices, fabrics, and metals. To find and trade for such items required ships and to build them, wood had to be imported as well, for the Greeks had depleted what forests they had.

Merchants who lacked sufficient funds could borrow money to finance expeditions from which they hoped to make a profit. Contracts were drawn up for a short term, such as the time period of a single voyage, and the terms of the interest to be paid to the lender. In the town markets, peasants and artisans generally sold their own products, although there were also retail merchants' guilds that sold fish, olive oil, bread, and vegetables. The process of minting silver coins appeared in Greece about 550. Bronze coins of lesser value appeared at the beginning of the fourth century. The state looked after the safety of the merchants in the harbors and the markets. No matter where a merchant was from, he was safe in both those places and in return, the state charged duties on imports and exports. This helped the Greek economy, while trade helped to improve the lives of the people.

FOUNDING OF MARSEILLES

The Phocaean Greeks founded Massalia (Marseilles) about 600, after the Persians destroyed Phocaea in Asia Minor. The city prospered as a port and trading center, doing business with the new trading posts they set up in the coastal towns of Agde, le Brusc, Antibes, Nice, and the Hyères Islands, as well as on the Rhône River at Arles and Avignon, and inland at Cavaillon and Glanon. In the following centuries, the Greeks administered Massalia as a republic. Major trade routes followed the Rhône and Saône Rivers into the heartland of Celtic Gaul (France). Marseilles became a major emporium for trade not only with Iberian communities on the Hispanic Peninsula, but also with Celts along the valley of the Rhône and beyond.

BATTLE OF ALALIA

Fierce trade competition between Greeks, Etruscans, and Carthaginians resulted in war about 535. At Alalia (today Aléria), a colony in Corsica established by Greeks from Massalia, a sea battle took place in which the Greek fleet, although victorious, was badly mauled by the combined forces of Carthaginians and Etruscans. They withdrew from Corsica, which soon passed into Etruscan hands while Carthage retained Sardinia. Carthage would fight two more major naval battles with Massalia, losing both, but still managing to close the Strait of Gibraltar to Greek shipping about 480, thus containing Greek expansion in the far western Mediterranean.

SICILIAN TRADE WARS

Rising success in commerce and a powerful navy brought Carthage into mounting conflict with the Greeks for control of the central and western Mediterranean; the island of Sicily, where both had colonies, became the focus of conflict. Three wars were fought over Sicily. The Greek cities of Syracuse and Agrigentum jointly challenged the Carthaginians in Sicily, setting the stage for the Sicilian Wars (480–307) between Carthage and the Greek forces that engaged in constant skirmishes, with each at times controlling most of the island.

IBERIAN PENINSULA

At the extreme western end of the Mediterranean the Iberians left extensive remains of settlements extending along the coasts and inland from eastern Andalucía well into southern France. They lived within walled towns in stone houses along narrow stone paved streets. The Iberians occupied towns in southwestern France from about 600 to 100, when they fell to the Romans. The Greek colony at ancient Agde at the mouth of the Herault River is thought to have been a direct trading partner with Iberian towns and villages.

The Turdetani, situated in southwestern Andalucía and southern Portugal (the Algarve and Alentejo), pertained to the kingdom of Tartessos where their undeciphered stone inscriptions have been found. In both cases, Iberians and Turdetani were of unknown provenance. About 900 BCE, Celtic peoples began moving onto the Iberian Peninsula, occupying regions north of the Turdetani and the Iberians. The Basque have dwelt in the northeast corner of the peninsula since time immemorial. The extent of trade between these diverse groups is unknown. The first substantial evidence of trade in this part of the world is that of long-distance seafaring commerce with the eastern Phoenicians and with the Greeks. The Phoenician colony at Gadir near Tartessos continued in use as a trading post for several centuries, leaving a variety of artifacts indicating its presence.[13]

Tartessian trade routes in tin, gold, and silver may have already been established when the southwestern Iberian Peninsula became a focal point of trade of eastern Mediterranean societies. Tin was particularly sought after, and Iberia had an abundance of it. In exchange for Iberian metals, Phoenicians supplied finished bronze

products, swords, knives, helmets, and luxury goods (rings, bracelets, and necklaces).

The Tartessian civilization disappeared sometime after the sixth
century, perhaps destroyed by Carthage in order to take over the
sources of trade. In the fifth and fourth centuries, the arrival of
Celtic peoples into southern Portugal began to fill the void left in
the wake of the Tartessian decline.

ULLASTRET AND EMPORION

Just across the Pyrenees Mountains from France, a little inland
but once closer to the coast, Greeks and Iberians established the
town of Ullastret on an old Paleolithic site. The inhabitants lived
behind thick stone walls, in stone houses on the top of a hill that
were well supplied with cisterns hallowed out of the bedrock to
collect rain water.[14]

The first permanent Iberian settlement here dates to the end of the
seventh century. Trade is evident from the appearance of Greek
ceramics of about 575, along with Etruscan amphora. During the
fourth century, numerous ceramics in the style of southeastern
Iberia indicate that the coastal Mediterranean Iberians carried on
internal trade along the 1,000 kilometers and more of their coastline
as well as with Carthaginian and Greek merchants.

As depicted on their painted pottery, Iberian women had a penchant for personal adornment in the form of ornate brooches, ear-
rings, and long-sleeved belted tunics. The men, warriors, are often
shown wearing short tunics and a kind of armor and helmets while
carrying javelins and round shields. How much of the jewelry and
weapons or armor was introduced by the Greeks is uncertain, but
Greek influence is clear in the writing system, some of the sculp-
ture,[15] the artwork, and the introduction of the olive to the Iberians.

A little north of Ullastret, the Greeks built the city of Emporión
on the Bay of Rosas. The historical name of Empúries comes from
the Greek term "Emporion," which means "marketplace" or "commercial center." The natural harbor in front of Emporion offered
protection to trading vessels, and close contacts existed between
the two cities. Emporión rapidly became one of antiquity's most
important commercial ports of the western Mediterranean.

RISE OF ROME

After subduing the Etruscan peoples of the northern Italic peninsula, the Romans conquered the Greek territories of southern Italy

in 272 BCE and began to challenge Carthage in the western Mediterranean.

With the Etruscans and Phoenicians out of the picture, trade in the western sea was contested by three powers: Greece, Carthage, and Rome. Rome could not tolerate the commercial control that Carthage held in the western Mediterranean and tried to ameliorate the situation with treaties. With the first treaty of 509, for example, Rome and its allies promised not to sail into the Gulf of Carthage, unless driven there by storm or by enemies. In such cases, they could buy only what was necessary for repairs or religious ceremonies, and had to leave again within five days. In Carthaginian Sicily, Romans were to be allowed the same rights as Carthaginians. Carthage was also restricted to terms: it was not to attack any town subject to Rome and its citizens could not stay the night in Rome if armed, and so forth. This and similar treaties did not allay the suspicions that both major Mediterranean powers had for each other. The Greeks, confined to northeastern Spain and France after the Battle of Alalia, left most of the region in dispute between the bitter enemies Rome and Carthage. The expanding ambitions of Rome and its trade requirements to support a growing population, and Carthage, entirely dependent on commerce, were, at least in hindsight, leading to an inevitable struggle for control of the western Mediterranean.

Roman and Punic Wars

Carthage considered Sardinia, North Africa, and non-Greek Sicily its domains. To feed its growing population, Rome coveted Sicily and its vast grain-growing regions. The First Punic War (264–241) resulted in a victory for Rome that acquired both Sicily and Sardinia. Carthage hence concentrated more of its commercial activity along the coasts of the Iberian Peninsula.

Rome exploited Sicily's vast production of wheat and imposed a treaty on Carthage that restricted Carthaginian trade to south of the Ebro River in northeastern Spain. However, when the Iberian commercial town of Saguntum (Sagunto) asked Rome for an alliance, although well south of the River Ebro, Rome responded favorably, perhaps looking for an excuse for another war with Carthage. As far as Carthage was concerned, the treaty was broken.

Under the command of Hannibal (248–183), a Carthaginian army, mostly recruited in Spain, besieged Saguntum in 219, captured it, and went on to cross southern France and the Alps to attack Italy

Merchants from Carthage selling slaves and wares in a Roman villa.
(North Wind Picture Archives.)

itself. In 218, Roman legions landed at Emporión under Gnaeus
Cornelius Scipio to cut off Hannibal's resources, and the Second
Punic War was underway. Hannibal raised havoc in Italy until the
Romans gained the upper hand. He fled to Carthage, where on the
nearby plains of Zama, in 202, the Romans defeated him. In the years
between the Punic wars, ambitious Rome undertook the conquest of
the Hellenistic lands to the east. The primary enemy, however, was
still Carthage. The Roman statesman Cato the Elder (234–149) always
ended his senatorial speeches with the words "Carthage must be
destroyed." Throughout the first half of the second century,
Carthage had recovered much of its trade prosperity. Nervous of its
growing commercial propensity that again challenged Rome for the
western Mediterranean, the Roman Senate demanded that the
Carthaginians give up their port city of Carthage and move inland,
a requirement that would have been tantamount to Carthaginian suicide. A Roman army besieged the city in 149 massacred most inhabitants and sold survivors into slavery. The city was leveled to the
ground. Rome was now free to assert its dominance over the entire
western Mediterranean.

Ostia, Port of Rome

Imports and exports by sea, for a time, were channeled through the port city of Ostia situated at the mouth of the river Tiber, some 22 kilometers from Rome. Crowded with people from many nations, the city supplied the needs of Rome. Replete with warehouses, the waterfront employed numerous workers such as cargo handlers and manifest checkers who examined the quality and quantity of goods for their owners, shipwrights, rope makers and caulkers, sailors, and soldiers—the latter to guard the coastline around Ostia. Slaves unloaded ships' cargo onto barges and moved it up river to Rome. The streets were crowded with food-sellers and hawkers, and were lined with inns, taverns, brothels, workshops, private houses, and tenements for workers. The latter formed organizations known as collegias (guilds) in which they had some say in their own occupations. There were over 50 attested collegias in Ostia, most having to do with trade, transportation, and ancillary jobs.[16] Ships sailed between Ostia, North Africa, the Iberian Peninsula, Gaul, and eastern Mediterranean ports. In the fourth century CE, the city faded into oblivion as other ports became available.

Roman Fleets

Cargo in bulk such as grain from Spain or France (later from Egypt) was transported by sea at cheaper rates than overland. Transport carriers were generally broad beamed with a single mast and large square sails. Ships sailed close to the shore for lack of navigational skills, making them vulnerable to pirates lurking in hidden coves along the hundreds of miles of uninhabited coastline. Sallying forth to plunder its contents when a ship was sighted, the pirates either killed the crew or sold them into slavery. Anyone important who was discovered on the vessel would be held for ransom. The Roman navy exerted some efforts to eradicate pirates in the Mediterranean, but wealthy Romans who found the pirates—from whom they bought slaves—useful sometimes hindered these efforts.

Fugitives and brigands from many countries swarmed to the Balearic Islands, which became a haven for buccaneers who preyed on the great grain ships that carried wheat to Italy. The situation became so bad that in 67 the senate gave Gnaeus Pompey the authority and resources to sweep clean the entire Mediterranean of anyone threatening Rome's wheat supplies. The mission was accomplished, but pirates soon returned to action when the pressure let up. To make sea journeys safer, the Romans built lighthouses on dangerous coasts, and constructed good harbors and sturdy docks. Only one currency was used, and there were no customs duties. Essential to the success of Roman expansion and a growing population, commerce was made as little encumbered as possible.

CELTS

A people of Indo-European origin, the Celts, appeared in Europe in the later years of the second millennium. During the first millennium, these diverse tribes often settled in hilltop fortified towns and generally lived in circular houses constructed of wood and thatch, beds placed around the walls, one entrance, and the hearth in the middle. Elevated outhouses (to foil rodents) were used to store grain. In their westward expansion, Celtic peoples introduced the use of iron in Europe, perhaps one of the reasons for their mastery over local Bronze Age tribes. Excavated villages exhibit workshops where iron was smelted, coins were minted, and weaving and pottery were produced. Iron swords and tools that were in great demand in trade circles as well as other items such as furs, metals, and slaves (usually captured prisoners of war) helped bring a semblance of wealth to the Celts.

Celtic clans eventually occupied regions from Eastern Europe to the Atlantic coasts of present-day Portugal; worked with iron; worshipped natural objects such as rivers, mountains, and forests; and followed the teachings of their priests—the Druids. As fierce, brave warriors, they were also reported to be fickle, irrational, and cruel. The Celts did not write and the Romans, their bitter enemies, often recorded their barbaric nature and brutality with, perhaps, some exaggeration.[17]

In the first century, the Greek historian Diodorus Siculus presented an account of Celts in France:

> They are exceedingly fond of wine and sate themselves with the unmixed wine imported by merchants; their desire makes them drink it greedily and when they become drunk they fall into a stupor or into a maniacal disposition. And therefore many Italian merchants with their usual love of cash look on the Gallic craving for wine as their treasure. They transport the wine by boat or on the navigable

rivers and by wagon through the plains and receive in return for it an incredibly high price, for one amphora of wine they get in return a slave—a servant in exchange for a drink.[18]

Mediterranean cities needed raw materials, salt, flour, hides, and slaves and the Celts—who desired luxuries such as wine and drinking vessels—found common ground for exchange. One of the centers of this trade was the hill fort of Mont Lassois in Burgundy, residence of powerful Celtic chiefs who traded along the Rhône and Saône Valleys and with Marseilles. At Mont Lassois, excavations have revealed numerous examples of long-distance Iron Age trade. Nearby at Vix, the skeleton of a 30- to 35-year-old bejeweled princess was uncovered, along with the Vase (Krater) of Vix, the largest vessel ever found from the Celtic period weighing over 200 kilograms. The Krater may have come from Sparta or Greek Tarentum in southern Italy, probably in pieces and put together by Greek craftsmen on the spot.[19]

The village of Vix is the highest navigable point on the Seine, and the Celtic chieftains who controlled it received tin from mines in Cornwall shipped south from Britain via Vix on its way to the Adriatic.

Finds also included bracelets, brooches, a necklace, a gold diadem, and a bronze cup from Etruscan Tarquinia, dating back to 520 BCE. Rich grave artifacts indicate a developing social hierarchy among the Celts in place by the sixth century BCE. The Celts never achieved a unified state but remained in tribal associations.

Bibracte

Goods traveled up the Rhône to present day Lyon and then continued up the Saône. They passed through the territory of the Celtic Aedui, whose major city was Bibracte, on their way to the Seine and Loire Rivers for trade with the Atlantic coastal peoples and England. The Aedui taxed the commerce entering their land. Celtic tribes sometimes fought each other for control of the rivers. They had developed skills in metalworking, farming, mining, and trading. The Hallstatt salt mines southeast of Salzburg produced vast quantities of salt for local consumption and for trade. Celtic miners, working deep underground by torchlight, hammered out the salt, placed it in baskets, carried it to the village, and sent it further afield by river. As a preservative, salt was an important trade item.

Manching

One of the most important Celtic centers of commerce, the site of Manching, was positioned at the crossing of north-south and east-west trade routes on a plain. Another advantage was its closeness to the Paar and Danube Rivers. Nearby were iron and gold deposits. The well-excavated Iron Age Celtic site at Manching in upper Bavaria, Germany, has yielded extensive information on industry and commerce during the life of the ancient city from about the fourth century to the middle of the first century BCE. The settlement, in the midst of agricultural land, served as a central depot for foreign trade and housed a number of craftsmen and a mint. It was the scene of a sizable iron working industry with ore mined locally. Besides iron tools, the workshops of the town produced jewelry, ceramics, and textiles. Trade over long distances was evident by the discovery of amber from the Baltic Sea, and amphora from the Mediterranean that contained wine. Local bronze coins were used for regional trade, while long distance commerce employed gold and silver coins.

In antiquity, wealthy Celts controlled trade routes along the river systems of the Rhône, Seine, Rhine, and Danube. They moved into the Balkans around 335, and Alexander the Great received delegations of Celts living near the Adriatic, presumably concerning trade. Julius Caesar in 58 began the campaigns that led to the Roman annexation of the whole of Celtic Gaul. In 43, the conquest of England began, while the Celts of Spain resisted Roman occupation for nearly two centuries, or until the time of Augustus. To facilitate the movement of armies, and incidentally, merchants and their goods, the Romans constructed great roads and bridges of stone, meant to last, throughout much of the conquered lands.

Britain and Gaul

The Celtic Veneti who inhabited today's Brittany (then Amorica) controlled the English Channel. According to Caesar:

> They have a great many ships and regularly sail to and from Britain. When it comes to knowledge and experience of navigation they leave all the other tribes standing . . . Since the Veneti control (these seas) they are able to exact tolls from almost all who regularly use these waters.[20]

Caesar wasted little time in eliminating the Veneti. Their leaders were put to death and the people sold into slavery.[21]

A major port on the British side of the Channel, Hengistbury Head (on the south coast), carried on extensive trade around the turn of the millennium. Imports consisted of wine, yellow and purple glass ingots, and figs, whereas exports were grain, cattle hides, iron extracted from nearby mines, copper, shale, lead, and probably hunting dogs and slaves.[22] Merchants to Ireland came away with Irish wolfhounds in exchange for trinkets, bronze vessels, or coins.[23] Today, Celtic peoples and their language are largely confined to Wales, Ireland, Scotland, and Brittany.

NOTES

1. Walker, 13.
2. Aubet, 95.
3. There is some debate as to who first reached Iberia from the East— Greeks or Phoenicians. According to Herodotus, the Greeks first reached the western extremes of the Mediterranean by sea. Boardman, 214.
4. Roman soldiers were often paid in part in salt, from which comes the saying "worth your salt" as well as the word "salary."
5. Some scholars believe that they sailed around Africa.
6. Some researchers believe they came from western Anatolia; others consider them indigenous to the region.
7. Trump, 277.
8. Macnamara, 23.
9. Macnamara, 145.
10. Macnamara, 29.
11. Macnamara, 130.
12. Palmer, 50–52.
13. No city of the Tartessian kingdom has yet been identified, but documentation of its existence is reasonably plentiful both from ancient authors and inscriptions.
14. Similarly, in France the ancient hilltop city of Ensérune near Béziers, inhabited by Greeks and Iberians, was a productive market and trade town.
15. See the Dama del Elche.
16. Aldrete, 213.
17. In Celtic Spain some documents written in Celtic using the Iberian writing system have been found.
18. quoted from Cunliffe, 88.
19. Aston and Taylor, 66; Chadwick (1981), 35–36.
20. Quoted from Cunliffe, 101.
21. Beckwith, 79.
22. Cunliffe, 102–3.
23. Cunliffe, 169.

4

EASTERN EMPIRES: EARLY CE

SASANID EMPIRE (NEO-PERSIAN EMPIRE 226–651 CE)

At the beginning of the third century, the province of Fars in southwestern Persia came under the control of a local Sasanid dynasty that was primarily agriculturalist. The dynasty consisted of disparate peoples ruled by a Persian elite. In the year 224, the first ruler, Ardashir (211–241), defeated the Parthians and took control of Persia, beginning a new era. Under the Sasanids, the Silk Route flourished. The government controlled trade and imposed heavy taxes on all goods passing through its lands. The Sasanid extended their domains from the eastern end of the Black Sea to India, taking in modern-day Iraq, Iran, Afghanistan, and Pakistan. It was the last Persian Empire before the Muslim conquest, and it was a major Western Asian power that competed with the Roman Empire over some four centuries. Sasanid commerce and influence extended far beyond its borders to Western Europe, Africa, India, and China. Its most important asset, the province of Fars, was its location along the eastern coasts of the Persian Gulf, and the northern coast of the Arabian Sea.[1]

By the late Sasanid period, the Persians in control of the Arabian Sea came into conflict with the Romans. Both competed and disputed trade concessions as far as Sri Lanka. The Roman emperor Justinian (483–565), residing in Constantinople, retaliated when

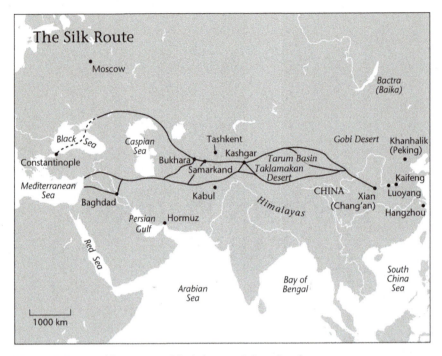

The Silk Route. (Courtesy of Leinberger Mapping.)

the Persians raised tariffs on silk and other exports by disallowing the sale of iron and copper to the Persians. Justinian refused to purchase Persian silk, and sought a route through the Red Sea (rather than the Persian Gulf) to India and China that would circumnavigate the Sasanid Empire. The Romans solicited the aid of Ethiopia to buy silk and then sell it to the Roman merchants, making Ethiopians—instead of Persians— middlemen. For the Ethiopians to buy silk from India was difficult, however, because the Persian merchants were always on hand at the ports when Indian ships arrived and purchased the entire cargos.

SOGDIAN MERCHANTS

In the east, the Sasanids shared the role of middlemen with the Sogdians, who were also of Persian stock. Both developed silk-weaving industries as well as decorated metal bowls and jugs that were highly prized. Other vessels made from thick, clear glass with elaborate cut decoration are typical Sasanid products and were traded as far as Japan, where the imperial family used them. East of the Caspian Sea, the people of the kingdom of Sogdiana, on the

Silk Route, warriors for the most part, turned their energy to commerce and their language became the *lingua franca* of trade. The ruling classes of the major cities, especially Samarkand (Uzbekistan), a commercial headquarters, and Bukhârâ, became wealthy as depots of exchange. Sogdians were well known in Chinese markets and trading circles.

The Turkish Khagans on the Asian steppes somewhat supported the Sogdian rulers, protected Sogdian trade, and employed them as officials and diplomats. The Chinese were considered distant overlords. During the seventh century, rapid development of the capital at Samarkand took place along with an expansion of trade, as evidenced by the abundance of coins. There was progress in silk weaving and handicrafts, and Sogdian merchants not only thronged the Silk Road east to west, but also the "Fur Road," north to the Urals. The many silver and gilded vessels found throughout Central Asia and in China are now believed to have been manufactured in Sogdiana. The warrior Sogdians needed to trade in order to bestow riches on their followers, whom they depended upon for political purposes and war with surrounding nomadic peoples.[2]

FARS PROVINCE

Far to the south, caravans departed the province of Fars for India, with some goods going on to China. The location of Sasanid Fars made it an important place of transit for land and sea trade. Fars was the original homeland of the Persians, who call themselves and their language Farsi.

Sasanid coins found in ports of southern China, and others discovered in northeastern China, indicate trade with Fars by the Silk Route and by sea. Chinese goods reached the Sasanid Empire by the fourth century, but the coins are generally from the late fifth to the early seventh centuries. Many were minted in Fars, whose merchants looked eastward to India and China to increase trade. Fars' importance rested on its linen, wool, cotton, perfume, and pearls from the Gulf as well as brocades and carpets that were exported to China. Because of the wars with the Roman Empire, the Silk Road declined in traffic and, as a result, the sea trade made Fars more influential, and the Persian Gulf became of greater commercial significance.

KUSHAN EMPIRE

The Kushan Empire benefited from trade between the West and China both by land and water, the latter from ports on the

Arabian Sea. It seemed to have had a profitable commerce with Rome, acting as an intermediary between Rome and China handling silk, fur, jewelry, and other luxury goods. The Kushan Empire, with its capital at Begram, controlled territory from the Aral Sea south, as far as central India, and east to the borders of China north of Tibet. This empire of mixed ethnic groups was ideally located for trade. East Indian merchants carried on commerce with the Roman Empire—much of it pepper—and Indian port cities became the emporia for such trade. Silk and porcelain from China, spices from southeast Asia, and slaves, ivory, and gold from Africa were significant items that generated wealth in Indian coastal cities. Indian craftsman also took advantage of the increase in demand for cotton textiles, leather goods, handwoven carpets, sugar, and cinnamon. They were also well known for steel production, and the demand for Indian knives and swords increased. With the rise of the Kushans, there were four great powers along the Silk Route: the Chinese, the Kushans, the Persians, and the Romans.

INDIAN TRADE WITH THE ROMAN EMPIRE

Roman communities of merchants composed of various ethnic groups—including Jews, Greeks, East Indians, and Arabs, who had long traded on the Indian Ocean—handled the cargos and sailed the ships that brought goods to and from India. The Roman trade network extended down the coast of east Africa and as far east as southern India.[3] Romans traded gold and silver for the luxuries from India first by the overland caravan routes via Anatolia and Persia, though in relatively small quantities compared to later times by sea. Most commerce was carried out with the Tamil kingdoms of southern India and Sri Lanka. With the fall of the Western Roman Empire in the fifth century, the trade routes remained operational. The Roman demand for silk, pearls, spices, cotton, dyes, and ivory continued to grow, stimulated by Roman mercantile investment.

GUPTA EMPIRE (AROUND 320–540)

Unlike the earlier Mauryan Empire's centralized bureaucracy, the Gupta Empire was less extensive but allowed defeated rulers to retain their kingdoms in return for tribute or military assistance. The efficient rule of the Guptas had an emphatic impact on India and is sometimes known as India's Golden Age. Under the later rulers, peace and prosperity increased and foreign trade flourished, especially with Rome in the latter part of the fourth century, that brought in vast amounts of gold and silver. The kingdom exported more commodities to the Roman Empire than they imported, thus amassing an immense amount of Roman coinage. Hindu traders were also aggressive in Southeast Asia. The Indian beneficiaries of this commerce were, as usual, the elite and the court, although the general populace could enjoy the beautiful public buildings erected with the money flowing into the country. At the time, Hinduism was the favored religion and the caste system was becoming entrenched, although Buddhism was accepted. Gupta craftsmen were excellent in producing dyes, soap, cement, and fine tempered steel. Through trade, these skilled craftsmen enjoyed a better life than the farmers or agricultural workers.

The middle classes seemed to have prospered, although the rich became richer. Slave labor helped build great estates. Charities existed, and hospitals supported by the rich offered free care to the needy. Rest houses for traders and travelers were built along India's highways and merchants, and travelers on the move there had little reason to fear robbery. The Chinese visitor Fa-hien (Faxian), who traveled in India for 11 years, recorded that he was never molested or robbed. Wealthy and middle-class people in the cities found pleasure in their gardens, from music and dancing, and from plays, baths, social activities and various foods, the most common of which were rice, bread, fish, milk, fruits, nuts, and juices. Gupta rulers acquired much of the land previously held by the Mauryan Empire, and peace and trade flourished under their rule. Sanskrit was the official court language.

SEA ROUTE: DHOWS, CREWS, AND CARGOS

During the Chinese Han Dynasty, a sea route opened up an alternative to the West for trade. From the Red River (near Hanoi) and the Gulf of Tonkin, ships sailed southward through the South China Sea then westward through the Malacca Strait and across the Bay of Bengal to India. Further voyages sailed around India and then northwest to the Persian Gulf, the Red Sea, or the east coast of Africa.

From the Red Sea towns, Chinese goods such as jade, silk, and porcelain went overland to the Nile River and were carried by riverboat downstream to Alexandria. Here they were transshipped to Mediterranean ports, including Ostia, the Port of Rome.

Ships employed in the Persian Gulf were generally dhows of around 175 tons with a single mast and a lateen sail. Timber for ship construction was imported from the Malabar Coast of India, and a voyage to China and back took nearly 18 months due to the directional flow of the monsoon winds. About 30 sailors manned the larger dhows, whereas smaller boats required about a dozen. For navigation, an instrument was used that measured latitude from the angle of the horizon and the polar star.

Dhows were used in trade to near or distant shores. Voyages were often fraught with danger, however, as ships were lost at sea when unknown shoals and storms took their toll. Further, there was always danger of disease spreading in the close quarters. Small boats traveled along the coastlines, larger ones, up to 180 feet long, ran before the monsoon winds across the open ocean to India.

Arab crew aboard dhows generally wore turbans and robes, and spent the leisure time at sea sleeping, talking, singing, smoking hashish or tobacco, making music, drinking tea, and sometimes weaving baskets. They rigged up fishing lines for fresh food. Most were illiterate. Crews were selected from different places so that they would not easily band together and perhaps threaten the captain. They slept on deck with a blanket if needed. Unleavened bread, rice, goat stew, ghee (clarified butter), and fresh fish made up their diet. Cargos for China and Southeast Asia comprised linen, cotton, woolen clothes, iron ore, and metal objects that were exchanged for silk, camphor, spices, and musk. From the Persian Gulf to East Africa, they carried dates and fish and returned with mangrove wood. Paying passengers were generally asked to contribute an animal such as a goat for consumption on the voyage.

The seafarers who traveled in Arab vessels must have spent a good deal of time bailing water out of the bilges, for the planks of the hull were stitched together. The stitches from coconut fiber were passed through holes drilled in the adjacent planks that were either teak or coconut wood.[4] Foreign observers noted the frailness of the ships and the constructions without nails, iron, or caulking, although some, according to various sources, employed pitch or resin and whale oil to block up holes and caulk the planks. Leaky seams, lack of decks, and constant groaning and creaking of the hull must have been at best uncomfortable for a voyage of any distance. Marco Polo later described ships at Hormuz as having no decks, but the cargo was covered in hide.

Rudders consisted of a side oar, one on each side in seagoing ships. A stern rudder was not introduced in Arab ships until the thirteenth century.[5] There was generally one mast of teak or coconut wood, and lateen sails were woven from coconut or palm tree leaves. This type of sail was used throughout the Indian Ocean, whereas the square sail was at the time employed in the Mediterranean. Navigation was always a problem for early mariners, and most ships stayed within sight of the coasts. Arab vessels were cheaper to construct, iron nails were expensive, and the ship offered more flexibility if it encountered a reef or was carried ashore by adverse currents or large waves.

ARMENIA

Annexed early on by the Medes, then the Persians until 330 BCE, when the Persian Empire fell to Alexander, Armenia was ruled by the Parthian Arsacid Dynasty until 428 CE, followed by the Sasanid Persians (enemies of Rome) until 642.[6] Situated around Lake Van and between the Black and Caspian Seas, the Armenians were in a position to participate in extensive trade. Its capital city was Yerevan.

Eventually surrounded by Muslim societies, Armenians maintained their own form of Christianity and became long-distance traders passing through Islamic territories. Commerce east and west often went through Armenia, when the route skirted the southern end of the Caspian Sea to later hook up with the Silk Road to China. The steppe lands to the north of the Caspian were more dangerous for travel due to unpredictable nomadic tribes. An alternative was a more southerly route through Afghanistan.

Whatever route was taken, Armenians were well represented as camel drivers and traders. Routes chosen generally depended on the political situation at the time. The Armenians rose to political power in the tenth and eleventh centuries due in part to the weakness of the Byzantine Empire and that of the Abassid Caliphate in Baghdad. The Byzantines, revitalized, stopped Armenian advances to the Mediterranean by cutting off their trade routes, and by 1070, the Seljuk Turks conquered Armenia and the Levant, ending the Armenian state. The conquest left pockets of Armenians in almost every port city of the eastern Mediterranean and Black Sea, where they continued to engage in commerce.[7]

Armenian merchants were found throughout the Persian Empire, and from their main colony at Julfa, a suburb of Isfahan (Iran), they made their way across India and into Tibet, trading from Lhasa with the Chinese. Sponsored by wealthy men of Isfahan, Armenian agents traveled to Anatolia, Russia, Europe (even Sweden), and the Indian Ocean, collecting one quarter of the profits for themselves.[8]

JEWS AND ARMENIANS

The Armenian merchant was to be seen throughout the Turkish Empire as a formidable competitor of Jewish and other merchants. They were not always welcome, as is evident from a letter to the king of France from the consul in Marseilles in 1623 that complained of "an invasion of Armenians with bales of silk."[9] The letter mentioned their greed and pursuit of money. In spite of a general dislike of Armenians, they were imminently successful due, perhaps, in no small part, to their closeness and loyalty to one another. Not unlike the Jews, the stateless Armenian traders could count on their associates. In the late Middle Ages, Jews could be found on almost every continent engaged in long-distance trade. Even more unfortunate than the Armenians, they had no solid base such as Julfa but were extirpated from their homeland, Israel, and scattered to the four winds. Most had little choice other than to become traders, bankers, money-lenders, or tax collectors, as most professions were closed to them. Expelled from England in the fourteenth century, then from France, Spain, Portugal, and Sicily at the end of the fifteenth and beginning of the sixteenth centuries, they nonetheless kept the faith, and many prospered.[10]

NOTES

1. *Past Worlds*, 186–87.

2. Beckwith, 77. See also http://www.silkroadfoundation.org/artl/sogdian.shtml.

3. Curtin, 100.

4. Hourani, 92.

5. Hourani, 98.

6. Lockwood, 175.

7. Curtin, 185.

8. See Braudel (1985), 122–23 for the commercial travels of an Armenian agent.

9. Quoted from Braudel (1985), 156.

10. Braudel (1985), 154–60.

5

THE ROMAN EMPIRE
(44 BCE–476 CE)

COMMERCIAL LIFE

Commercial enterprises were of great importance in Roman life. Traders supplied most of the slaves for government projects, for the great farms (latifundia), for households that could afford them, for the ships and harbor workers, for the mines, and for any other suitable work. Merchants also provided the prodigious amounts of food for the growing cities, the wild animals for the arenas throughout the empire, the spices that many demanded, and the fine apparel the upper classes favored. They furnished horses for sport, farming, transportation, and the military, that showed a marked preference for Arabian and Spanish horses due to their endurance, speed, and strength. In the forums of cities such as Rome, businessmen and merchants often gathered to promote their agendas and carry out transactions.

The aristocratic elite looked down on commercial enterprises but nevertheless engaged in them and reaped large profits. The Piazza of the Corporations in Ostia appears to have been the place where many shipping companies had their headquarters, each defined by a plaque showing the products they imported that included wine, grain, horses, elephants, and so on. Celebrations in Rome and major imperial cities were big business: conquering generals, wealthy patricians running for public office, and emperors

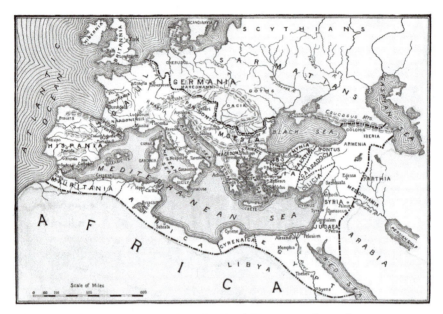

Map of the Roman Empire. (North Wind Picture Archives.)

soliciting the goodwill of the people all provided lavish festivities in the arenas and amphitheaters at their own expense, and for which admission was free. Suppliers of the required animals, gladiators, wine, and food for the many and heavily attended events were in a position to do well financially. Bloody gladiatorial spectacles disappeared only in the fifth century CE, and those employing the cruel use of animals about a century later.[1]

ESSENTIAL GRAIN

Of supreme importance to the empire, grain, produced in the western provinces in abundance, helped feed a growing population in the second century of about a million Romans (not counting slaves). Massive amounts were required, benefiting the landed estates that grew it, shipbuilders and owners to transport it, bakers and bread vendors to sell it, and merchants to make the arrangements to deliver it. Much of the wheat came from the provinces of Hispania and Gaul, Sicily, and North Africa. Long-distance trade from the provinces required contracts, invoices, and facilities. No news of a ship's whereabouts after it sailed out of sight led to anxious times for the merchants and investors, since agents in foreign ports might or might not be dependable. Coming from distant places, grain (and other commodities) might change hands a number of times before reaching Rome, and traders not only had to figure costs, but the possibility that the ship might never arrive due to destructive storms, pirates, mutiny or other unforeseen events.

For most Romans, meals were centered around grain, oil, and wine. The staple food, cereals, were in the form of husked wheat made into porridge or bread. Bread was the most often eaten food in ancient Rome, but cereals were also consumed in a variety of cakes, pastries, and tarts that were baked commercially or at home. As land in Italy for plantations became scarcer, the wealthy acquired property in the provinces for their own benefit. Latifundia developed as soon as a territory was secured by the legions, and supplied Rome with a variety of comestibles including beef, wheat, barley, olive oil, fish and fish oil, and wine, while other significant imports were glassware, iron, lead, tin, leather, marble, perfumes, purple dye, silk, gold, silver, and wood. Also imported were vegetables of various kinds, fruit and nuts, spices, and herbs.

LOCAL AND PROVINCIAL TRADE

Various regions supplied essentials to the population of Rome, as was the case with the port city of Pompeii in south-central Italy, an important wine center surrounded by extensive vineyards and dedicated to the god Bacchus. The eruption of Mount Vesuvius in 79 obliterated the region's wine industry by burying vineyards and warehouses replete with grapes and wine for sale under a cloud of ash, not to mention the complete destruction of the city and the nearby town of Herculaneum, also a wine emporium. The repercussions of the disaster were soon felt, and wine prices rose sharply. New vineyards sprang up around Rome, uprooting grain fields in the process to make land available. Soon there was a surplus of wine, depressing prices to the detriment of growers and merchants. Meanwhile, a shortage of grain caused the cost of bread to increase, and in 92, Emperor Domitian prohibited the establishment of further vineyards and ordered others destroyed in the provinces. Now less available, wine prices stabilized, and the land produced more wheat. The edict, not always adhered to, remained until its repeal in 280 CE.

WINE

Strong, pure wine was considered bad form; Romans drank their wine watered down, some of it spiced, and heated. Wine concentrate diluted with water was common; and low-quality wine, beer, and mead were popular among the lower classes. Milk, generally from sheep or goats, was considered barbaric as a drink and was reserved for making cheese. Once an exporter of wine from the surrounding vineyards, Rome became a major importer as the city and the empire grew. The provincial wines from Spain, France, Sicily, and North Africa were shipped in amphorae by sea to the thirsty Romans; although there were many sizes, a common measure was 39 liters.

Greek and Roman merchants distributed the containers and their contents even further, to Britain and central Russia. River routes were used extensively, including the Rhône, Danube, Dnieper, and the Don, to bring Mediterranean wine to Northern Europe, often in exchange for Baltic amber and furs. Demand for wine also came from the Christian Church and Jewish communities for ritual purposes. As Christianity spread into Northern and Eastern Europe, so did the wine trade. However, the use of amphorae began to disappear in the seventh century as wine barrels came into use in the western Mediterranean. Amphorae continued much longer in the Black Sea regions until they were replaced with barrels in the fourteenth century by Italian merchants who then dominated the trade.

SLAVES

Many slaves were taken in war from Spain and Gaul, or bought in Slavic and African countries. They were also products of Roman society when people were forced into slavery through debt, or sold their children. Slaves formed the vast majority of manual labor workers. Those purchased in foreign countries and resold in Rome or other cities were a steady source of income for traders. Slaves could be sold to the state as workers in the construction of public roads, baths, temples, arenas, and a host of other projects, where they labored in chain gangs and were locked up at night. Encased in an iron collar, they had little chance of escape. Some might be skilled and expensive, and were treated well, as was often the case with Greek slaves, who performed functions as teachers or physicians to wealthy families.

MERCHANT HOUSES

Affluent homeowners throughout the empire, often merchants, lived in grand one-story houses. In a city, they might use one room facing the street to display and sell merchandise. The most

Iberians driven under the yoke and sold as Roman slaves. (North Wind Picture Archives.)

important space was the atrium, where guests were entertained and business deals were conducted. Open to the sky, the atrium allowed rainwater to drain from the sloped tiled roof above and flow into the pool in the center. The tile floor was often decorated with mosaics, and there was usually a small shrine dedicated to the household god. Bedrooms were arranged around the central atrium. In the back of the house would be a garden with standing columns, and around the enclosure were the baths, toilets, kitchen, and a cool summer dining area. These single-family homes, attended by slaves, might house several or more generations of one family. Plebeians, lower class people, lived in tenement houses, often three to five stories high. A merchant might choose to live in an apartment building above his shop. In such a case, he might have ample space and running water, but most tenement dwellers and their families—including grandparents, parents, and children—squeezed into a one-room apartment and had to carry water from the public fountain and use public toilets.

Merchants' shops situated on the street front of houses or tenements were generally single rooms, but some also had workshops in the back or space for storage. Imported goods were available in some. Those engaged in selling food might have stone counters facing the street and ceramic basins imbedded in them. From these, the servant dished out wine or food to customers passing by.

ROMAN HISPANIA

Metals (including gold and tin), came from northwest Spain, silver from the Sierra Morena in the south, iron from the hills of Toledo, copper from the Río Tinto mines, lead from Cartagena, and mercury from Almadén. Olive oil was imported from around Gadir (Cádiz), and wine from the vineyards of Tarraco (Tarragona).

Mining was lucrative for Roman owners, but for slaves working in them, the circumstances were appalling. In the province of Granada, for example, a vertical shaft a meter wide was hewn as much as 200 meters into the rock with tunnels that radiated off it at different levels for a kilometer or so, to the ore deposits. Branded and fettered slaves worked in these narrow, low passages with pick and shovel. They placed the ore in esparto grass baskets tied around their necks, crawled back to the main shaft, and sent it by rope and pulleys to the surface.

The miners never saw the light of day. Hauled up at sunset, they were marched off to miserable barracks, given some bread and a little wine, and settled for the night. Seven days a week, the gruesome task went on. Miners' lives were understandably short.

For the extraction of gold from Hispania, hundreds of thousands of slaves washed away entire mountains. At Las Médulas, in the present-day northern province of León, mining continued over the second to the fourth centuries, and children of slaves and their children, through generations, were born into slavery and carried on the work. Galleys were bored into the mountainsides into which great gushes of water were released from aqueducts, flushing out the rock and minerals. The water carried the ore to panning lakes where the gold was sifted out. Slaves slow to leave the tunnels were washed out with it to their death. The precious metal was then dispatched to the south along the *Camino de la Plata* to Sevilla, and on to Cádiz for shipment to Ostia and Rome. The voyage to Ostia for cargo-laden ships was about nine days.

Besides metal, slaves, and grain, the Iberian Peninsula also satisfied the demand of Italy and Rome for other products, especially wine and olive oil in exchange for Roman and Greek pottery, highly prized by Iberians and Romans living in the provinces. Olive oil, a major import for Rome, was used in a variety of ways: cooking, lamps, medication, and rubbing down athletes.[2] Merchants became wealthy on sales of the oil that went to both private individuals and to the state. Amphora kilns and olive plantations worked in harmony to produce and ship the oil. A ship from Spain that went to the bottom near Marseilles in the year 14, on its way to Ostia, carried a notation on one of the amphora that 71.29 liters of oil was bought by the Merchant Lucius Antonius from the estate of Charitianus and was registered by Primus.[3] The oil was probably shipped by barge down the Quadalquivir River in southern Spain to the Atlantic Ocean and then transferred to a larger seagoing ship owned by a rich merchant, for the voyage to Italy. A few wealthy families generally owned the Spanish olive oil business. The voyage to Ostia was always in some peril; however, a ship that went down off the southern coast of France in about 50 was loaded with a cargo of olive oil, garum, kitchen pottery, glass, and metal objects. Wealthy merchant families bought or sold contracts for goods and shipping space aboard the vessels. They had commercial establishments in Rome, Ostia, and the provinces. The rich olive oil business in southern Spain began to dry up in the fourth century as competition from North Africa began to undercut its price.

Mostly in the hands of wealthy families were the production, distribution, and sales of expensive garum that was shipped throughout the Mediterranean basin and inland in Gaul and England. Affluent families with enough money to underwrite the initial costs also controlled wine and pottery from Spain along with wool and flax. Esparto grass, found in great abundance in southern Spain, was used for footware, chairs, mattresses, ships' ropes, baskets, and clothes. Dyes, too, were important exports made from the murex shells that were found on both the Mediterranean and the Atlantic coasts. Marble quarries also helped supply the Romans' penchant for building. Sometimes marble columns were produced in Spain and shipped to Rome in one piece.

Mérida, then the capital city of the province of Lusitania (Portugal), was a Roman trade hub with a theater, arena, amphitheater, temples, monuments, and river docks on the Guadiana for transport by boat of cattle and horses from the Alemtejo. Most of the previously mentioned resources, sought long before by Phoenicians and Greeks, and now by the Romans, were the cause of many battles on the Iberian Peninsula between native peoples, generally Celts, and the Roman legions.

GARUM

From Portugal came the best garum shipped from Lagos to Rome, but numerous factories on the southern coasts of Spain also produced vast amounts for the Roman market. Garum consisted of the entrails, heads, and fins of fish, salted and placed in large outdoor vats, where it was left to liquefy and ferment under a hot sun for up to three months. Poured into amphorae, the sauce was dispatched to Rome and other Roman cities by ship. It was popular spread on bread and added flavor to monotonous food. The making and shipping of garum was big business, as it was enjoyed all over the Mediterranean except, perhaps, by the people that lived near the open-air vats where it fermented.

ANCIENT GAUL (FRANCE)

In 125 BCE, the Romans took possession of Massalia (Marseilles) and constructed the Via Domitia in 118 across southern Gaul from Italy to Spain, founded the city of Colonia Narbo Martius (Narbonne), and built the Via Aquitania to Burdigala (Bordeaux) near the Atlantic coast of Gaul and from where wine was transported to the Roman military in Britain. Much wine traveled these roads to Gaulish clans who paid dearly for it. Up the Rhône River from Marseilles, merchants established trading centers in the first century CE at what are today Vienne and Lyon. Metals were produced in the south, wine in the area around Bordeaux and Marseilles. The province also exported wool, copper, glass, bronzeware and slaves, mostly shipped down the Rhône River to Marseilles and on to Rome.

ROMAN BRITAIN

With the colonization of Britain in 43 CE came the exportation of various products that were exchanged for wine, pottery, and olive oil. Roman security on the roads and seas gave men of commerce confidence that their products would reach their destinations. Under the empire, the northern province exported lead, wool, slaves, tin, some gold, and hunting dogs that traveled along the excellent Roman roads to cities and coastal ports. When these roads were established on the island, internal British trade rose considerably. Goods were ferried across the channel and made their way overland to Italy or to the Mediterranean, where again they were loaded onto boats for Rome. Sometimes, they were shipped around

Spain and through the Strait of Gibraltar directly to Italy. From a ship carrying much first century pottery from France and the Mediterranean, and sunk off Britain, trade contacts with the continent seem to have been ongoing before the Romans came to Britain, where they ruled for over four centuries. Archaeological finds, especially pottery and Roman coins, show that trade was an important feature of the occupation. Other artifacts such as brass, pewter, and jet show items that were exported; imports into Britain in Roman times included silver cups and plates, glassware, and silk. Before and after the Roman invasion, wine was perhaps the most important item of commerce, for which the Romans received slaves, furs, animal hides, beef, gold, and silver. After the Roman conquest, trade with Ireland and Scotland picked up, but with the collapse of the empire, and the safeguards of Roman power, trade dwindled as merchants could no longer be confident their products would reach their destinations.

NORTH AFRICA AND EGYPT

The ancient provinces of Mauretania and Numidia (today Morocco, northern Algeria, Tunisia, and Libya), sparsely populated by Berber tribes, provided Rome with wild animals for the arenas, marble, olive oil, copper, grain, and slaves. Once the items were collected at the depots near the old city of Carthage, the sea voyage to Italy took only four days. Animal trade was big business in Rome and throughout the provinces as audiences flocked to the arenas to see lions from Africa or tigers from India tear their victims, sometimes Christians, to pieces. Special ships were constructed to transport the animals.[4]

THE INCENSE TRADE

The incense route traversed the western edge of the Arabian desert parallel to the Red Sea coast, about 100 miles inland. Pliny the Elder stated that the journey consisted of 65 stages divided by halts for the camels.

Two fragrances of antiquity, frankincense and myrrh, both greatly sought after, derived from trees found only in Ethiopia, Somalia, and the southern portion of the Arabian Peninsula. They were brought north by Arab merchants on camel caravans that from southern Arabia ended in Gaza on the Mediterranean Sea. This route made up a trade network that transported not only the

fragrances, but also gold, ivory, spices, pearls, and some textiles
from distant places such as India and the Far East. Arab merchants,
the Nabataeans, acquired substantial wealth from this trade that,
once it reached the Mediterranean, crossed the sea to European
destinations. The trade began in the third century BCE and continued into the second century CE.

ROMAN TRADE IN THE EAST

Roman commerce with India and the Far East was little known
until recently in spite of references to it by contemporary Roman
writers. Pliny the Elder, for example, complained in the first century
that some 25 million *denari* left Rome annually to pay for imported
spices, perfumes, and silk from the East. Located on the Red Sea in
southern Egypt, about 800 kilometers south of Suez, with a good
harbor, and settled in the third century, Berenike (also Berenice)
was from the beginning a trading site linking India, south Arabia,
Sub-Saharan Africa, and Rome. Once the ebb and flow of the monsoon winds across the Indian Ocean were understood, the city
became a gateway to the subcontinent. It was also south of the fierce
northerlies that were so troublesome for boats under sail making
their way up the Red Sea to ports nearer the Mediterranean.
Through Berenike, Romans conveyed their eastern and African luxuries. The seaport town was deserted in the sixth century and was
left to the desert sands after many centuries of thriving trade.
Recent archaeological excavations show intensive trade and many
Indian goods, including coconuts, pepper, beads, mats, pottery,
cooking utensils, and teak.

Items exported by the Romans, some of them from Roman Egypt
to the port at Berenike for shipment further afield, included clothing, flint, copper, iron, wine, and olive oil. Highly desired by
Indians were emeralds, usually found in Ethiopia, to be set in the
headgear of Indian rulers, and Indian women were attached to
red coral, much of it retrieved from the Red Sea beds for which they
might pay as much as 20 times its weight in gold.

The ever popular silk from China, especially for Roman women
who found it lightweight, cool, and comfortable in the heat of a
Roman summer, was expensive and it is easy to see why. Chinese
merchants had their coolies load the ships in ports such as Canton,
and the vessels made their way south along the coasts of what is today Vietnam. They then turned westward and either sent it overland
across the Malay Peninsula or continued further south before

turning northwest through the Strait of Malacca. Either way, the silk went on to Sri Lanka, where Indian and Tamil merchants bought it and reshipped it to southern Indian ports on the Malabar coast. Arabs and Greeks then took over the fabric and sent it to the semi-desert-like islands of Socotra near the entrance to the Red Sea, where traders of many diverse nationalities and shades of color clamored for business. Generally transshipped on Greek vessels for the last leg of the journey, the goods finally reached Berenike. Camels then carried the precious cargo, which became more expensive with each change of hands, overland across the desert sands to the river Nile. Reloaded on ships or rafts, the silk traveled downstream to Alexandria, where it was transferred to Roman or Greek ships bound for Ostia. By the time it reached its destination, the cargo was worth about 100 times what it cost in China.[5]

The stages of commerce were pretty much established: the Chinese seldom sailed beyond Sri Lanka, Indians were happy to unload their burdens at the mouth of the Red Sea and transfer them to Arabs for shipment north, and the Roman merchants found Alexandria far enough away from home. Greeks, in the employ of Rome, manned many ships carrying merchandise from India to Italy. Roman maritime commerce to the East fell away as the empire declined, and it was brought to a halt in the seventh century by the spread of Islam.

Generally, only wealthy patrons could afford to import luxury items from faraway places, and Roman trade seems to have declined after about 200. Bubonic plague decimated the populations of many cities, and the upper classes seemed to be more intent on an urbane life in government or on their estates. With slaves to do their bidding, incentive was wanting. Commercial stagnation began to set in, and commerce diminished by around 50 percent by the middle of the third century.[6]

COLLAPSE OF THE WESTERN ROMAN EMPIRE

Numerous factors contributed to the general decline of the Western Roman Empire: debasement of coinage; lavish living; official corruption; prodigious use of German mercenaries, who owed little allegiance to Rome to defend the borders; and Germanic tribes swarming across the frontiers of the empire causing havoc and destruction. When the Western Empire expired, the Mediterranean Sea reverted to a dangerous place for merchants and their ships, as there was no strong central power to control the activities of buccaneers who marauded as far north as the English Channel. As so-called barbarians overran Europe, traders had little assurance that their goods would be safe. Without the policing power of Rome, few merchants were willing to buy what was produced in far-off provinces and entrust it to the dangers of the road, or to ship goods to markets via the Mediterranean. Land routes became vulnerable to marauding bands of brigands no longer in fear of Roman garrisons, or to invading Germanic tribes intent on plunder. By the fourth and fifth centuries, the empire collapsed under the weight of Germanic invasions and internal divisions. In 476, the last emperor to reside in Rome was deposed by Odoacer, a German general. The Eastern Roman Empire, with its capital at Constantinople (sometimes called New Rome), carried on the traditions of the old imperial city.

NOTES

1. Aldrete, 211.
2. Keay, 98.
3. Keay, 101.
4. Arête, 222.
5. Bernstein, 4.
6. Cantor, 43.

6

WESTERN ASIA: MIDDLE AGES

BYZANTINE EMPIRE (330–1453)

Founded in the seventh century BCE, Byzantium, once a Greek colony, commanded a strategic position between East and West. It became a Roman province in the first century BCE. The Roman Emperor Constantine (306–337 CE) made it the capital of his empire in 330, when it became known as Constantinople. About 482 to 565, the emperor Justinian restored for a time much of the old Roman Empire and had great monuments built in the new capital. Trade was not neglected, as he sought ways to circumvent the Persians through whose lands came Chinese silk, Indian spices, and other Eastern products. An attempt to establish a sea route through the Red Sea and Abyssinia, where products from India and China arrived, was unsuccessful due to Persian interference, but another route north of the Caspian Sea and through the lands of the Turks was more viable.

By 522, the Byzantines obtained silkworm eggs that had been smuggled out of China, and within two decades, Constantinople produced its own raw silk, thus eliminating the Persian taxes and middlemen.[1] The excellent location of the city attracted merchants from all corners of the world, although the government fixed prices and charged for licenses to trade. State-run workhouses produced the silk that enriched the city throughout the seventh to the tenth centuries, after which other Greek cities produced their own.[2] With few exceptions, the purchase of silk outside the empire was prohibited.

The Byzantine economy was the most advanced in Europe and the Mediterranean for centuries. The city was a major hub in a trade network that at various times extended across much of Eurasia and North Africa, and it was the primary western terminus of the Silk Route. The Byzantine Empire exhibited an image of splendid opulence, and travellers were impressed by the wealth accumulated in the capital.

Imports into the city included spices, with pepper and ginger being two of the most important. Wheat imported from Egypt helped feed the people, but this source was lost in the seventh century due to the expansion of Islam. The city became one of the great entrepôts of the time, its maritime trade controlled by merchants from Italian cities such as Venice, Genoa, and Pisa. Byzantine wine also travelled north to Kiev and was reexported to Sweden, Poland, and northern Germany. Large quantities were exported for liturgical purposes after the Russians converted to Orthodox Christianity in 988.

Commercial life in the empire was a state concern, and the imperial government regulated trade and oversaw the building of factories, workshops, imports and exports, prices of goods, customs duties, wages, and so on. Responsible for the welfare of the citizens, the state inspected the quality and quantity of imports. Surpluses were exported for the benefit of the state coffers. The system provided the emperor, nobility, and church with desired luxury products.[3]

Constantinople's most prosperous period in the ninth century was mostly due to luxury goods. Corporations formed into various guilds were state controlled; bakers, for example, had to sell bread and pastries at a fixed price. Breach of guild rules could result in fines, banishment, or worse, but workers were not forced to belong and the door was open for freelancers to produce and sell their products. Slave labor was used extensively in imperial workshops and on government projects.

Luxury items were imported from India and China, and were considered state monopolies. Before the Chinese secret of its production became widely known, only members of the royal family were permitted to wear silk. Byzantine nobles were not averse to trade, and many were successful owning carpet or perfume factories, or selling produce from their estates.

A 10 percent tax was charged on items entering and leaving the city but much more on the small amounts of silk destined for export.[4] The restrictions persisted until silk manufacture became more widespread in the tenth century, when it was produced in provincial towns.

Both men and women were skilled workers, the latter often employed at home in the crafts of weaving and embroidering. Constantinople sometimes usurped trade from other cities: Antioch, for instance, once the center of the finest jewelry, gave way to the city on the Bosporus as the leading manufacturer of items of this nature. The gold coins of high value, minted in Constantinople, had much to do with the stability of the state. The coin maintained its worth until the ninth century.

The ships of the Byzantine Empire were of great importance to its prosperity. Space on the vessels was allocated equally between passengers and crew, although men were entitled to three times the space allotted for women.[5] Ships often sailed in convoy to offset the threat of Arab pirates. Merchant sailors who manned the ships often jointly owned them, unlike in Europe where wealthy merchants were generally the proprietors. A steward earned about two gold coins a month, enough to keep him and his family from starving, but little more. Italians were instrumental in the trade to and from Constantinople. About 24 days at sea were required for a Venetian galley to make landfall at the city's docks.

In the tenth century Constantinople became the recipient of a good deal of Slavic trade from Russia and the Ukraine. It came primarily down the Dnieper River and across the Black Sea, bringing furs, honey, wax, leather goods, and caviar to exchange for horses, wine, glass and metal objects, pepper, and church paraphernalia (after conversion to Christianity). Strict rules were imposed on the Russians, more so than other traders due to their belligerence when they attempted to conquer Constantinople in the previous century. The Russians, unlike other foreigners, of which there were about 60,000—mostly Italians—in the city, were forced to live outside the walls and were allowed in only when unarmed, through one gate, and accompanied by a Greek official. The most privileged traders were the Genoese.[6]

Merchants from Kiev were looked upon favorably due to a treaty signed in 907 that allowed them to forgo entry and exit duties. They received bread, wine, and other food gratuitously while in the city, special bath houses were assigned to them, and when they departed all equipment for their ships was provided. Like all other foreigners, they registered when they arrived and were allowed a three-month stay. Any goods not sold before the time of departure were given over to officials, who then sold them and handed over the money the next year the traders reappeared.

Life in Constantinople was pleasant enough for the upper classes and the well-to-do merchants who built fine houses with interior courtyards, gardens, baths, and servants' quarters, and were cut off from the noise of the streets by solid, windowless walls. For the poor, it was a different matter: they occupied tenement buildings and lived in crowded conditions. Squatters were common, erecting hovels wherever they could. In some of the worst slums, unbridled crime presented the authorities with unmanageable problems. By the ninth century, about a million people lived in the city.[7] The hippodrome, which could hold 40,000 spectators, and where sporting programs took place as well as more sinister events such as torturing prisoners, was the center of attraction for rich and poor.

Between the ninth and eleventh centuries when the empire was at its height, the country people remained no better off than in previous centuries. Generally living in a state of indigence, they detested the landlords and the tax collectors. Riots were not uncommon. These very people produced the food that major cities relied upon, yet they were little better off than slaves on the large estates of the rich. Country people, rich and poor, were always subject to raiders and crusaders, the latter supposed friends but who lived off the land with little thought for the farmer. The men and women who tilled the soil and the poor and the impecunious town dwellers saw little or no benefit from the greatest trade metropolis of the Western world. Jews, already persecuted in Christian lands, strongly participated in Constantinople's commerce, and although afforded equal civil rights with Christians, they were required to live in a special section of the city.

RISE OF ISLAM

To defend the empire, Byzantines often found themselves at war. Outposts in Spain and North Africa, inherited from the Roman Empire, were lost to Germanic tribes in the sixth century; Italy soon followed. Jerusalem fell to Persians in 613. By 640, Egypt, Palestine, and Syria were in Arab hands and Constantinople was attacked in 678 but weathered the storm and regained much of the Levant. At the same time, the Byzantines fended off Slavs and in the eleventh century, the Seljuk Turks posed an ominous threat to the Anatolian Peninsula from the East, while in the twelfth century, crusades from the West imperiled Constantinople and its surroundings, undermining its power. These struggles, coupled with murderous palace intrigues, slowly enfeebled imperial strength. With the rise of Islam in the seventh and eighth centuries, the Middle East and Central Asia became acquainted with the teachings of the Prophet and the Koran through Muslim merchants. Inroads into India and Southeast Asia followed. Islamic armies of the Umayyads and the later Abbasids contested the region of Western and Central Asia.

Umayyad Caliphate (661–750)

The death of Mohammad in 632 ushered in the Orthodox Caliphate and a sequence of four caliphs who were all close to the founder of Islam. Before his death in 644, the second, Omar, conquered Syria, the Levant, Egypt, and much of Persia. The last three Orthodox Caliphs were all murdered, sowing the seeds of dissension among Muslims. Upon the death of the last, Ali, the office of caliph passed to the Umayyad family, who set about further expansion of the faith among the Berber tribes of North Africa before crossing the straits into Spain in 711. In the East, Arab warriors pushed on to the Indus River, creating a huge empire. Many Muslims did not accept the Umayyad as successors to the Prophet due to the unpardonable sin of having slain in battle, in the year 680, Huysan Ibn Ali, the grandson of Mohammad.

In 750, a rebellion broke out, and the entire Umayyad family was slaughtered, save one, who escaped to Spain where he began a new Islamic kingdom. The destruction of the Umayyad dynasty was led by a descendent of Abbas, an uncle of the Prophet, hence, the name Abbasids. The consequences of the violent beginnings of Islam led to a schism in the religion. Those Muslims who believed that Huysan Ibn Ali was the rightful heir to the Prophet became known as Shi'ites; those who favored the Abbasids denied this and became the Sunni, or Orthodox, Muslims.

Abbasid Caliphate (750–1258)

The Abbasid power lay mostly in Persia, where they built the splendid city of Baghdad on the Tigris River. Baghdad developed a large business section where merchants gathered and sold perfumes from Arabia, silk from China, Syrian glassware, Indian rubies and silver, slaves from Russia and Africa, leather hides from distant Spain, and swords from various other places. The wealth

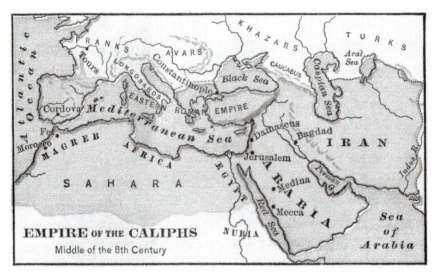

Map of the empire of the Arab caliphs, middle of the 700s. (North Wind Picture Archives.)

that flooded Baghdad was due to the city's fine location along caravan routes from China and India, and the Tigris River that accommodated ships from India and Arabia. Muslims encouraged trade, and moneychangers set up banks that offered merchants letters of credit called sakk. Throughout the Muslim world, the sakk from one bank could be turned in for cash at another, even one in a distant land. The word was taken into European languages as "check."

In Central Asia, the influence of the Abbasid Caliphate was at its height in the late eighth century and reached from North Africa to Transoxian, today's Uzbekistan. The commercial interest of the caliphate extended all the way to China and was due in large part to tolerance of nonMuslim subjects. From the capital at Baghdad, the caliph appointed a vizier to administer the government, who in turn selected governors to run the provinces and collect taxes. Qadis, or judges, were appointed to interpret Islamic law. A body of religious scholars helped decide public policy in accordance with Islamic principles. The Abbasids also established a large bureaucracy to handle commerce and security, making both internal and long-distance trade easier and less dangerous on the roads.

Increased commerce brought in more money in taxes, much of which was spent on ostentatious projects but also on improving trade and trade relations. One Abbasid caliph, Harun-al-Rashid (reigned 786–809) sent a number of presents, including an elephant, to Charlemagne of the Carolingian Empire in Europe.[8] To facilitate trade, banks were established through which men of commerce could secure loans, change currency, and cash bills of exchange, which allowed them to avoid carrying large amounts of coinage. Gold and silver dinars as well as silver dirham were used both at home and in long-distance trade.

Unrest in the provinces, civil war, and political intrigues weakened the empire after 809, and Turkish mercenary soldiers for the Abbasids became a strong and menacing force. By later in the tenth century, the caliph had become little more than a powerless symbol of Sunni Islam while real control lay among the tribes in the provinces. Turkish influence grew and came to a head in 1055 with a Seljuk revolt and the capture of Baghdad. They took over an enfeebled empire, but trade continued to flourish as local rulers promoted it, anxious to enhance their income. The rise of the Abbasids and the contemporary rule of the trade-friendly T'ang in China made East-West commerce much more expeditious. The T'ang capital at Chang'an (present-day Xian) developed into a great urban center, and Chinese westward expansion (for a time as far as Afghanistan) and the Abbasid eastward territorial enlargement facilitated the travel of many foreigners to China who could make the entire journey in the seventh and eighth centuries relatively free of unpleasant incidents along the way such as robbers or numerous customs posts. Not since the first century CE at the time of the Han, Parthian, and Roman trade network across Asia was the Silk Route so accessible.

KHAZARIAN EMPIRE (AROUND 650–960)

Farmers, craftsmen, nomads, merchants, and fishermen made up diverse ethnic groups but were all ruled by the Turkish Khazar clan that had converted to Judaism. Workshops throughout the kingdom manufactured numerous products for trading. Khazars controlled the rivers Don, Volga, Dnieper, and Severskya Donets. The capital city, Atil, on the Volga delta at the northern end of the Caspian Sea, was in an excellent position to capitalize on the trade route from the Baltic to the Byzantine and Islamic empires, and the east to west branch of the Silk Road.

Land routes connected the empire to Kiev, Baghdad, and Volga Bulgaria. Black Sea routes connected it to Constantinople and the

Levant, and the Caspian Sea route led to Baku and numerous ports in Persia. To the vital Khazarian junction came Vikings, Arabs, Turks, Chinese, Jews, and Persians. Ten percent of the value of goods was the normal import tariff collected by the king. Goods included such items as silverware, honey, candle wax, weapons, pottery, fur, silk, jewelry, cotton clothes, mirrors from China, paper from Samarkand, and coins from the Byzantine Empire. Goods exported to other locations were glass, fish, pottery, silver and gold wares, wine, jewelry, mirrors, spears, leather, slaves, cows, and sheep. Trade declined in the ninth and tenth centuries, taken over by the growing Islamic state of Volga Bulgaria and by the state of Kiev.[9]

While traders of many ethnic backgrounds engaged in commerce across Central Asia, the Jewish communities along the routes, tolerated by the Abbasids, played a large role in commerce. Called Radanites, they paid a special tax along with Coptic Christians within the Abbasid Empire, and their communities existed all along the trade networks. For a time, Jews pretty much controlled the East-West trade.[10]

Little is known about the state of affairs at the time of this somewhat obscure kingdom.[11] The Radanite trade diaspora lasted only about a century. It disappeared as the Chinese T'ang Dynasty turned inward and persecuted foreign religions, Abbasid power declined, and Tartars moving westward through Asia obstructed trade routes.

SELJUK TURKS (AROUND 1000–1300)

A Turkish tribe previously converted to Sunni Islam, moved westward out of Central Asia (Turkmenistan) in the latter part of the tenth century, and united under the leader Seljuk, taking their affiliation from his name. They established the Sultanate of Rum in Anatolia, with the capital first at Iznik and then at Konya. As cities on the Black Sea and the Mediterranean were seized from the hands of the Byzantines, the Seljuks prospered, especially during the twelfth and thirteenth centuries. Encouraging trade, they repaired old Roman roads for the benefit of travelers and offered a kind of state insurance for losses that traders might suffer along the routes.

They made efforts to protect traders by building caravanserais along the roads, including the ancient Silk Route. These were large walled rectangular precincts with space enough to give shelter to traders and their animals, and secure their goods from thieves. A small mosque was available for prayers. Repair shops and baths were also available. At the end of each day, caravans were received into the enclosure and were permitted to remain three days without charge. The caravanserais greatly facilitated the flow of goods from Central and western Asia to the Mediterranean port cities for further distribution. Along with other towns, Konya gained great wealth during the heyday of trade in the eleventh and twelfth centuries. Wealth pouring into the Seljuk Sultanate coffers gave them the means to subdue other states established in Asia Minor.

The Seljuk capture of Jerusalem, a most holy city for Christians and Muslims alike, inspired the First Crusade in 1095[12] and opened a new focal point in the history of trade. Christian pilgrims had, since the beginning of the faith, visited Palestine, but under Arab jurisdiction it became more difficult. With the Muslim Seljuks in possession, it was almost impossible.

CRUSADES

In 1095, Alexius I Comnenus, the Byzantine emperor, asked the Catholic Church synod taking place in Piacenza, Italy, for Western aid against the Seljuk Turks who were closing in on Constantinople from the east across Asia Minor. The pope called for a Holy War to recapture Jerusalem and the sacred places of Christianity. The European response was positive; nobles, knights, and the common people gathered in large numbers throughout Europe and set off on various routes to meet in Constantinople, where a force estimated at over 100,000 took the vows of a crusade.[13] They marched from the city through the hostile and sun-baked land of the Sultanate of Rum to the Levant, and on to the holy city of Jerusalem. Many died on the way from Seljuk ambushes, as well as from thirst and starvation. A mixture of religious fervor against Muslims and secular considerations of land and riches drove them on. Jerusalem fell in 1099, after a long siege, and the first Latin kingdom of Jerusalem was established under Baldwin I, a French nobleman. Further crusades followed to strengthen the Christian hold in the Levant. In 1104, the city of Acre, on the Mediterranean coast, fell into the clutches of the crusaders and became their main port in the region until the Muslims, under Saladin, retook it in 1187. Four years later, it was back under Christian jurisdiction. As the last stronghold of the crusader kingdom, it fell back to Muslims in 1291.

Meanwhile commerce was carried on across the Mediterranean and in Asia during the two centuries in which the Latins (or Franks, as the crusaders were called) struggled to maintain their hold in the Levant. Vessels carrying commercial cargo, pilgrims, or both set sail from European ports in early spring and returned in late summer before the winter weather arrived. The human traffic was highly regulated to ensure the safety of pilgrims, so much deck space was allotted to individuals for sleeping and for their luggage. The ships were regularly inspected, food and cooking were watched over, captains' duties were specified, and so forth.[14] In the Levant, crusaders created a feudal state in Palestine and Syria while the Italian cities shipped men and European goods to them for huge prices. They arranged with the new Christian crusader kings of Asia Minor to establish trading centers, and secured monopoly rights over trade and trade routes. Italian vessels returned from the East loaded with silks, spices, dyes, gems, carpets, and other goods for distribution throughout Europe.

The land route to Palestine was fraught with danger from Muslim Turks even before reaching Antioch. The army had to be supplied over this inhospitable ground by Venetian and Pisan ships. When important cities fell back into Muslim hands, a new crusade was begun. The Second Crusade in 1147 accomplished little and suffered an ignominious defeat at Damascus, and the third was initiated in 1189 and also accomplished little. One result of the Third Crusade was the conquest of Cyprus in 1191 that gave the crusaders a well-located base of supply to support their armies in Palestine.

To rescue Jerusalem from the Muslims, the Fourth Crusade was launched in 1202, but in 1204, instead of continuing their trek to fight the Muslims in the Holy Land, the rabble of crusaders occupied Constantinople and razed the city. These so-called Latins remained masters of Constantinople and its surroundings until 1261, when the imperial but nearly destitute Palaeologues family managed to regain the throne.

The looting and destruction of Constantinople has been attributed to Venetian avariciousness and treachery. Venice furnished ships for a price that the crusaders could not pay, but a deal was struck and the crusaders helped the Venetians destroy the city of Zara on the Dalmatian coast—a commercial competitor with Venice. This accomplished, the crusaders, with the connivance of Venice, went on to sack Constantinople, from which Venice acquired much of the spoils while diminishing the trading capacity of the city. This, in turn, allowed Venice more direct access to Eastern products.

Meanwhile, having been excluded from the fabulous booty of Constantinople, Genoa backed Enrico, Count of Malta, in his desire to become king of Crete. Crete was an ideal location for trade, and the Genoese were promised commercial sites in the Cretan towns. Before this could happen, however, the island passed to Venetian control and prompted the first of the hostile encounters between Venice and Genoa, which would result in fierce trade rivalry on the sea lanes to Acre.

ACRE

The port city of Acre, under the Arabs after 638, taken by crusaders in 1104 became the primary port of call in Palestine. Except for a brief interlude, it remained in crusader hands until 1291, when it again fell to the Muslims. Most traffic in goods from the West was unloaded in Acre, ranging from cloth to metals in exchange for precious stones, ceramics, spices, perfumes, and dyes. European products traveled from Acre throughout the Middle East.

Intermingling of Franks and Arab traders led to mutual distrust and animosities but generally did not break out into open conflict. Both converged on Acre in great numbers by ship and caravan as reported by Ibn Jubayr, who said[15] "Its roads and streets are choked by the press of men, so that it is hard to put foot to ground. Unbelief and impiousness there burn fiercely, and pigs [Christians] and crosses abound. It [the town] stinks and is filthy, being full of refuse and excrement." Ibn Jubayr lamented the fact that mosques had been turned into churches but found some solace in that Muslims were left a small corner of the churches for their own use. Friendly relations between Muslims and Christians often prevailed, and Christian ships were considered safer to travel in than others by both sides of the religious divide. On board, Muslims and Christians occupied their own parts of the vessel and refrained from interfering with one another. Passengers of both religions, unused to sea travel, often found themselves short of provisions after a short time, but as Ibn Jubayr mentioned, they could buy almost any kind of food on the ship from fish, bread, and cheese, to watermelon and figs, and most certainly water. Sailors expected shortages and came aboard with extra supplies to sell to a captive assembly.[16]

COMMERCIAL INDUCEMENTS FOR CRUSADERS

Although many crusaders went to the Holy Land to liberate it from the Muslims, there were at times other than religious motives. Two later crusades, one aimed at Egypt and the other at Tunisia, seemed to have been inspired to a large extent by economic motives. The King of Cyprus, Peter I, regarded the Mamluks of Alexandria as a threat to his commerce because they undercut Western trade that passed through Famagusta, the eastern Cypriot port city. He mounted a crusade that wreaked havoc on Alexandria but was forced to abandon the city a week later when a Mamluk relief army arrived. In 1389, a delegation from Genoa arrived at the French court and proposed a crusade to capture the Muslim Berber Hafsid port city of Mahdia in Tunisia, a pirate stronghold. A French army was assembled and transported to Mahdia in Genoese ships. Once landed, they unsuccessfully besieged the fortified city and were forced to withdraw. Before so doing, the Genoese signed a trade treaty with the Muslims of the beleaguered city.[17]

Both Muslims and Christians profited from mutual trade and although the term "holy war" was still much in vogue during the European occupation of the Holy Land, neither group was anxious to disturb the profitable incomes made from commerce. Truces, which often did not last long, were made for the sake of mutual trade.[18] Crusaders in fortified towns and castles in the thirteenth century controlled the coastal strips of the Levant. They were able to meet their needs from the fertile coastal lands and from the income generated by trade. Luxury items from the East sent overland to Muslim cities such as Damascus were then passed on to the Frankish ports for transshipment to Western Europe. The Frankish rulers of the Levant sustained military power through the profits of commerce, and paid their retainers and followers in cash rather than grants of land.[19]

Although Constantinople had been on the verge of collapse by the Fourth Crusade, commerce continued and grew. The fourteenth-century visitor to Constantinople Ibn Battutah noted that the Franks dwelt in the western section of the city and included Genoese, Venetians, Romans, and French—all men of commerce. He saw about 100 galleys in the port and small ships too numerous to count.

With the ejection of the crusaders from the Holy Land in the thirteenth century effectively ending the crusades, the Muslims reached their pinnacle of power in Asia. The arrival of Mongols in the thirteenth century, the devastating plague in the fourteenth, and the exploits of the Portuguese in the fifteenth, brought an end to Muslim domination of the commercial lanes east and west by land and sea.

NOTES

1. Previté-Orton, 199.
2. *EWT*, 218.
3. Rice, 121.
4. Rice, 128.
5. Wise, 138.
6. Wise, 140.
7. Wise, 14.
8. *EWT*, 1.
9. *EWT*, 559.
10. Curtin, 106.
11. Beckwith, 412.
12. Franck and Brownstone, 72.
13. Hallam, 17.
14. Hallam, 298.
15. Hallam, 185.
16. Abulafia, 311–13.
17. Hallam, 284.
18. Hallam, 284.
19. Hallam, 248.

7

MONGOL AND OTTOMAN EMPIRES

MONGOL EMPIRE (1207–1360)

About the beginning of the thirteenth century, Mongol tribes began to unite under the leader Genghis Kahn, who assembled the largest empire and controlled more land than any previous ruler. Genghis and his grandson, Kublai Khan, controlled lands from China in the East to the Levant in the West.

Destructive military campaigns by the Mongols gave no quarter when resistance was encountered, but little harm came to communities that chose to capitulate. The conquerors established administrations, invigorated trade, and assisted craftsmen. They patrolled the Silk Route, keeping banditry by rival nomadic tribes to a minimum, and in the cities were diligent about maintaining order.[1] Such protection came at a price through taxation. With the roads made safe, and foreign traders such as the Polo brothers welcomed, merchants felt secure. On their second trip to the East, along with young Marco Polo in 1271, the latter upon returning to Venice published his accounts of the journey that were read throughout Europe. The sojourn of 17 years related in his accounts describing the riches of the East stimulated the commercial appetite of Europeans.

Nomadic Mongol tribes had always depended on trade items to demonstrate rank and status, for instance, body ornaments or horse accouterments. The invasion of China in 1211 seems to have been the result of the Chinese limiting of trade with the Mongols in the hopes of gaining better terms.

Although initial offensives led to utter destruction of city, village, and farm, and trade slowed to a trickle as centers of commerce were devastated, the Mongols nevertheless valued trade and especially the taxes and tolls that could be collected from it. After the conquest of China, trade picked up again. One European observed that "a virgin riding a mule loaded with gold could travel the length of it [presumably the Silk Road] unmolested."[2] Post stations were established along the roads, as were caravanserais for merchants and travelers. Settlements again appeared across Asia whose inhabitants—Jews, Muslims, and Christians—fostered trade. The Mongols were impartial. They were equal opportunity tax collectors at 5 percent on all transactions.

Life in China under Mongol Rule

Areas devastated by war were rebuilt by the Mongols and furnished with storage buildings for surplus grain. Laws were promulgated prohibiting animals of nomads to trample on and feed in the peasants' fields. Mongol overlords helped peasants organize into cooperatives for better agricultural output and encouraged land reclamation, control of water resources, and (of great importance) more production of silk. Mongol initiatives to aid the peasant farmer seem to have been based on generating a surplus that in turn would lead to more taxable trade. In this connection, they engaged in public works such as improving the Grand Canal in China. The schemes alienated the peasants, however, since they were forced to labor for these projects. The situation for artisans was different. Considered an inferior class under Chinese rule, artisans were esteemed by the Mongols, who valued their work in painted ceramics, jade, porcelain, and metal, all of which were items of decoration in Mongol palaces, as well as for trade. Artisans were exempt from forced labor.

Break-Up of the Empire

In the fourteenth century the so-called Pax Mongolica began to disintegrate as trade dwindled due, in part, to seizure of lands in the western regions of the Silk Road by Turkish nomads from the Caspian Sea region. Internal feuds throughout the empire were not uncommon and contributed to its demise as trade networks suffered and became less secure. Insecurity on land also gave a boost to seaborne trade that further eroded land commerce through Mongolian territory. In the late fourteenth century, Mongol hegemony and power ended.

OTTOMAN TURKISH EMPIRE AND TRADE

Around the beginning of the fourteenth century, the Ottoman Empire was established under the leader Osman. This empire inherited the Seljuk trade routes and caravan stops. The significance of commercial enterprises and their importance to the empire were not lost on the Turks.

Government controls in the field of commerce were extensive, and taxes were levied on each transaction. Businessmen, including traders and captains of cargo vessels, were required to have licenses; the government even demanded to know when an employee departed a company for any reason. A *kadi*, or judge, watched over the marketplaces with authority to immediately discipline anyone caught deceiving the public or making more than 10 percent profit. Government priorities included fair trade and safety along the routes. Permits were required for foreign traders, and exports were carefully scrutinized and monitored.

Along with wool, skins and leather were primary exports, but specific items required for military use such as lumber for ship construction, certain minerals, and food products were seldom sent out of the country. Immigrants, many of whom were Jews driven out of Spain in 1492, were thought to be useful and were gladly received.

Travels of Ibn Battutah

Firsthand information on the Turks was recorded by the fourteenth-century Moroccan traveler Ibn Battutah on a visit to Anatolia (al Rum). He praised the people, saying:

> Wherever we stopped ... hospice or private house our neighbors, both men and women (who do not veil themselves) came to ask after our needs.[3]

He visited the city of al-Alaya (now Alanya, Turkey) on the Mediterranean coast where traders from Syria, Cairo, and Alexandria came to do business. The plentiful forests in the region provided much wood that was exported to Egypt.[4] From al-Alaya, he moved on to the city of Antaliyah (now Antalya on the coast of southwest Turkey), a large populous city for the time, where the inhabitants lived in separated sections: European Christian merchants occupied Al-Mina, where they were encircled by a wall whose gates were shut from the outside both at night and during the Friday Muslim prayer service. Other separated walled sections contained Greek Christians and Jewish traders. The ruler and his guards lived in still another compound. The Muslim population occupied the center of the town.

The city of Constantinople fell to the Ottomans in 1453, an accomplishment that dismayed and frightened Europeans, although the city was no longer of great importance since the Turks controlled most of the Anatolian peninsula to the east and the Balkans, including Greece, to the west. Between the fourteenth and sixteenth centuries, the Ottoman Empire came to encompass southeastern Europe, Anatolia, the Levant, and much of North Africa. Suleiman I the Magnificent, considered the greatest of the Ottoman rulers, completed the Ottoman expansion in 1559 by conquering most of Hungary. Further conquest was stopped by the unsuccessful siege of Vienna. Under theocratic Ottoman rule, Christians were not given equal status with Muslims. The head of state, the sultan, was also caliph, or supreme religious authority—God's representative on earth. Non-Muslims paid higher taxes, Christian churches had to be inferior in height to mosques, Christians could not wear the sacred color green, any kind of proselytizing was forbidden, and Christians could not carry arms. In some communities, they were obliged to dismount from their horses when a mounted Muslim approached from the other direction.[5]

Aspects of Trade

In general, Istanbul—previously Constantinople—and other cities were maintained by trade caravans whose departure and arrival dates were set to avoid too many goods at one time, which would affect local prices by swamping the market. Some caravans, however, functioned by regular schedules. There was one between Istanbul and Izmir every week, and another between Georgia and the capital every three months. Two a year arrived from Basra, and at various times from Aleppo and Persia.[6] The primary focus of the government was on food products for the people of the cities, especially Istanbul, and collecting as much duty as traffic would bear. Trades were generally composed of guilds and distinguished by their dress code. They were licensed and set standards, and the number of workplaces was regulated. Disputes were settled in their own guild halls. Money might be loaned by the guild to members in need. Five-year apprenticeships were normal and the neophytes, upon completion of the term, presented examples of their work to guild elders for approval in order to be accepted as a master. A government inspector collected the dues, supervised the work, and turned down and destroyed anything considered substandard. Guilds generally had a religious component as part of the initiation rites. A penchant for innovation seems to have been lacking, however, and they were often far behind their European counterparts in generating new products. France obtained trade rights with the Turks in 1534, as did England some three decades later. Queen Elizabeth chartered the Turkish Company to carry on exclusive commercial rights with the Ottoman Empire.[7]

Ottomans in the West (North Africa)

Turkish fleets became supreme in a Mediterranean that in the sixteenth century had become a dangerous place. The Barbary Coast, a name derived from the Berbers who inhabited the region, extended from Egypt (conquered by the Ottomans in 1517) to Morocco. The southern shores of the Mediterranean were occupied by semi-independent Muslim states under the sovereignty of the Ottoman Empire. The most important cities—Oran, Algiers, Tunis, and Tripoli—were hotbeds of pirates who preyed upon the commerce of European nations whose governments paid them protection money to refrain from attacking their ships.

Algiers became a primary center of corsair activities. Pirates dominated the sealanes and gained much wealth from stolen cargo, ransom money for kidnapped seafarers (whose families could pay), and bribes. Captured sailors with no means for ransom were made slaves. Although unknown at the time, Miguel Cervantes, whose fame would come later, was taken captive by pirates in the Mediterranean and imprisoned at Algiers. The city teemed with Berbers, renegades, adventurers, Spanish Muslims who had fled the country after the fall of Granada in 1492, work gangs of Christian prisoners, and—of course—seasoned pirates. Mistaken for a person of substance, Cervantes was put aside for a ransom that was beyond his family's ability to pay. He spent five years in captivity before family and friends could redeem him.

In the late eighteenth century, improved firepower and ship construction enabled Europeans to challenge corsair domination. By then, the days of Ottoman Algiers were fading, and international agreements to outlaw piracy made collective action feasible. In 1815, the United States, after paying protection money for years, sent a naval squadron against Algiers. The following year, an Anglo-Dutch fleet destroyed most of its defenses, and in 1830, a French army captured the city.

BLACK SEA AND CAFFA (KAFFA)

After the fall of Constantinople, Ottomans acquired control over Black Sea commerce and a large source of the food trade. They exported from Anatolia to the Black Sea ports of Caffa, Kilia, and Akkerman silk, cotton, copper, hemp, woolen cloth, figs, olive oil, and manufactured items. In return, they imported agricultural and animal products, slaves, salted fish, wheat, honey, beeswax, and alum. Caffa was one of the most important of the Ottoman depots. Before, in the thirteenth century under the Mongols, the city's trade was carried out by Venice. The Genoese arrived in the second half of the century and bought Caffa from the ruling Mongols. Genoese trade flourished as they monopolized Black Sea commerce with Caffa as the main port and center of administration for all their Black Sea trading colonies. It also became one of Europe's biggest slave markets. Caffa fell to the Ottomans in 1475 along with the small states and colonies around the region. By gaining control of the water routes between the Black Sea and the Mediterranean, the Ottoman sultan Mehmed II was in a position to demand that the Genoese colonies on the Black Sea recognize his authority and pay him tribute. Ottoman control terminated when the expanding Russian Empire acquired the Crimea in 1783.

The district of Galatea on the European side of Istanbul harbored Genoese and Florentines. Along with Istanbul, other Ottoman cities such as Izmir, Smyrna, Aleppo, and Alexandria attracted Venetians, French, Dutch, and British merchants, who came in significant numbers. Sicilians established colonies of merchants in the Balkans in such cities as Belgrade and Sarajevo. With the conquest of Egypt, Syria, Palestine, Rhodes, Aden, and Cyprus, the Ottomans controlled the eastern Mediterranean cities in the sixteenth century. Many European countries signed commercial treaties with them between the fifteenth and the eighteenth centuries.

Decline of the Ottoman Economy

Among the many reasons for the waning of the empire (demands for independence by non-Turkish ethnic groups such as Greeks, Albanians, Armenians, and others; government corruption; and wars), one was changing patterns of trade. During the heyday of the Ottoman Empire, most trade between Asia and Europe passed through Ottoman territory, but innovations in shipping allowed European traders, with the Portuguese as pathfinders, to bypass the empire by circumnavigating Africa by sea. The Ottoman Empire shifted from being an exporter of manufactured and Eastern goods to a producer of raw materials for European industry. Diverse parts of the empire provided different commodities: Lebanon became a center of silk production; Syria, once a great steel producer, grew foodstuffs; and Egypt became one of the world's major producers of cotton.

Throughout much of the nineteenth century, European states were eager to keep the Turkish empire as a producer of inexpensive raw materials which fed European industries, and to sell finished products back to the empire. [8]

After World War I, with Turkey on the losing side, the Treaty of Versailles dismantled the empire, and Turkey lost all its possessions. Under the leadership of Mustafa Kemal Ataturk, the country made significant economic progress and remained neutral during most of World War II. With the threat of Communist Russia after the war that had designs on Turkey's eastern provinces and the Dardanelle Straits, the Turks entered an alliance with the United States. In 1952, it became a member of the North Atlantic Treaty Organization (NATO) and in 1995 a member of the World Trade Organization.

Currently, Turkey's major exports include clothing, agricultural products, oil, gemstones, tobacco, and electronic equipment. Imports embrace appliances, optical instruments, and pharmaceuticals. Major trade partners have been the United States, European countries, and Russia. Since the 2008 financial crisis, Turks have stepped up trade with Central Asian, Middle Eastern, and African countries. Trade with the Organization of Islamic Countries (OIC) has also been increasing.

NOTES

1. *EWT*, 558.
2. *EWT*, 675.

3. Mackintosh-Smith, 102.
4. Mackintosh-Smith, 102–3.
5. Crampton, 30ff.
6. Lewis (1971), 177.
7. For more detail, see, http://ottomanempire.info/economy.htm
8. See http://www.countriesquest.com/middle_east/turkey/history/ era_of_modern_reform/european_sabotage.htm.

8

RED SEA AND GULF OF ADEN

Two Arabian cities were prominent in ancient times, Aden (Yemen) on the Gulf of Aden near the southern entrance to the Red Sea, and Petra (Jordan) near the northern end. The city of Aden was a collection and transfer point in the early trade diaspora that commercially united Africa, Asia, southern Arabia, and Europe. Similarly, Petra (of the Arab Nabataeans) was a dispersal point for goods from the south headed for Egypt, the Levant, and Europe. The Incense Route (mentioned earlier), about 2,000 kilometers long, connected the two cities, one route overland by caravan, another by maritime transport.

INCENSE ROUTE

From the third century BCE to the fourth century CE, control of overland commerce in resins (mostly incense and myrrh) from Somalia and transported north overland along the Arabian side of the Red Sea, brought prosperity to the ruling elite and many merchants. Incense was extensively used throughout the Middle East for religious rites and in Egypt for the process of embalming. Both had a variety of other uses, including in perfumes and medicines, to disguise unpleasant odors and drive away malevolent spirits, and in religious ceremonies to please the gods with their aromas. Both were burned on altars in temples, public and private, of which there must have been many tens of thousands. Both resins were in steady demand.

Overland routes that connected the northern and southern sections of the Red Sea were mostly dusty desert trails between poor villages and watering holes. To attract traders, some rulers paved a few kilometers of road over the worst patches. Trade was not only good business for the merchants, but it also brought great profit for the rulers who collected entry and exit fees on goods passing through their kingdoms.

SABAEAN KINGDOM

During the first century BCE, Egypt and Syria had fallen to Rome. Ever more desirous of luxury goods such as silk, pearls, spices, dyes, cotton, and ivory, trade with the East was inhibited by Rome's enemy, the Parthian Empire. The Red Sea route to the Gulf of Aden and on to India and beyond to China was one way to circumvent the Parthians and their substantial tolls on goods passing through their lands. However, the Sabaean kingdom in ancient Yemen, with the capital at Ma'rib, controlled the lucrative trade at Aden. The Romans referred to the region as Arabia Felix due to its comparatively high level of civilization and prosperity, most of which came from trade. Arab and Indian merchants carried out much of the sea trade with India across the Indian Ocean. Indian ships sailed to Aden but generally no further, where Arab traders took over the cargos and sent them north to Cairo and Petra, whence they were shipped on via Gaza to Alexandria at the mouth of the Nile River and where they might cross the Mediterranean to Europe.

With Egypt in their clasp after 30 BCE, the Romans established a foothold on the Red Sea near Jiddah, took Ma'rib briefly, and attacked Aden along with taking command of direct trade with India and thus eliminating the Arab middlemen. The Roman military was soon forced to withdraw from southern Arabia back to Egypt due to disease, Arab resistance, and overextended supply lines.

Roman ships, at least those financed by Romans, sailed from Egypt to India directly. The Greek geographer Strabo reported that 120 ships left Egyptian ports for India annually. Trade contacts between the West and East declined during the third century CE with the demise of the Han Dynasty of China in 220, along with the Kushan Empire in northwest India.

YEMEN AND ADEN

During the summer months with the winds from the north favorable, merchants sailed down the Red Sea to the Gulf of Aden, where they sold their goods, or sailed with the summer monsoon winds across the Indian Ocean to India. Sailors and merchants frequently risked their lives to travel this dangerous route, for a successful voyage could mean significant wealth. During the first millennium CE, prosperous states arose along the commercial corridor of the Red Sea. After the fall of Rome, the Byzantines held sway over some Red Sea ports such as Berenike, but in the sixth century, they abandoned them and withdrew north to Sinai.

ISLAM

With the rise of Islam in the seventh and eighth centuries, Muslim merchants took control of Red Sea commerce, the Gulf of Aden, and the routes across the Indian Ocean to India, Ceylon, and beyond to Southeast Asia. They spread Islam and Arabic culture across the vast stretches of the southern seas and along with converted Indian merchants and Hindu traders, maintained a tight grip on commerce until the sixteenth century.

With regard to Aden, Marco Polo wrote:

> ...Aden is ruled by a sultan. The people are all Saracens, worshippers of Mohammed and mortal enemies of Christians. There are a great many cities, but Aden is the port where the ships put in from the Indies, laden with merchandise. At Aden, cargos are transferred into smaller boats capable of sailing up-river for seven days. After seven days the goods are loaded on to camels which carry them on for a further thirty days until they reach the Nile, down which they sail to Alexandria. This is how the Saracens of Alexandria are supplied with pepper, spices and other rare goods, which cannot reach them more safely or more quickly by any other route.[1]

Marco Polo also wrote about other aspects of trade along the shores of the Gulf of Aden from which a great number of ships laden with cargo left for India. Arab horses were one of the popular items, as a horse sold in India for an exorbitant 100 silver marks. Polo also mentioned the Sultan of Aden, who made a great deal of money by taxing the many ships sailing in and out of the port.

Situated about 700 kilometers northeast of Aden, the city of Shirhr also had a fine port from which merchants sent many ships to India with cargos of horses. The local people had an abundance of dates and cultivated fine white incense, but they needed to import grain. They lived mostly on rice, meat, fish, and milk. Since there was little vegetation, the cattle, sheep, camels, and horses were fed small fish. Large tuna abounded in the sea and could be purchased from fishermen for very little money. They were chopped up and mixed with a kind of flour and then dried in the sun to make biscuits. Wine was made from dates, rice, and sugar. Incense was purchased by the local sultan on behalf of his overlord, the Sultan of Aden, who resold it for four times the price he paid for it. Marco Polo considered the Sultan of Aden one of the richest men in the world.

Further along the coast to the northeast lay Dhofar (now in Oman), also under the rule of the Sultan of Aden. It, too, was a busy commercial city involved in shipping incense and horses to India. Still further along this coast lay Kalhat, also once a bustling port engaged in the Indian trade. According to Marco Polo, the residents lived off salted fish and dates, although the rich had access to more refined food.[2]

Just across the Strait of Hormuz was the strategic city of Hormuz (now in Iran), also with a fine port where Marco Polo witnessed Indian ships laden with cargos of spice, precious stones, pearls, gold cloth, and elephant ivory. In addition, he mentioned the unbearable summer heat from which residents escaped by standing in the river and streams, and the leaky, dangerous boats constructed with planks sewn together. Other visitors found the city to be a den of iniquity where every imaginable vice was practiced and every conceivable sin committed. Saint Francis, who visited the city, was shocked.

Meanwhile, the Red Sea was growing more dangerous. Besides the many uncharted reefs that could quickly scuttle a ship, pirates lurking in coves had few scruples about doing what the reefs did not. Pilots who knew the waters, as well as armed men, were needed for a safe voyage. While pirates may not have been plentiful there compared to many other places, the crusader Reynauld de Châtillon built a small fleet at Aqabah in 1182 and terrorized the coasts of the Hijaz. He plundered the city of Aydhab, where he slaughtered a merchant caravan and commandeered ships.[3]

Sailing north against the prevailing winds was time consuming, which was the primary reason that land caravan routes ran parallel to the sea on the Arabian side. It was easy for sailing ships to travel south with the winds, but Jiddah was about as far as large ships cared to go northward. The Muslim hold on trade, first by the Arabs and then by the Ottoman Turks, remained firm until the sixteenth century when better built Portuguese ships with superior firepower made Muslim control of the Indian Ocean untenable. The rise and decline of cities and states, from grand prosperity to poverty-stricken backwaters was often due to shifts in trade.

Muslim trade diminished in the sixteenth century when the Portuguese set out to control seaborne commerce with the East, turning the Red Sea region, and especially Yemen, into an economic backwater. The only world commodity left to Yemen at the time was coffee, a monopoly that continued for several more centuries.

To contain Portuguese progress in the Indian Ocean, the Turks seized the port of Massawa (now in Eritrea) at the entrance to the Red Sea on the African side. Portuguese access to trade in the Red Sea and Ethiopia was thus cut short. The Ottomans failed to gain hegemony over the Indian Ocean, however. In 1513, the Portuguese under Albuquerque attacked Aden with 20 ships and over 2,000 men. After four days of siege, they were repulsed, and the admiral departed after sinking the Muslim ships in the harbor.

ADEN "HOSPITALITY"

In 1609, Aden, under the Turks, was visited by the *Ascension*, a ship of the British East India Company. At first pleasantly welcomed, the captain was then escorted off to prison, where he remained while his ship was stripped of all goods. The Dutch East India Company sent Captain Van den Broeck to the city, where he was warmly received but soon understood that he, too, was not wanted and hastily departed back to India. In 1609, Henry Middleton, a director of the British East India Company, landed in Mokha (Mocha) on the Red Sea, where he seemed to be welcomed but was subsequently arrested by Turkish officials and imprisoned. Some of his crew were killed. Fear of the British stemmed from the idea that they would take over the trade from India, thus depriving local merchants of their livelihood. Middleton escaped and sailed away.[4]

In 1618, the English obtained permission to set up a trading post at Mokha. Four years later, in 1622, the Dutch East India Company also entered the coffee trade at Mokha.

MOKHA (MOCHA) COFFEE

Coffee trees appear to have originated in the highlands of Ethiopia, and the beans seem to have been first brewed in the

Yemeni port city of Mokha in the late fourteenth century. In Arabia, it was considered medicinal and used in religious rites, but eventually it passed into the public domain as a desired beverage. Pilgrims to Mecca spread coffee throughout the Islamic world, and coffee houses began to flourish in Muslim societies where there were no taverns, since the use of alcohol was prohibited in the Koran.

At first, the Arabs refused to allow the seeds to leave their domains without first being boiled or parched so that they would not grow elsewhere. According to Indian folklore, an Indian Muslim pilgrim called Babu Budan smuggled some back to India where they grew, matured, and spread. There is no documentary proof of this, however.[5] Dutch traders carried seeds from the Malabar Coast in India to Java and established coffee plantations there.

Turkish emissaries to France and Austria introduced wealthy Europeans to the exotic drink about 1665. In 1683, when the Ottoman army hastily abandoned its futile second siege of Vienna, leaving behind sacks of coffee beans, the Viennese gathered them up and, by adding milk and honey to the thick, black, bitter brew, made it more palatable to European tastes. Coffee houses sprang up and soon became popular meeting places throughout the city.

In 1708, the Frenchman Jean de la Roque, in command of three ships of the French East India Company, sailed around the tip of Africa to Mokha and returned with a cargo of coffee beans—the first French direct purchase of coffee, which eliminated high overland costs and middlemen. Blended with coffee beans now grown in Java, brought there by the Dutch, the drink was then called Mocha-Java.[6]

The Dutch supplied Louis XIV of France with an entire tree from Mokha, and the first greenhouse in Europe was constructed to contain it. (The tree cannot resist frost.) Seeds from this botanical garden in Paris were then transported to slave plantations in Haiti, where they could be cultivated at less expense than those in Mokha. The price of coffee, as to be expected, fell dramatically, and consumption of the drink, well within reach of the common purse, rose substantially.

The trees eventually found their way to Central and South America about 1720 via Martinique in the Caribbean. There is a story, unverified, that on the transatlantic crossing, the ship ran low on water and all the seeds but one died. The Frenchman caring for them, Mathiew de Clieu, shared half his meager water ration with the one remaining seed. The spindly shoot reached Martinique to become the ancestor of millions of coffee trees.

The self-pollinating trees were later introduced into Brazil, Mexico, the Indian Ocean region, East Africa, and elsewhere. Each country zealously guarded its treasured trees and seeds. The emperor of Brazil, for example, wanting to cash in on this trade, sent Francisco de Melo Palheta to French Guiana to obtain seeds, but he was refused. Undaunted, he seduced the French governor's wife, who then gave him, upon departure, all the seeds he needed, buried in a bouquet of flowers, to begin Brazil's huge coffee industry.[7]

Slave coffee plantations in the New World produced coffee cheaper than Yemen's artisans, and the price fell in the British North American colonies from 18 shillings a pound in 1683 to one shilling in 1790. Brazil then became the leading producer and with good harvests, stored the surplus beans in warehouses to maintain prices. During the depression of the 1930s, excess Brazilian coffee was dumped in the ocean or burned. Columbia then stepped in and expanded its world market share.[8]

WORKERS AND TRADERS

The current major world-producing coffee countries (in order of importance) are Brazil, Vietnam, Columbia, and Indonesia. By the end of the 1980s, retail coffee sales were about $30 billion, of which coffee exporting countries received $10 billion. In 2002, exporting countries received less than $6 billion from retail sales that totaled $55 billion annually as figured by the International Coffee Organization. While traders, wholesalers, and retailers made money, the producers remained at or near poverty. Higher prices to growers and environmentally friendly conditions have been the goals of the proponents of Oxfam and Fair Trade.

Estimates concerning the number of people dependent on the coffee trade vary widely. The *Wall Street Journal* estimated some 124 million in 2002; Fair Trade reported 100 million, and the World Bank gave a figure of direct and indirect involvement at 500 million throughout the world. Calculations of the Dow Jones Commodity Services concluded that 300,000 people have jobs in Italy's 110,000 coffee shops serving 70 million cups of coffee per day.[9] In the United States, the coffee trade, worth $19 billion a year, has 150,000 full- or part-time employees serving 161 million consumers. Counting related industries such as companies that make Styrofoam cups, coffee machine servicers, and others, the number jumps to about 1.5 million. Whatever the exact figures amount to, it is clear that coffee occupies an enormous place in world markets. When the price of coffee drops significantly, it leaves in its wake hundreds of thousands of unemployed people, leading to impoverishment and social disorder.[10] The coffee companies now reap enormous profits making the coffee trade second only to that of the petroleum industry.

COFFEE PLANTATIONS

While the Spanish conquest of Central and South America was underway, coffee was introduced in the early eighteenth century by the Dutch in Surinam and the French on Hispaniola. Its cultivation required workers, and the near extinction of the indigenous people through war, diseases, and abuse left a gap that was to be filled by black slaves from Africa, ferried across the ocean by the millions to the New World beginning in the sixteenth century. Slave laborers on the plantations—first sugar and cotton—mostly lived in abject misery. Human life was worth little; profit was everything. When coffee seeds arrived, black slave labor was already entrenched. Coffee trees spread throughout the Caribbean quickly—by the English in Jamaica in 1730, the Spanish in Cuba a few years later, along with mainland Central and South America. In 1572, the Portuguese introduced it in Brazil, where more slaves were imported from Africa to work the plantations that grew and proliferated. For every slave sent to North America, 15 went to Brazil.

Slaves who survived the sea voyage worked from sunup to after sundown and were severely whipped for any show of idleness. Torture or death awaited those who were particularly recalcitrant. The horrors of the lives of slaves were repeated on plantations everywhere, whether they were sugar, tobacco, cotton, chocolate, or coffee.

COFFEE HOUSE CULTURE

From its lowly origins in Ethiopia and Yemen, coffee changed the nature of European society. An inevitable outcome for such a popular drink was the large number of coffee houses that were established to attract specific clientele, the first opening in London in 1652. In Vienna, London, and Paris, people met in these establishments to discuss the topics of the day and read the newspapers, their conversation stimulated by mind-enhancing caffeine. Men of similar interests gathered in coffee houses and began associations, for example, the insurance underwriter Lloyds of London arose from informal meetings in Lloyd's coffee house. The East India Company used the Jerusalem coffee house as its unofficial headquarters.[11]

In Paris, the aroma of fresh coffee emanating from a Turkish stall at the market of Saint-Germain attracted the curious to sample what they already knew the aristocrats enjoyed. Soon, refugees from the Ottoman Empire set up coffee houses throughout the city. The first shipment of coffee beans from Mokha by the Dutch arrived in Holland in 1616, and the first commercial shipload was sold in Amsterdam in 1640 by a German merchant.[12] Most of the coffee beans used in Northern Europe came via Amsterdam until about 1660.

DEMISE OF ADEN

With its corrupt governments and avaricious officials, cargo ships looking to offload their wares came to see Aden as an option less attractive than other Red Sea ports such as Mokha. The once fortified and trade-rich city degenerated into ruin. The British seized Aden in 1839, claiming it was a nest of pirates that threatened maritime trade with India. The English Captain Haines described its condition when it became British:

> The little village (formerly the great city) of Aden is now reduced to the most exigent condition of poverty and neglect. In the reign of Constantine, this town possessed unrivalled celebrity for its impenetrable fortifications, its flourishing commerce, and the glorious haven it offered to vessels from all quarters of the globe. But how lamentable is the present contrast! With scarce a vestige of its former proud superiority, the traveller values it only for its capabilities, and regrets the barbarous cupidity of that government under whose injudicious management it has fallen so low.[13]

Yemen is now one of the poorest and least developed countries with over half the population unemployed. The economy relies heavily on the little oil and gas it produces from rapidly diminishing oil fields.

SADANA ISLAND SHIPWRECK

A large ship capable of carrying some 900 tons of cargo sank off Sadana Island in the Red Sea in the reef-studded waters a little after 1764. European ships such as this one brought Chinese or Indian goods to trade at Mokha or Jiddah for coffee. Transferred to Muslim vessels, the coffee was then taken to Suez and on to further destinations. The cargo excavated from the wreck confirms what was traded at the time and the course of the ship. It was carrying thousands of fragile porcelain cups and saucers from China, goods such as spices and shells from the islands of the Indian Ocean, and coffee beans and incense from southern Arabia. Judging from personal items found, the ship was Egyptian and sailed by a Muslim crew. It was probably headed for Suez.[14]

As navigational techniques improved, so did confidence in maritime commerce on the Red Sea as well as elsewhere. Trade diminished considerably for the southern kingdoms as the expensive land route gave way to the cheaper sea route. Goods that once arrived from India to be transported by land along the coast of the Red Sea no longer needed to unload and shift to pack animals—they sailed straight up the Red Sea passage.

OTHER ITEMS OF TRADE

In ancient times, much of the trade across the Red Sea from Africa to Arabia was in the form of raw materials and slaves. The busy port of Adulis, now a ruined site in Eritrea, lies about 30 miles south of Massawa. From Adulis were exported spices, ivory, rhinoceros horn, and tortoise shell; received in exchange were cloth, spears, axes, and swords. In medieval times, thousands of slaves were exported from Abyssinia (Ethiopia) to Arabia. Slaves, including many Nubian women, were the principle export from Africa to Aden. This commerce continued into early modern times of the fifteenth and sixteenth centuries. More than slaves and animal products were shipped from Africa to Arabia, however, and other goods included food substances such as many types of grain that were grown in Ethiopia and carried to the coast at Massawa and shipped to Jiddah, Mecca, and other Arabian cities.[15] Arabian exports to Africa arrived primarily at Massawa, some originating in Egypt, India, and Europe.

NABATEAN KINGDOM

One of the beneficiaries of the north-south trade along the early caravan route were the Arab Nabateans who earned their living from the trade they controlled at the northern end of the Red Sea.[16] Nabataean commercial settlements were found as far away as Damascus and south along the Red Sea. Their capital at Petra grew prosperous between the fourth century BCE and the second century CE. The Nabatean kingdom was annexed by Rome in 105 CE to become the province of Arabia Petra. Its good position relied on land-based commerce to and from Gaza and Alexandria, the cities of the Levant, and from Mesopotamia and southern Arabia. As Red Sea trade picked up at the beginning of the Common Era, Petra capitalized on it with its port city of Eilat at the end of the Gulf of Aqaba and the port of Leuce Come down the Red Sea coast. From the latter, goods from the south and from India could be conveyed to Petra by camel, donkey, or mule caravans. Ancient writers refer to Leuce Come as a busy Red Sea market town that served as a major transit hub for spices, gems, and other goods en route to the Mediterranean from Arabia Felix or modern-day Yemen. Its ancient location is still unknown.[17]

Petra's merchants sold products in the West that included sugar and spices, exotic animals, ivory, metals, oil and medicines, perfumes, pearls, cotton, silk, and gold. The Nabateans exported to India and China gold and silver, glass, orpiment, asbestos, henna, storax, cloth, and damask, among other items. Romans and Nabateans jointly established a few troops and a customs office at Leuce Come, where duty on luxury goods was set at 25 percent.

The successful commercial empire of Nabataea kept trade routes and sources as secret as possible, holding a monopoly on many of the trade goods. According to Strabo, the Nabateans were governed by a king and royal family, all people shared in needed work, and no slaves were kept. Some maintained sheep, goats, and camels. Suddenly, building stopped due to unknown reasons except that Palmyra (Syria) grew in importance as it attracted trade away from Petra. In the first century BCE, Palmyra flourished as a caravan stop and by the middle of the first century CE, the city became wealthy from trade. It controlled the Indian silk trade on the caravan route, linking China, India, Persia, and the Roman Empire. It continued to amass wealth until its decline began in 212, when the Sasanids took control of the Persian Gulf. Petra was overrun by the Muslims in the seventh century and gradually fell into ruins.

The construction of the Suez Canal (completed in 1869) revitalized the Red Sea route between Asia and Europe, thus giving the British, who controlled the canal and Aden, great influence over Red Sea shipping with a presence at both ends. Even in the twenty-first century, pirates are still a threat to shipping in the Gulf of Aden.

NOTES

1. Quoted from Waugh, 179.

2. Waugh, 182.

3. Lunde and Porter, 13.

4. Wild (2004), 79–80.

5. Wild (2004), 98.

6. *EWT*, 186.

7. Davids, 15–19; Wild (2004), 172. This story seems to be a Brazilian invention.

8. *EWT*, 186.

9. For these figures see Wild (2004), 1–2.

10. Wild (2004), 2–3, looking at world statistics from the 1990s, concludes that from coffee sales of around $55 billion, only $7 billion, or thirteen percent, goes to the exporting nations.

11. Wild (2004), 86.

12. Wild (2004), 82.

13. See http://www.globalsecurity.org/military/world/yemen/aden -history.htm.

14. The above is taken from Lunde and Porter, 165–170.

15. Pankhurst, 19–22.

16. Hourani, 20.

17. Schoff, 101, 103.

9

MEDIEVAL EUROPE

By about 500, the Western Roman Empire had splintered into numerous Germanic kingdoms: Ostrogoths ruled in Italy, Visigoths in Spain, Franks in Gaul, Vandals in North Africa, and many smaller Germanic geographical political entities controlled areas throughout Europe. Roman armies and administration were no longer available to police the seas and roads, and Germanic tribes were often at war with one another, seafaring pirates grew in strength, highwaymen increased in numbers, commerce on land and sea faded away to a trickle, and towns, no longer centers of trade, were abandoned. With little in the way of commercial exchange, people left the towns to seek a living in the countryside and support themselves from the land.

Along the rivers and trade routes, local petty chieftains imposed duties on whatever goods might pass through their domains; and with the high costs of tolls, plus those of armed men to accompany and guard commercial travelers and their products, long-distance trade stagnated in the West. The Romans left behind a system of excellent roads crisscrossing the landscape, however, that helped maintain trade contacts between cities.[1]

Even the great city of Rome shrunk to about 5 percent of its highest population after the city was sacked in 410 by Visigoths and in 455 by Vandals.[2] In the ninth century, an increase in trade began to take place in Northern Europe between the British Isles, the Baltic Sea communities, and the Carolingian Empire under the Franks.

By the eleventh century, travelling along commercial routes once again became more secure. Mediterranean commerce gathered momentum as Amalfi, Genoa, and Pisa began to control the seas around them in the western Mediterranean, to the detriment of both Muslim and European pirates. Venice extended its contacts in the eastern Mediterranean, carrying on commerce with Alexandria, Constantinople, and Beirut. After a long period of decline, Eastern goods, such as spices, began to appear once again in Europe as far north as England.

Trade routes stretched from Northern Europe to the Mediterranean: from the forests of the Baltic came timber, furs, and skins; the English sold woolen garments, the Dutch offered salted herring, Spain produced wool, and France exported salt. Southern Europe was rich in wine, fruit, and oil, and Italian and German cities straddling trade routes promoted and financed the business.

By the late Middle Ages, some enterprising men were able to make fortunes: Francesco Datini (1335–1410), Italian banker and merchant, lost his family to the bubonic plague. He moved from Italy to Avignon in 1350, where he remained for 32 years and amassed a fortune from trade. At the time, the papacy resided in Avignon, and Datini made his fabulous wealth providing religious articles, cloth, armor, jewelry, and imported Florentine paintings that were in great demand. In 1378, he moved back to Italy along with the pope and opened a cloth manufacturing business, establishing his headquarters in Florence. In time, he opened other offices in Italy, Barcelona, Bruges, and London and opened a bank to underwrite insurance contracts, and made money in the silk trade. As a banker, he inevitably ran into conflict with the Catholic Church, which resisted the idea of profiting from interest charged on a loan. His commercial empire ranged from the Black Sea to the north of England.[3]

ENGLAND

When the Roman armies abandoned England at the beginning of the fifth century to protect against invading Germanic tribes closer to home, they left the Celtic tribes on their own.

From northern Germany and southern Denmark, Angles, Saxons, Jutes, and some Frisians settled in southeastern Britain, driving the

Celts into remote western and northern regions of the island (Cornwall, Wales, and Scotland). The new settlers were mostly farmers and carried on local trade. Clans fought among themselves, but eventually the country was somewhat pacified and united under Alfred the Great, King of Wessex (871–899). Fishing was an important industry in coastal towns, which fostered trade. As elsewhere, slaves, often Celtic prisoners of war, provided a lucrative business, with a major slave trade center at Bristol whence they were often sent to Ireland.

For monasteries and farms alike, a surplus of produce in a good year allowed the monks or farmers to take it to the local market and exchange it for needed items that they could not make themselves such as salt, metal implements, pottery, building blocks, and certain spices. Seafood from streams or the coast, salted or otherwise, was usually available on a local basis, along with vegetables and meat. Exotic items, including spices, wine, glassware, jewelry, and weapons, came from beyond the shores and were too expensive for the average person.

Marketplaces were generally established by the king or the lord of the district, and fees were collected for stall space. All transactions were taxed. In the countryside, highwaymen were often lurking along the roads ready to rob the trains of packhorses unless armed guards accompanied the merchandise. More appealing than soggy country roads for distance transport, the rivers offered cheaper and more secure passage, and many market towns were founded in the vicinity of such waterways. Before the advent of credit, merchants paid cash or traded in kind for the goods. Most buying and selling took place on a seasonal basis between spring planting and fall harvesting. Silver pennies were minted in a few places, but not many filtered down to the lower classes, whose trading was primarily for needed items and not for profit. Merchants were employed by estate owners to perform transactions for cereals, livestock, required tools, and sometimes luxuries.

Geographical considerations played a role in demography and commerce. The north of England, for example, was more sparsely settled and less suitable to agriculture than the south. By the time of the Norman invasion of England in 1066, London was again a thriving commercial city after earlier Viking raids had destroyed it. English seaports traded with the European continent, and desirable Anglo-Saxon coinage was employed far afield. Products traded across the channel were cheese, pottery, wool, textiles, salt from tidal flats, silver, lead, and iron.

TRADE FAIRS

A great attraction during the Middle Ages for merchant traders, peasants, and aristocracy were the commonly held trade fairs. Merchants came from far and wide to sell and buy at these functions that were held on special days of the year at designated locations. At these large markets, one could buy just about everything from livestock, kitchen ware, spices, clothes, shoes, and fabrics to leather goods, cooked food, and farm tools, and be entertained by musicians, puppet shows, fortune tellers, acrobats, jugglers, competitive games, gambling, and much more. They were colorful affairs with banners flying, flag-draped stalls, and cheap wine and ale readily available. For financial aid to recover from some disaster, towns were sometimes granted a fair that would bring in revenue. It might be held on the village green or in nearby fields, but the primary goal of any fair was to promote commerce. In Paris, pilgrims came by the thousands every June to see a piece of the "true cross" in Notre Dame Cathedral. To take advantage of this mass gathering, merchants set up their stalls in the nearby streets and in open spaces, in effect, creating a large exhibition that attracted performers from all over the country. As early as 629, the king of France, Dagobert, granted the monks of the abbey of Saint Denis near Paris the right to hold a fair. The monks collected dues levied on transactions, and no trade could take place except at the fair.[4]

Merchants often traveled between villages and towns to peddle their wares at the gates or in courtyards, and fairs were no doubt a welcome opportunity. After the eleventh century, a time of economic growth in Europe, fairs began to proliferate along well-used routes, at river landings and in port cities. Some of the most prominent were established in Champagne in the heart of Europe, where the royal court protected traders, charged low taxes, and set up law courts where disputes could be promptly resolved. To these fairs in the twelfth and thirteenth centuries, merchants came from as far away as the Middle East and Africa. Also of great importance were the six-week fairs of Provins and Troyes, where just about everything from gold to fish and beer was available. Italians introduced the bill of exchange in the twelfth century—a written promise to pay a debt at some future time.[5]

Some towns regulated space for fairs outside the town limits, but elsewhere it took over the entire city as it did, for example, at Medina del Campo in north central Spain. Held three times a year, the premises of the fair were the town itself. Merchants did not carry large amounts of coin to the trade fairs where, as at Medina del Campo and other important fairs such as Frankfurt, Lyon, and Beaucaire, bankers turned up and kept track of the transactions on paper and debited or credited the merchants' accounts accordingly. About 2,000 merchants were in regular attendance at Medina del Campo along with about 15 bankers. In a similar manner, millions of *scudi* (Italian coins) changed hands at the great fair at Piacenza in northern Italy. Letters of credit, bills of exchange, and standards of weights and measures greatly facilitated transactions at these sites. Trade fairs continued on into modern times, boosting regional economies. It was important to hold them at regular times and places, not only so buyers and sellers could arrange their schedules, but also so sponsors could prepare security and costs.

Mediterranean sea trade, much reduced after the fall of Rome, continued along the coasts but in the seventh century, with the rise and spread of the Muslims who came to control the sea, even this small amount of commerce came to near ruin at the hands of pirates from North Africa. Another reason for its decline was the feudal system that took hold in Europe by the eighth century, which had little use for a merchant class. Almost everything needed on the fiefs of the nobles could be made or grown by the serfs. Self-sufficient estates often preferred warring with each other to mutually beneficial exchange. Some necessary items, such as salt, continued to be traded, however.

As feudalism declined in the eleventh century, trade revived. The crusades opened up a new interest in luxury items from the East, money instead of land was becoming increasingly sought after, peasants moved into cities to break away from miserable lives on the estates, and monasteries became involved as they cleared land and improved their agricultural techniques, often producing a surplus of crops to trade at local markets for money or needed items. Long-distance trade was revived by the Italian city-states of Venice, Genoa, and Pisa despite Muslim control of the sea lanes.

THE TOWN CHARTER AND MERCHANT GUILDS

Merchants formed guilds or corporations both to manage their own affairs, and to confront the seigniorial and ecclesiastical lords of the land. Guilds arranged town charters or contracts with the landed aristocracy, who were often anxious to obtain luxury goods. Many charters allowed the land rented by merchants to become free land, and town members became free subjects unhampered by seigniorial restrictions on movement and labor. Special courts were created to hear complaints, and merchants controlled local police, and elected mayors and aldermen. During the later Middle Ages, roads were cleared and rebuilt, bridges reconstructed, and rivers policed, all for the benefit of commerce. The merchant class established communities at crossroads and river landings, where they built homes and warehouses. These sites attracted laborers, and many towns developed where merchants formed a distinct class of their own, controlling traffic of goods. They established regulations that ensured monopolistic control over merchandise. Traders from outside the town were forced to pay special tolls and taxes to sell goods in the town markets and to adhere to standards of quality. Town merchants could thus protect themselves from unwanted competition.

Returning from the crusades in the thirteenth century, Teutonic Knights staked out lands that included much of the southern shores of the eastern Baltic, with the purpose of Christianizing the pagan peoples of the region. Seizing opportunities for making themselves rich, they monopolized the amber-covered beaches, forbade private collection under penalty of death, and maintained control of the amber trade until the early sixteenth century.

In 1533, they transferred control of the amber trade to a family of merchants in Danzig. It underwent a severe blow during the Protestant Reformation in the Baltic countries when Catholics refused to purchase amber beads from Lutherans. The trade was renewed when the beads became popular with Muslims in the Near East. People living along the Baltic shores improved their financial state by collecting it clandestinely and selling it to dealers.

The Prussian government of Frederick Wilhelm purchased rights to the amber trade in 1642 and closed the beaches to individuals. Not finding the investment profitable, however, it reopened the beaches to individual collectors in 1811, and mining operations for amber buried underground began in 1870. Mining produced so much amber that the Prussian government again took over operation of the trade.

CAROLINGIAN EMPIRE

At the time of the demise of the Roman Empire, Gaul consisted of scattered petty Germanic kingdoms. Franks, of Germanic origin, occupied northern Gaul from the channel to the Rhine River.

Clovis, king of the Franks, controlled most of Gaul and succeeded in unifying the various tribes by the end of his reign in about 511.[6] Frankish silver pennies were minted and circulated along with English coins and Arabic *dirhams*. In 744, the monarch, Pepin, ordered the bishops of the country to establish and maintain at least one marketplace in every diocese. The crown also encouraged the great market fair at Pavia in Italy that fell under Carolingian jurisdiction, and at Piacenza where trade was so animated that the four-day fair held once a year was extended to five times per year with a total of 43 days.[7]

Under Charlemagne, the Frankish kingdom grew into an empire that, at his death in 814, comprised all of modern France, the Netherlands, and a large part of Germany and Italy.[8] Land was still the most important component of wealth, but most of the population lived on the edge of subsistence. The imperial estates of this Holy Roman Empire, as it was called, both secular and monasterial, produced surpluses in agricultural products and craft items that were traded locally and that supplied the towns with food. Merchants came from England, Spain, Italy and throughout the empire.

The Carolingian Empire's local and imperial officials promoted commerce for regional benefits but also for their own purposes. The court, aristocrats, and high clergy created a demand for luxury goods and accordingly maintained ports, bridges, and roads in good repair. For the use of coastal shipping, Charlemagne rehabilitated from the ruins the great Roman lighthouse at Boulogne in 811.

Included in the many fees merchants were forced to pay was a wheel tax, a carriage tax, bridge tolls, and ferry fees across rivers. If freight was moved on the numerous rivers of France, merchants paid tolls and mooring fees when the water passed through or alongside a noble's land. The Rhine River was especially noted for its tolls every few kilometers. Merchant vessels were at the king's command for carrying troops and military supplies.

In 828, Louis the Pious granted merchants the special privilege as imperial vassals that exempted them from tolls and other charges.[9]

HUNDRED YEARS' WAR

Between 1336 and 1453, England and France engaged in intermittent warfare. The cause of the conflict was ostensibly England's claim to the French throne. Apart from dynastic disputes, however, underlying economic factors were present; both sides desired control of the lucrative trade in Flanders that at the time was the industrial focus of Northern Europe due to its cloth manufacture. It had long-standing trade relations with England but was under French jurisdiction.

Wool imported from England helped supply the factories and contributed immensely to the country's foreign exchange. It also supplied the English crown with hefty export taxes. English wool was exchanged for Flemish cloth that in turn was traded for French wine in lands under the English crown in southwestern France. Both Flanders, the primary export market for English wool, and Gascony, a major wine producing area and exporter of wine to Britain, were contentious issues in the long and costly war.

MEDIEVAL SPAIN: JEWS AND MUSLIMS

The arrival of the Visigoths in Spain in the late fifth century brought about a new epoch in Hispanic affairs. About 300,000 Visigoths united most of the country from their capital at Toledo and ruled a population of about 4 million Hispano-Romans.[10] A militant warrior class like their Germanic predecessors, the Visigoths were not much interested in commerce, and trade diminished greatly. They did not build ships, had no navies to patrol the Mediterranean, had no means to keep pirates at bay, and copper and gold mines, from earlier Roman times, degenerated into ruins. What commerce there was, was mostly in the hands of individual Jews. Although greatly persecuted by the Christian Visigoths, and banned from nearly all occupations, they were useful for voyages to North Africa to bring back precious goods for high government and church officials.

Not until the Muslim conquest of Spain in 711 were Jews allowed to shake off the legal restrictions that restrained them and engage in all activities. As the land was retaken from the Moors by Christian kings in the north of Spain, the Jews again came under heavy persecution. They were excluded from commercial guilds that controlled trade and nearly all other activities, including agriculture, leaving few alternatives except money lending,[11] a big risk at the best of times because law courts were unsympathetic if a client defaulted on a loan from a Jew.

Commerce was one niche Jews could universally fill, and although it was looked down upon, the money was not; kings and princes were often only too eager to borrow it. Jewish family members or acquaintances in distant places could be trusted to fulfill their trade obligations, and Jews involved in the shipping trade in the Mediterranean and Indian Ocean could and did accumulate riches. Although conquered by Muslims in 640, Palestine was still the home of many Jews whose primary occupations were glass-making, tanning, and dyeing, and whose connections with Jewish merchants facilitated overseas trade.

By the twelfth century, Jews were involved in silk production in Constantinople and held monopolies on it in Palermo and other Italian port cities since silk veils and gowns were much in vogue. Jews formed commercial partnerships among themselves, sometimes with Muslims, and prosperous Jewish families controlled much of the commerce. Their communities flourished in most North African ports, and they carried on trade over caravan routes with western Sudan. Similarly, trade with India seems to have been worthwhile; Jewish merchants from Muslim Spain, Portugal, Egypt, and other communities made sea voyages to India via the Red Sea or Persian Gulf, or travelled overland through Persia. The profits were large, but Jewish traders were heavily taxed at ports and border crossings with tolls and import duties. The head of the Jewish merchant community in Aden was said to have sent several camel-loads of merchandise to Egypt but had to include eight camel-loads of pepper and 100 valuable robes for payment of custom duties.[12]

The Mediterranean city of Almería was the major port of Hispano-Muslim commerce, with an economy based on shipbuilding and silk manufacturing.[13] Also of commercial importance were Málaga, Denia, Sevilla, and later Valencia—all with access to the sea. Ships sailed from these ports to Alexandria in Egypt and returned with Eastern goods. Some 70 kilometers inland from the Atlantic Ocean, Sevilla was well situated on the Guadalquivir River, an important waterway for transport to and from inland markets such as Córdoba. Goods from al-Andalus (now Andalucía) were often shipped across the strait to the Maghrib for the market there, or for transshipment to other southern Mediterranean ports. There were many routes such as Denia to Algiers that took about one week, or faster voyages from Algeciras to Ceuta, of less than a day. From Ceuta to Fez with loaded camels took six or seven days. From there, the route might continue on to Marrakesh. Almería to Alexandria by ship might take anywhere from one to two months. Jewish merchants also carried out trade with Syria and other places in the Levant.

While al-Andalus became well integrated into the Muslim Mediterranean world of trade, it was much less involved in that of Christian Europe. Some Jewish merchants and a few Muslims carried on commerce with European Christian merchants who appeared in al-Andalus ports. They were generally Italian, from Genoa or Pisa. As the Christian reconquest of the peninsula slowly edged southward, cities such as Burgos, Leon, and Santiago de Compostela, falling back into Christian hands, became important market towns, the latter attracting pilgrims to the shrine of Santiago. In demand in the north were Muslim textiles, paper, spices, resin, ceramics, and leather goods along with gold coins; slaves, raw metals, and furs went in the opposite direction. Muslims and Christians would not sell slaves of their own faith but readily engaged in buying and selling those of different religions.

On voyages to al-Andalus from the eastern Mediterranean, Muslims naturally chose to sail along the coasts of Africa, whereas Christians preferred the northern littoral. Jews too traded with both, but along the African coast, where they were no doubt better respected. Muslims sometimes considered Christian merchants gullible, naïve, and unenlightened, and they preferred trade with "people of learning and refinement." Leaders of Christian lands often opposed trade with Islamic countries as tantamount to dealing with the enemy. Nevertheless, commerce continued while the degree of cooperation and negotiations shifted with the changing conflicts in Spain as the Christian reconquest advanced southward. In general, Muslim, Jewish, and Christian traders operated side by side in the Mediterranean and cooperated with one another even if informally. Commercial partnerships, on the other hand, seldom crossed religious lines.

In the twelfth century, Christian trading enterprises in al-Andalus picked up substantially. Italian maritime pursuits grew rapidly; Genoese, Pisan, and Provençal merchants appeared in southern Spain in growing numbers. Up until the thirteenth century, the balance of trade was in the Muslim's favor; afterward, the tide turned as Christian ships came to dominate in the Mediterranean. Around the middle of the thirteenth century, Iberian trade had shifted in favor of the Christians.

The medieval demand for spices included medicinal drugs, aromatics, mordants, dyes, and flavorings, and shipments of such items were well suited to merchants, since they were easily transported and yielded high profits, as did pepper, indigo, cloves, ambergris, myrrh, frankincense, saffron, camphor, and cinnamon, amongst others, that were imported into al-Andalus from as far away as India and Southeast Asia. Some of these spices served multiple purposes in cooking, cures for ailments, and perfumes to sweeten breath and clothing. Some mordants, such as alum, indispensable to bind dyes, were costly, and the best came from Egypt, Chad, and Anatolia. Imported were raw wool from the Maghrib and thousands of bales of Egyptian flax that were shipped westward annually, a bale weighing about 300 kilograms. One of the most productive trade commodities exported from al-Andalus across the sea was textiles, including cotton, silk, woolens, and finished carpets.

Among the various Mediterranean foods, only those of a nonperishable nature could travel over distances, for example, dried fruit and olives along with their oil, were international exports while little wheat was shipped from al-Andalus except in times of famine elsewhere when prices for it were high enough to make it worth transporting a bulk cargo. Successful traders maintained correspondence with associates abroad concerning markets and the value of commodities, since demand was sometimes fickle. After sending a shipment of a certain item, it was periodically discovered that no demand existed for it at its destination.

In general, nonprecious metals moved from west to east, whereas diamonds, rubies, and pearls went from east to west. Ivory was shipped from East Africa along the Red Sea to Egypt and then transshipped to al-Andalus. A merchant in al-Andalus might write a colleague in Egypt requesting him to keep a sharp eye in the marketplace for a certain item selling at a low price and ship it to al-Andalus, where it was going for more. The most productive source for gold at the time was western Sudan (now modern Senegal, southern Mali, western Niger, and adjacent regions), from where it crossed the Sahara Desert by caravans to the Maghrib and transshipped across the sea to Spain.

Al-Andalus produced and exported ceramics as well as imported them from North Africa. Other items treasured by foreign merchants were beautifully made Córdoban leather shoes, furniture, harnesses, bookbindings, and paper—the latter from Játiva and in high demand. Spain was known for great pine forests along the Mediterranean coasts and the foothills of the Pyrenees, and timber from al-Andalus was exported to the Muslim world. Among the many uses for wood were fuel and construction, but the greatest use was for shipbuilding.

SLAVES

Slaves were imported from Eastern Europe or from the Christian north of Spain and France into al-Andalus and shipped out again to many regions of the Islamic world. Warfare and border raids in

Spain between the Muslims and Christians generally provided captives for this trade. An early thirteenth century Islamic jurist, Saqati, described a situation in which some confusion arose from the interchange of Christian and Muslim slaves. An out-of-town buyer came to Córdoba to purchase a Christian slave girl, said to have been captured in the north of the country. He paid a high price for her, bought her expensive clothes, and prepared to take her home. She then spoke up and declared she was a free Muslim woman, a fact verified by her perfect Arabic. Fearing the possibility of being taken before a magistrate, the man acceded to her wishes to go to Almería, an important trade port with the Islamic world. Once there, she apparently kept silent, and her purchaser sold her to another Muslim buyer for a higher price, since slaves for export were more expensive. Presumably, the girl then received some of the profits and was in a position to repeat the process.

A major commodity, slaves passed through al-Andalus for distant markets. Basques, Galicians, and Slavs were a good target for the trade. Male slaves destined for markets in Islamic lands were castrated in order to offer no threat to a prince's harem. The slave market declined on the Iberian Peninsula as Muslim cities such as Córdoba fell to the Christians in 1236, and a new, lesser trade took hold in which Christian buyers bought Muslim slaves. The market dried up altogether as slaves became Christianized and Muslim dynasties in the East found it expedient to take slaves from places closer to home. At this time, too, black slaves from Africa became more plentiful, replacing white ones. Muslim and Jewish slave traders in Spain now found themselves out of a job.

SHIFTS IN TRADE

Until the early eleventh century, al-Andalus commerce with the East was carried on through Tunisian coastal towns, and merchants operating there received Egyptian or Syrian goods and either sold them there or in Spain if the market was thought to be more favorable. Genoese merchants were well entrenched in southern Spain, while in the north, Castilian merchants were dominant.

In the twelfth century, sales of agricultural products rose significantly, especially wool that was sold at fairs where contacts were made with agents of European industrial centers situated in France, Flanders, and Italy—countries where raw wool was made into fine garments and carpets.

Besides wool, iron deposits in the southern Sierra Morena and in the northern regions of the country yielded ore for export. Sometimes it was refined into steel for swords and cutlery manufactured in towns such as Toledo. Al-Andalus copper, too, was important both for export and to be locally pounded and beaten into utensils. Most traders also dealt in high-value silk. Large and small kingdoms developed in Christian lands, leaving the Muslims only Granada, which also was being whittled away. Buyers in the Near East and North Africa looked for sellers elsewhere, while Christians sought new markets in Europe. Ports on the Bay of Biscay such as Santander became important for the shipment of iron, wool from Merino sheep, wine, and Muslim slaves to Flanders and England instead of Egypt and the Maghrib. The remaining kingdom of Granada, although it had an abundance of fruit and vegetables, no longer had trading partners in neighboring Muslim territories and now had to seek staples such as wheat from North Africa, and enter into agreements with Christians.

Trading patterns also changed to the effect that shipments of raw timber to Muslim ports dried up. Hispanic Christians were not eager to supply the timberless regions of Muslim lands with wood to build ships.

Christian slaves could no longer be exported from Christian domains and gold imports discontinued, since Muslim traders could buy gold in North Africa where it was brought from sub-Saharan Africa by the desert caravans. Highly praised olive oil from Sevilla did continue as a major export even after the city was taken by Christians in 1248. Much of this trade was handled by merchants from Genoa. Spanish ceramics, the best from Málaga, also continued in a more or less unbroken line as objects of trade into Europe and England. The once profuse silk trade diminished; although some continued to be produced in Granada for the Muslim world, Iberian consumers were switching to imported Italian, Flemish, and French woolens and linen.

The growing demand in Europe for iron, much of it supplied by northern Spain, was needed for weapons, plows, horseshoes, and ships' fittings among other things. Northern coastal cities and Barcelona thrived on iron exports. Horses and mules were another primary export but were restricted by various Christian kings, as they might fall into enemy hands. In 1237, Pope Gregory IX decreed that Catalan traders in Tarragona (a little south of Barcelona) should not sell timber for ships to Muslims in the pirate-infested

Balearic Islands. The shifts in trade caused an imbalance of Muslim and Christian naval power in the western Mediterranean.

As the reconquest of Muslim territory in Spain progressed between 1212 and 1348, commerce shifted from Muslim to Christian control. Whereas the Muslims catered to markets of North Africa and Islamic states in the Middle East, Christians began to pay more attention to the markets of Northern Europe. The Muslims in Nasrid Granada (the last major stronghold along the southern coasts of Spain until 1492) still exported silk, fruit, and other foodstuffs to North Africa or surrounding Christian territory through local arrangements. The large market of al-Andalus rapidly dried up, however, as Christian forces closed in and the ports of Málaga, Almería, and others fell under their control. The axis of exports from Spain shifted from east and west under Muslim traders to north and south under Christians. Spanish figs, once so welcomed in Baghdad, were now enjoyed in the Netherlands while qirmiz (a red insect dye) was sold in England rather than in Egypt. New Christian exports included olive oil from Sevilla that was previously traded by Muslims and mostly carried in Genoese and Venetian ships to both Egypt and Northern Europe. A thirteenth-century document from Bruges shows olive oil shipped from Sevilla, and those of the fourteenth and fifteenth centuries show heavy traffic in this oil from Sevilla and Portugal to England.

OTHER SPANISH EXPORTS

Besides qirmiz, saffron and cumin were exported to the Netherlands and England in the thirteenth and fourteenth centuries, and from the mines in Almaden, a little north of Córdoba, mercury was exported to Mediterranean ports as well as Flanders and England. In the fifteenth century, these items were carried by Genoese merchants, who acquired from the crown of Castilla a monopoly on the trade. Córdoban leather was a big item in foreign markets, and pelts from diverse animals (rabbits, cats, sheep, and so on) made their way as far as England, as witnessed by the cargo of a wrecked ship off the coast of Sandwich in 1337.

The traveler Ibn Battutah visited Málaga when it was still Muslim and remarked on the wonderful pottery made there as well as the finest figs and raisins. Grapes, he reported, sold at eight pounds for a small dirham.

Islamic merchants brought silk to Spain where, by the tenth century, al-Andalus was Europe's primary silk-producing center. The industry declined in the thirteenth century as silk farming expanded in Italy and Sicily, and Byzantine silk became more readily available. In the second half of the thirteenth century, however, the wool industry was on the rise. By the fourteenth century, exports in wool were firmly established and dominated the Spanish economy. Ready markets for Spanish wool were also found in Italy and Flanders.

In 1273, Alfonso X, King of Castilla, created the Honorable Council of the *Mesta*, a powerful syndicate of sheep owners. Merino sheep produced high-quality wool that was funneled through Burgos to the northern ports and hence to awaiting markets. In 1447, there were 2.7 million head of sheep in Castilla.[14] Not only was the export of wool advantageous for the king, who collected taxes on it, and aristocrats, who owned the land on which the sheep grazed, but also for those who invested in them. The *mesta* was of great benefit to the poor northern export towns (once fishing villages) such as Santander, for shipbuilders, sailors, and shepherds, cargo handlers, carters, and other auxiliary enterprises. The *mesta* was a huge commercial activity.[15] Millions of sheep were grazed in the north of the country in summer and herded south to Estremadura in winter, where the climate was milder and the grass greener. They began the northward trek again in spring. The sheep also produced quantities of milk and butter, cheese, and meat. While passing through cultivated areas, the great mass of animals were supposed to follow designated pathways, but with so many it was not easy to police them. Complaints of peasant farmers who had their fields overrun and ruined generally fell on deaf ears. The corporation was a powerful and wealthy entity backed by the crown.

Wine was shipped to England from Spain as early as about 1228, as attested by a shipment to Bristol in that year, although there was always competition with wines from France. In the thirteenth century, as the Muslims were driven from their Iberian cities, Christian Spain was becoming an integral part of European trade networks, and honey, salt, grain, sugar, and alum joined the export market. Trade patterns shifted along with religious demographics of the peninsula.

ITALY

The Italian peninsula underwent radical changes as Germanic tribes settled there. First came the Ostrogoths, who were followed by the Lombards. The latter settled in the north while the south underwent difficult times under competing Arabs, Byzantines, and Normans. Papal states rose in the center and made their presence known by popes hungry for power and wealth. Northern cities such as Venice, Milan, Genoa, and Pisa developed into city-states that were not under the immediate jurisdiction of popes, Byzantines, or others.

The city of Venice became a republic in 697 with an elected doge (chief magistrate), and in 991 signed a commercial treaty with the Muslims. The crusades and trade with the East made the city an influential commercial center with a powerful presence in the Mediterranean. It transformed into an oligarchy in the thirteenth century, and Genoa was its chief commercial rival. In the fourteenth century, the two cities engaged in a number of wars over trade. After a naval battle near Sicily with the Venetians in 1373, Genoa was forced to yield to Venice. In the mid-fifteenth century, the Ottoman Turkish invasions brought an end to Venetian commercial ambitions. The Turks soon dominated the Mediterranean sealanes, took Venice's island holdings in the Mediterranean, and compelled the Venetians to pay them a tax each year for the right to trade in the eastern Mediterranean and the Black Sea. The island city declined further when the Portuguese discovered a sea route around Africa to India in 1498, depriving the city of much trade in spices from the East.

HOLY ROMAN EMPIRE

Among other towns in Flanders, Ghent, Bruges, and Ypres had their share of artisans and were important places for the manufacture of cloth. Such towns prospered in medieval times on the wool trade and built a reputation for the finest linen and woolen fabrics that were sold throughout Europe. Flax came from the region, and the best raw wool was brought in from Spain and England. The finished cloth was sold at all major fairs. Envious of the wealthy cities of Flanders, French kings made territorial inroads into the region, bringing parts of it under their control.

Flemish towns specialized in material goods, some producing garments, others tapestries or textiles. These high-quality products were expensive but much in demand. Skilled craftsmen spun the English wool into yarn and then wove it into cloth that other workers finished and dyed. Guilds controlled the work, and merchants sold the product in their shops, which were often attached to their houses with the workshop behind.

In the center of Europe, Germany was active in both local and international trade. Its rivers were a big asset for transporting goods. Towns were generally governed by the merchant class, and sometimes they banded together to resist foreign encroachment on their trade. Some towns were under the jurisdiction of local nobility while others, free towns, owed allegiance only to the emperor of the Holy Roman Empire. A major trade product, salt, came from mines in the north around Lüneburg, and was carried to various destinations by horses and wagons. Expensive, dangerous, and arduous, the land route was replaced in part by the Elbe-Lübeck Canal in Schleswig-Holstein, begun in 1390, that connected the Elbe and Trave Rivers, and made goods cheaper to transport and in greater bulk.

NOTES

1. For details see Wood, 410.
2. *EWT*, 645–647.
3. www.britannica.com/EBchecked/topic/152262/ Francesco-Datini.
4. *EWT*, 349.
5. *EWT*, 646.
6. Todd, 197.
7. *EWT*, 150.
8. Elcock, 296.
9. *EWT*, 151.
10. Payne, Vol. 1, 9.
11. Cantor, 365.
12. Roth, 181.
13. For more detail on the following, see Constable, passim.
14. Payne, 156.
15. Payne, 76.

10

BALTIC REGION

The majority of the population in the Middle Ages in Scandinavia comprised farmers who produced wheat, barley, oats, and rye, and raised cattle. Other occupations included hunting, trapping, fishing, and iron mining. Specialist craftsmen made objects of walrus ivory, soapstone, wood, and amber that were traded in Northern Europe.

As farmers, most people lived outside of the confines of the villages in wooden, stone, or turf houses that had a single room that could be partitioned off for various functions. The buildings were often in the form of a hall with benches along the walls for sleeping and sitting, and a hearth in the center with a hole in the roof to vent the smoke. Many dwellings had an adjacent bathhouse. Extended families tended to occupy the same house, and the women ran the farm when the men were away hunting or trading. Wealthy families had slaves to do the manual labor. Young girls married between the ages of 12 and 15 with no input as to who was to be the husband. A dowry was expected, but it remained her property. Women had more rights compared to others throughout Europe; they could, for example, divorce an abusive husband by calling witnesses and proclaiming their separation.

AMBER

In abundance along the shores of the Baltic Sea, amber was an early item of long-distance trade. To the people living around the seacoast it was commonplace, readily available, and perhaps of little importance. To people in faraway lands such as Mesopotamia or Asia, amber had mystical qualities and burned, it had the aroma of pinewood; sculpted, it made exquisite figurines, as decorative beads it could be worn as a necklace or bracelet and bring good luck. The confinement of an ancient insect caught in the sticky resin of the pine tree as it hardened made amber even more precious. It was traded as early as the Neolithic period, and Baltic amber has been found among Mycenaean cultural artifacts of ancient Greece. It was transported from the north by the Vistula and Dnieper Rivers and the Black Sea, and overland to Italy, and it made its way as far as Egypt. The Romans, fond of amber, used it for imperial decoration. Not until the eighteenth century did people realize that amber was the organic fossilized sap of ancient trees. In medieval Europe, it was in high demand for rosary beads.

VIKINGS

Comprised of Danes, Norwegians, and Swedes, Vikings ranged the northern world from the shores of Newfoundland in the west to the Caspian Sea in the east, and to the Mediterranean in the south. Viking voyages were made possible by their sturdy, shallow-bottomed ships powered by oars and sails that performed well at sea and along rivers.

On June 8, 793, Vikings appeared off the east coast of northern England, came ashore, and sacked the monastery at Lindisfarne, beginning a period of Viking raids and settlements in the west. They pillaged and terrorized the populace along the coasts of Europe and inland up major rivers. In 841, they founded the town of Dublin. In the tenth century, they established the duchy of Normandy in France, derived from the name "Norsemen." Europeans were so fearful of them that a new prayer in the litany of the church was devised: "From the fury of the Northman, O Lord deliver us."[1]

International trade was not an important feature of Scandinavian ambition until the ninth century when, apart from amber, their products gradually became known beyond their wintery world. Walrus ivory, furs, cattle, and iron ore from local mines became major trade items. The Norse discovery of Iceland in 860, and its colonization four years later, offered another source of products for trade with Scandinavia and other Viking communities.

DUBLIN

In the ninth century, there were two settlements where the modern city of Dublin stands, one Scandinavian and one Celtic. Vikings ruled Dublin for almost three centuries.There they had a large market for slaves who were captured and sold not only by the Norse, but also by warring Irish chiefs. Like slaves the world over, they were no better off among Vikings than were domestic animals, and they cost about the same. An owner could buy and sell them as he wished, and murder them with impunity. If a nonowner killed one, the dead man had to be replaced. When a female slave bore a child, it was the property of her master. Enslaved people, the majority of whom were Germans, Slavs, Irish, and Finns taken in the course of Viking raids, were also often sold in Europe. It was a profitable business.

The geography of Scandinavian countries somewhat dictated their conquests and trade ventures. From Norway they found their way to Britain, Western Europe, and beyond, whereas those from Sweden explored and traded along the rivers from the Baltic Sea inland into Russia and on to Constantinople. Danish Vikings raided and exploited lands east, west, and south.

Situated in southern Denmark, Hedeby grew into the largest trading city in the Viking age with its river access to both the Baltic and North Seas. At Hedeby, the Norsemen could meet foreign merchants and shape commercial arrangements. Northwest Europe benefited from products made there from silver, soapstone, amber, and wood, as well as articles produced by artisans from glass, bone, horn, and bronze. Norwegians destroyed the town in about 1050, but archaeological remains attest to rectangular wooden houses interspersed with craft workshops.

JORVIK (YORK)

A major center taken in 866 by the Viking Ivar the Boneless, where goods were made and traded, Jorvik was a Viking city that has yielded archaeological remains, including a variety of metalworking tools. It became the most important trading town in Britain at the time, a distinction that earlier belonged to Saxon London, which was devastated and burned by the Vikings in 851.

Besides glass and amber, other materials were used for making jewelry, including jet, copper, and precious metals. Woodworking was also an industry that produced cups, bowls, and utensils. Textile production and dying, leather goods such as shoes, belts, and harnesses, were all made in Jorvik along with carved and shaped bone and antler used for a variety of objects from pins to ice skates, to combs and decorations. Archaeological discoveries from Anglo-Viking Jorvik document soapstone receptacles that seem to have come from Norway, jewelry from Scotland and Ireland, cloth from Holland, pottery and millstones from the Rhineland, and amber from the Baltic.

The island of Gotland in the Baltic Sea was also a major center that derived its success from the handling of transit trade. Wealthy pagan graves and buried hoards of Viking treasure, found all over the island, suggest that even local farmers had a hand in the lucrative business. Hoards contained considerable quantities of Arabic and European silver coins, and pieces of jewelry broken into smaller pieces, perhaps for melting down. Similarly, weights and scales have been found in Viking sites.

NORSEMEN IN THE EAST

About the time Danes and Norwegians were plundering Western Europe with their raids on coastal and riverine towns and villages, others, mostly Swedes, were making their way east and south in search of booty and trade, and in the process revitalizing existing trading zones in Eurasia. Bearing furs and pieces of bright, translucent amber, they penetrated the river systems of Russia and the Ukraine to the Black Sea and encountered Muslim traders eager to purchase northern products with silver coin, an exchange agreeable to the Vikings, who lacked silver. Muslim writers describe the Norsemen as heavily armed merchant-warriors primarily interested in trade for the silver *dirhams* minted by the Abbasids. The Muslims themselves ventured northward in search of commercial opportunities. Here, in the network of trading stations along the mighty rivers, the Swedes carried on active commerce with Arabs, Persians, and Greeks. From there, some of the Scandinavians sailed down to the Black Sea, toward the regions they called Sarkland, a name that may refer either to the lands of the Saracens (today Azerbaijan and northern Iran), or to the Khazar fortress of Sarkel, at the mouth of the Don on the Black Sea coast.[2]

The extent of Viking trade can be seen from gravesites in which have been found not only Arab silver, but Byzantine silk, weapons, and glass from the lands of the Franks and coins from Anglo-Saxon England.[3]

NOVGOROD AND KIEV

A place well favored as a commercial center, the city of Novgorod was close to Lake Ilmen and major Russian rivers that led to the Caspian, Black, and Baltic Seas. Goods ferried by water between these important regions converge on this area, and by the early ninth century, Viking tribes known as the Rus had a base on the site of Novgorod. For the Vikings, trade was the primary reason for their journeys deep into Russia during the ninth century. The river system of Eastern Europe, flowing north and south, made it relatively easy for goods to travel between the Baltic and Black Seas. Trade in transit, especially along the river Dnieper, the "Great Waterway," served the Vikings well. The name Rus was a Finnish word for the Swedish Vikings in Russia that came to be applied to all local people whether Nordic or Slavs, and eventually to the country of Russia.

The city of Kiev on the Dnieper River (in the Ukraine) was seized in 882 by the Vikings to protect the profitable Rus trade with Constantinople. Viking traders unified and fortified the upper and middle Dnieper waterway in the ninth century, replacing the faltering Turkic Khazars, who had earlier guaranteed safety on the trade routes across the steppe. The goods of the northern forestlands, including furs, slaves, and honey, were brought to the stronghold of Kiev on the middle Dnieper River and then transported by flotilla each spring down the river, over the portages, and by boat along the coast of the Black Sea to Constantinople. There they were traded for Mediterranean luxury articles such as wine, jewelry, and fine fabrics that were brought back to the land of Rus and beyond, to Scandinavia. The city was the center of commerce between Constantinople in the south, the steppes of western Asia, and the woodlands of the north. In the thriving market of Kiev goods came together from many and distant areas and included horses, slaves, gold and silver, clothes, fruit, wine, furs, wax, and honey.

The Volga River trade route linked Northwestern Russia with the Caspian Sea allowing Nordic peoples to trade with Muslim societies on the banks of the Caspian. The eighth and ninth century route was used at the same time as the Dnieper and Don River trade connecting the Scandinavians with the Black Sea, and to trade with the Greeks settled along its shoreline.

In 882, the Viking chief Oleg moved his headquarters to Kiev, where he concluded a treaty with Constantinople. Kiev became the center of trade between the Byzantine world, the land of the steppe, and the forested north. It has been said that in Kiev, one could find almost everything, emanating from all directions.

Early-ninth-century Arabic coins have been found along the Volga, attesting to this commerce. The Vikings brought furs, including sable and squirrel; hides; honey; and slaves to Atil, a busy commercial port on the Caspian Sea. They then crossed the sea to link up with caravans to Baghdad.

A CONTEMPORARY OBSERVER

A tenth-century traveler and diplomat for the Abbasid caliph of Baghdad, Ibn Fadlan, was sent on a mission to the Volga Bulgars in 922. He ran across Norsemen, known then as Rus, camped on the banks of the Volga River and engaged in trading furs from a long wooden structure. They set up the shop near a Bulgar camp. Ibn Fadlan's letters home reveal aspects of Vikings that are none too flattering. The essence of his comments were that the men were tall, blond, and tattooed all over their bodies, but extremely dirty. A slave girl brought them a bowl of water each morning, and they took turns washing face and hair, rinsing their mouths, spitting into it, and blowing their noses. The water was not changed throughout the entire procedure. When they left their boats and went ashore, each man carried some food, such as bread and meat, and took it to a large wooden stake with a human-like face, surrounded by smaller figures. They prostrated themselves before the large image and prayed for bountiful trade, after which a gift was presented. If the trading process moved too slowly, they returned to the statue to try again. The smaller, surrounding stakes were also appealed to if trade did not pick up. If the bartering process did go well, a goat or sheep was sacrificed, and its head was placed on the posts.[4]

Trade took place from large wooden houses erected beside the river Volga in which 10 or 20 people lived, each one with a couch occupied by the owner along with the beautiful girls he had for sale. If the Vikings decided to engage in sexual intercourse with one of the girls, it took place in full view of everyone.

Ibn Fadlan also described the funeral of a Viking chief. Days were spent preparing his funeral clothes and dividing up his possessions between his family, as well as dealing with the cost of his funeral garments and the drink on the occasion of his burial. His girls and attendants were asked who would accompany him. When one volunteered, she was committed to the flames with the dead man, his couch, and some of his possessions along with herbs and drink that were placed in a boat. While the men beat upon their shields, making a lot of noise, the person to die with the chief was given a strong drink and killed, and placed in the boat that was then set on fire. All was soon engulfed in flame.

A Norseman reputedly said to Ibn Fahlan,

You Arabs are stupid! You would take him who is the most revered and beloved among men, and cast him into the ground, to be devoured by creeping things and worms. We, on the other hand, burn him in a twinkling, so that he instantly, without a moment's delay, enters into Paradise.[5]

VIKING INFLUENCE

New items and ideas profoundly changed the Viking homeland. The kingdoms of Norway, Sweden, and Denmark took shape; silver flowed into the new sovereign entities, cities and towns grew; and new market places developed. Christianity made its appearance and spread throughout northern lands. One of the major sources of trade for the Vikings—slaves—diminished and disappeared along with the propensity for raiding as Christianity gained a firm hold.

Iceland was settled, developed, and prospered. Although abandoned by most Nordic people, Greenland also flourished for a time and was then left to the Eskimos. In England, Viking influence left its mark in place names and in laws as well as in the course of English political history. Similarly, the establishment of Viking Normandy and the Norman invasion of England in 1066 altered historical trends in both countries.

At the apex of the Viking period, their commercial diaspora stretched from Greenland eastward to the White Sea, and to Constantinople and the middle Volga River. The age of the Vikings faded away in the eleventh century. According to some accounts, in spite of their often bloody raids and much loss of life, Viking raiders had a positive economic impact in so much as they robbed the churches and monasteries, returning to circulation precious gold and silver that had lain dormant in them since the fall of the Roman Empire. In short, they became suppliers of money that helped stimulate Western economies.[6]

FRANKISH (CAROLINGIAN) EMPIRE

More or less contemporary with the expansion of the Viking world in the eighth to the tenth centuries, the empire of the Franks lay to the south and east, stretching at its height from the Pyrenees Mountains bordering Spain to Denmark.[7]

Intense competition developed between Franks and Norsemen for trade with the Arabs to acquire silver.[8] Frankish arms were exported to Scandinavia in the ninth century, especially swords. Viking graves often contain Arab silver, Byzantine silks, Frankish weapons, glass from the Rhineland, and other products of an extensive trade. Silver coins from the caliphate have been found in great abundance in Scandinavian countries, attesting to trade with the Arabs and minted in Samarkand and in Baghdad.[9] That all of these coins were not simply brought back by Vikings but that Arabs had reached the northern lands to purchase goods is verified by Arab accounts. One merchant stated, for example, that he reached a point north where the sun only shined one hour a day.

Charlemagne, King of the Franks (768–814), understood the importance of trade to maintain and strengthen the Frankish economy. He advocated commercial activity with Scandinavian towns and others along the Baltic coasts. The Franks extended their trade into Central Asia in search of Muslim silver and used it to create their own currency.[10]

HANSEATIC (HANSE) LEAGUE

After the demise of the Viking era in the eleventh century, the Baltic regions came to be dominated by a league of German merchants in the latter half of the twelfth and thirteenth centuries. Known as the Hanse, they formed a bond to protect themselves at sea from pirates and on land from highwaymen. The idea originated among merchants in Köln and spread to other cities in northern Germany such as Bremen and Hamburg. When Köln dropped from the association, Lübeck became the leading city of the league, whose members came to encompass some 100 towns and cities, mostly along the north German coasts. At its height, the influence of the league's power and wealth in the fourteenth and early fifteenth centuries stretched from London and Bruges north to Bergen and east to Novgorod. While it was a group of independent cities they followed, if not orders, at least suggestions set out from Lübeck.[11]

To protect their mutual interests, the Hanse established Visby on the island of Gotland as a major center for the transshipment of goods especially from Novgorod, the primary depot for Russian trade. Staples of Hanseatic trade were cloth generally from England, salt from France and German Baltic cities, wine from Alsace and the Rhine region, and perhaps, as important as anything, herring—the latter eaten throughout Europe but especially on Fridays when meat was forbidden by the church. There were, of course, other commodities for exchange that figured into the league's inventories such as furs, timber, grain, honey and wax from Eastern Europe, spices from the south, and luxury goods that included silk. Beer was a common item of trade.

Swedish copper and iron ore were traded westward. In Lübeck, Danzig, and a few other Baltic cities, the Hanse was also engaged in shipbuilding and sold vessels all over Europe. When the Dutch became competitors of the Hanse, the league attempted to prevent shipbuilding technology going from Hanse towns to Holland. The Dutch traded directly with north German principalities with non-Hanseatic League connections, and hostility arose because Dutch freight costs were considerably lower than those of the league.

The league's aggressively protectionist trading practices often aroused opposition from foreign merchants. It typically used gifts and loans to foreign political leaders to protect its commercial privileges, and when this proved inadequate, it threatened to withdraw its trade and occasionally became involved in embargoes and blockades.

A mercantile—not political—organization, the league nevertheless attempted to ensure peace and order among its members, and police the sea lanes and land roads.

Hanse Power

To safeguard its investment in trade and ships, the league trained pilots, constructed lighthouses, and sailed with armed ships. At the height of its power in the late 1300s, league merchants used their economic importance and sometimes their military strength to influence policy. Between 1361 and 1370, the league waged war against Denmark when the Danish king, Valdemar IV, attempted to wrest control of the southwest Baltic from Hanseatic control. Copenhagen was devastated, and the Danish king was obliged to commit 15 percent of Danish trade profits to the league by the peace treaty of Stralsund in 1370. The Hanse also waged war on pirates and with the Dutch in 1438, who wanted free access and trade in the Baltic. In 1422, Henry VI of England granted free trade to Hanse merchants in London and at the fairs throughout the country, a privilege that local merchants opposed. Money no doubt changed hands. Less welcoming, Ivan III of Moscow closed the Hanseatic trading settlement at Novgorod in 1494. In the fifteenth century, the Dutch too were able to oust German traders from Dutch domestic markets and much of the North Sea. By the mid-sixteenth century, Dutch ships had even won control of the trade from the Baltic to Western countries, dealing a severe setback to Lübeck.

Demise of the Hanse

Sweden began to exert greater influence in the Baltic, and Denmark regained authority over its own trade. Foreign trading ports of the Hanse closed one after another as competition increased and political problems mounted. League cities began to concentrate on their own particular commercial interests, paying less and less attention to the Hanseatic League. Amsterdam merchants gained unrestricted access to the Baltic fisheries and broke the Hanse monopoly.

English merchants, like the Dutch, forced inroads into Baltic trade. Europe at the time was undergoing major problems—the Protestant Reformation and the subsequent Thirty Years' War (1628–1648) greatly retarded trade and finally put paid to the once powerful Hanseatic League of German Merchants. At its formal meeting in 1669, few members came, and from then on it was all downhill. It was never formally dissolved, however, and Lübeck, Hamburg, and Bremen are still referred to as Hanseatic cities. A major result of the Hanse period can be seen in the establishment of new towns along or close to the eastern Baltic coasts such as Tallinn, Riga, and Elblag, where German migrants under the auspices of Hanse authority set up businesses.[12]

NOTES

1. Wallbank, 195.
2. For a list of Viking exports and imports see http://www.hurstwic .org/history/articles/daily_living/text/Towns.htm.

3. See also Newton, 75.

4. Brøndsted (1965), 64–65.

5. For more on Ibn Fadlan, see Sherman, 169; for a list of Viking exports and imports, see Judith Gabriel, http://www.saudiaramcoworld.com/issue/199906/among.the.norse.tribesthe.remarkable.account.of.ibn.fadlan.htm.

6. Braudel (1993), 312.

7. Beckwith, 135.

8. *Past Worlds*, 242.

9. Newton, 83.

10. Taylor, 92.

11. Curtin, 7.

12. See also http://mysite.verizon.net/~baronfum/hansa.html.

11

PORTUGUESE EMPIRE

King Afonso III of Portugal (1246–1279) completed the reconquest
of the realm in 1249 by expelling the Moors from the Algarve, the
southernmost portion of the country, and making Portugal the first
of the European nation-states. During his reign Lisbon, as the seat
of government, grew rapidly, along with international trade.
In 1279, Dinis came to the throne. He considered agriculture
a primary source of the country's wealth and did all he could to
promote it by turning over unused land to peasant farmers, drain-
ing marshes, and encouraging the planting of cereal and other
crops. Portugal soon found itself in a position to export not only
grain, but also dried fruits, almonds, raisins, olive oil, cork, grapes,
wine, and figs as well as salt from the ocean tidal flats. These
measures allowed the country to import linen cloth and other
much-needed items. Foreign trade was encouraged, and the king
had documents drawn up to provide for losses at sea, a kind of
early marine insurance. Besides agricultural exports to European
countries, Dinis ordered the exploitation of mines that produced
silver, tin, iron, and copper whose surpluses could also be
exported. In 1293, the king permitted the establishment of a fund
for the defense of Portuguese merchants in foreign cities.[1] The
shipbuilders' guild contributed money to a fund that was used to
reimburse unfortunate merchants who were robbed by pirates or

forced to pay foreign duties in other nations, and this also became a form of marine insurance. In addition, Dinis brought about agreements with Flemish and English commercial organizations for the mutual protection of traders.

Commercial relations with Flanders had already been established sometime before, as noted by Portuguese attendance at a fair in Lille in 1267. England and Portugal signed their first commercial agreement in 1308. Before Dinis died in 1325, he made a contract with a Genoese, Manuel Pesagno, who would become his admiral, and by which Portugal would have trading privileges at Genoa in exchange for 20 warships and their crews. Employed against pirates, the ships formed the basis of the Portuguese navy. The arrangement also gave rise to a Genoese trading community in Lisbon.[2]

Agriculture was Portugal's mainstay, and the country exported numerous farm products to Flanders and England. There was little industry, however, and guns and munitions, elegant clothes, and some manufactured products from Flanders and Italy were purchased. The ocean offered opportunities for fish and other seafood, most of which was consumed locally, but after about 1325, King Afonso IV raised a commercial fishing fleet with public money. When the bubonic plague struck in 1348, ravaging a good proportion of the population, land was left unattended and those people who could, migrated as commercial life came to a near halt. Laws were passed compelling men to work on the land. As the country recovered, a commercial treaty was signed in 1353, for 50 years, between Edward III of England and the merchants and maritime communities of Lisbon and Oporto. Commerce was not only on the minds of Portuguese merchants, the upper classes were also involved. King Fernando (1367–1383), greatly interested in building ships, encouraged their construction by exempting all duties on the cargo of the first voyage, and for shipwrights who built ships of over 100 tons, who were permitted to take whatever wood was needed from the royal forest at no charge.[3]

PRINCE HENRIQUE THE NAVIGATOR (1394–1460)

A son of João I and Philippa of Lancaster, Prince Henrique (called the Navigator) and his royal brothers, along with other nobles, devised a plan called the Enterprise of Ceuta, to attack the Muslim city of Ceuta across the Strait of Gibraltar. Henrique was a man of maritime interests, and although he was rich, he was concerned with amassing more wealth. He had a deep-seated hatred of Muslims and the prospect of taking Muslim-held Ceuta was attractive, as it would deprive the enemy of a trading port to which products from Africa were brought by camel caravans across the Sahara and then shipped to Europe, mostly by Genoese traders; and the wealth from trade for which the city was famous would fall into Portuguese hands. Another factor taken into consideration was that the Genoese and the Venetians, who controlled shipping in the Mediterranean, delivering goods from the Muslim African port cities to European destinations, had also shown interest in gaining more influence in Ceuta. Better under control of the Portuguese than Muslims or Italians. The Portuguese fleet transported the army across the strait to Ceuta and the city—surprised and unprepared—fell in one day. A Portuguese garrison was quickly installed. From the city harbor, the Portuguese navy was now in an excellent position to disrupt and even capture Muslim ships trading along the south coast of the Mediterranean. The Enterprise was expected to bring rich booty to the nobles of Portugal and in the longer term take over the commerce of the profitable Saharan trade route. On both accounts, the expedition was an unmitigated disaster, however. The great palaces and warehouses of wealthy Muslim merchants in Ceuta were so badly looted by Portuguese soldiers that few items of value remained. In a frenzied search for gold and silver, expensive vases, tapestries, furniture, bales of silk, and great stores of cinnamon and pepper were destroyed in the reckless scramble for loot, or consumed by fires that quickly ensued. There was little left to reimburse the crown for the huge expenditure laid out for the Enterprise. As for the Muslim merchants, they redirected their trade to other ports and Ceuta's commerce, amidst constant Muslim counterattacks, dried up. Instead of wealth pouring into the royal coffers, they were drained by the cost of maintaining the Ceuta garrison.

Not having learned an expensive lesson, Henrique—imbued with Christian fervor and a desire to profit from trade—agitated for an attack on Muslim-held Tanger, just east of Ceuta, and eventually got his way under the new king, his older brother Duarte. The Portuguese parliament, the Cortes, granted the money, but another disaster loomed: Tanger was prepared. Impotent sieges cost the lives of many Portuguese soldiers as the army became surrounded. Henrique was forced to sue for peace and for safe conduct back to Portugal. The Muslims demanded that Ceuta be given back to them and Henrique's younger brother, Fernando, was left as a hostage until the transfer of the city to the Muslims was completed. Back in Portugal the Cortes, with Henrique's approval, refused to give up Ceuta and Fernando perished in a Muslim prison. Henrique retired to Sagres on the southwest tip of Portugal to follow his interest in maritime ventures.

According to Eanes de Zurara, a man in the service of Henrique, the prince was immensely curious about what lay to the south in Africa, beyond the Muslims. How far did the Muslim lands extend? Were there Christians beyond with whom he could trade and find allies against Islam? A coordinated attack from north and south could rid Africa of his detested enemy, much to the glory of Christ and to the benefit of Portugal.

He sponsored voyages down the coast of West Africa partly motivated, it seems, by a monopoly on all profits gained from trade, curiosity, and a search for Christian allies. The thought that there might be Christians somewhere in Africa was fueled by stories at the time of a mysterious Christian kingdom ruled by a certain Prester John. Another inducement to explore southward was the fact that gold from sub-Saharan Africa was transported over the Saharan trade routes. To outflank the Muslims by sea and gain direct access to the mines would have been a major coup for the Portuguese economy.

Cartographers of the time realized that it was possible to sail around Africa and reach India and the Far East, an idea that also attracted Prince Henrique. In the explorations of the African west coast, the Portuguese captains traded trinkets, beads, grain, and other items of little value for gold. During the 1440s, as they explored the west coast, African goods began to appear in European marketplaces. In Bruges, parrots, lion cubs, and monkeys could be obtained from Portuguese merchants.

They were also beginning to bring black Africans to Lagos in southern Portugal to sell on the slave block. Merchants soon began to solicit the prince for a license to sail south and participate in the slave trade. In 1444, six caravels left Portugal, sailed south to Cape Blanco, and after killing a number of natives who resisted, the ships were filled with captives. As agreed beforehand, a fifth of the slaves were turned over to Prince Henrique, and the rest were sold in the market at Lagos.

Merchants and Henrique's captains were forced to extend their southern slave raiding parties further along the coast of Africa as the natives became increasingly aware of the danger of the vessels and their crews armed with muskets. But it was also learned that African tribes would exchange their own slaves captured in warfare for European goods, and in 1449, Henrique ordered a fort/trading post constructed at Argium a little south of Cape Blanco and leased it for 10 years to a private entrepreneur. Every year, caravels visited the post to exchange cereals, fabric, and horses for gold, slaves, and cotton.

Portugal became the first modern European nation to supplement its shortage of agricultural workers with black African slaves—some 700 to 800 a year—and for over a century, Portugal monopolized the European seaborne traffic in slaves. With a population of about 100,000 inhabitants in Lisbon, some 10,000 were black Africans. Sixty to 70 slave markets existed in the city, along with others in the southern ports.

In 1484, the Genoese Christopher Columbus called at the Portuguese court with his plan to sail west to reach Asia and, in effect, open a direct trade route with the Far East. After due consideration, his project was declined. It sounded too risky to the crown, already invested in the African venture, and to merchants who would have to finance the expedition. As is well known, Columbus had better luck at the Spanish court.

In spite of efforts to locate it, the hoped-for Christian kingdom of Prester John, or at least that of his descendants, was never found. The rumor that the kingdom existed had some basis in fact, as there were Christians in the vaguely defined region of Ethiopia, but when Pêro da Covilha, an agent of the Portuguese king João II, reached the mysterious land, the Ethiopians were not interested in an alliance with the Portuguese.

MADEIRA ISLANDS

When the Portuguese colonized the uninhabited islands of Madeira after about 1419, they brought slaves from the Canary Islands and Africa to tend the sugarcane plantations they began there with cane that was introduced from Sicily. The islands also produced wine, honey, wax, wheat, fish, and timber for export to the mainland. Some 70 vessels from Antwerp were engaged in the sugar trade by about 1480. Sugarcane production, a major component of the islands' economy, enticed not only Flemish traders, but also many Genoese to the islands. As trade increased, so did the demand for slaves to work the fields. The production of sugar on the islands quickly developed to the extent that sugar prices fell to nearly half in European markets, and island production was limited to offset the losses and maintain prices. Most of the Madeira sugar was bound for Flanders.[4]

SÃO TOMÉ E PRÍNCIPE

Discovered in 1471, the islands of São Tomé e Príncipe were discovered by the Portuguese and became a sugar-producing colony. In 1493, Portugal conscripted 2,000 Jewish children between the ages of two and 10 to work on the sugar plantations in São Tomé as slaves. Six hundred survived the year, yet none converted to Christianity. The Jewish population was expelled from Portugal in 1497.[5]

SAÕ JORGE DA MINA (ELMINA)

In 1482, the Portuguese erected the fortress called Saint George of the Mine to access the African goldfields that became one of the important trading posts established along the West African coast in present-day Ghana. The fact that the Portuguese were often their own worst enemy in trade arrangements is seen at Elmina as well as in a number of other places. They showed little respect for native peoples and generally tried to impose their own Christian beliefs on noncomprehending populations. Building the fort at Elmina entailed the destruction of village houses and a sacred rock worshipped by the local animists, and native assaults on the settlement followed. Finally, after further attacks, the Portuguese burned the village. The site later became an important stop for Atlantic slave traders and for the transport of African gold.

In the early sixteenth century, items such as beads, shells, and wine were traded for slaves and gold,[6] much of which was imported to Portugal through Elmina. Most was used to pay for European imported merchandise such as grain and manufactured goods.

TREATY OF TORDESILLAS (1494)

There has perhaps been no treaty as bold and arrogant as the Treaty signed at Tordesillas, a small town on the Castillan plateau. The Aragonese pope, Alexander VI, decided to clear up any possible confusion over the ownership of land between Portugal and Spain, two staunchly Catholic countries, and issued bulls in May 1494 that divided up the world's still undiscovered land between the two by establishing a line of demarcation that ran north and south through the Atlantic Ocean 100 leagues (or about 480 kilometers) west of the Cape Verde and Azores Islands. Spain would take possession of any newly discovered land west, whereas Portugal would take over unclaimed territories to the east of the demarcated line. Dissatisfied with the arrangement, King João of

Portugal protested in Rome and through argument and bribery had the rules changed.[7] The line of demarcation was moved west from 100 to 370 leagues (1,770 kilometers) in a bull of June 1494. This allowed Portugal to later claim Brazil.

VASCO DA GAMA

After much exploration of the African littoral, King Manuel I appointed Vasco da Gama to lead a voyage of four ships with three years' supplies to find the route to India by sea and open a new trade corridor, bypassing the land routes controlled by Muslims. Da Gama set out in July 1497, and the bold venture proved successful. After rounding Africa, he sailed up the east coast of the continent, whose ports were under the jurisdiction of Muslim sultans, stopping first at Mozambique, where the sultan looked at the Portuguese trade goods with disgust. Bells and trinkets excited native African chiefs on the west coast of Africa, but for a sultan dressed in fine silks and gold and silver ornaments, they were far from adequate. Further up the coast at Melindi, da Gama found a pilot and crossed the Indian Ocean to arrive at Calicut, India. The Arab and Persian merchants were not pleased to see European vessels anchoring in their traditional trade ports. After finally landing at Calicut, da Gama's journal records that the Portuguese were greeted with the words: "May the devil take thee!" The Hindu Samorin, the headman, sided with the merchants. The proposal to trade low-quality Portuguese products for spices was ill received, but da Gama was able to load some spices on board before the situation turned ugly. The Muslim merchants were not going to give up their monopoly to usurpers. The Portuguese left Calicut, explored further along the Indian coast, and then headed for home.

Already decimated by disease and accidents, the fleet spent three months struggling against adverse winds in the Indian Ocean. Scurvy took so many lives that upon reaching Mombasa, one of the ships was abandoned for want of a crew to sail her. The admiral reached Lisbon in September 1499. At the end of the 26-month voyage and 44,000 kilometers, 44 men out of the 168 returned home.

India was not the Orient that the Portuguese captain had expected. Instead of finding a single wealthy realm, he found many states with a vast and complex commercial network, and merchants who for centuries had been trading European metals and gold bullion for Indian spices via Venetian middlemen who traded at Aleppo (Syria), the Levant, Istanbul, and Alexandria.[8] To his surprise, in addition to European goods, da Gama also saw items from North Africa and Malaya, and gold and ivory from East Africa that arrived through Muslim networks. Prior to the appearance of the Portuguese, maritime trade in the Indian Ocean, established peacefully through the centuries between Muslim and Hindu merchants, resulted in a mutually beneficial relationship.

FURTHER EXCURSIONS

Another voyage, this one made by Pedro Alvares Cabral, took a wide birth around Africa, discovered and claimed Brazil, and went on to reach Calicut. The Samorin, this time pleased with the gifts brought by Cabral, offered to negotiate. The Muslim merchants would have none of it, however, and several Portuguese were killed. Cabral bombarded the city with the ship's cannon, sank some of the nearby vessels, and sailed away to Cochin and Cannanor, where the Samorins, enemies of Calicut, proved friendlier. Cabral departed from India in January 1501, leaving some men behind to establish a trading station in Cochin.[9] Of his 13 ships, less than half made it back.

Vasco da Gama made a second voyage with 20 ships in 1502. In the Indian Ocean, he caught sight of a ship carrying pilgrim families home from Mecca and set fire to the unfortunate vessel, sinking it with all on board. He then sailed into Calicut harbor. The Samorin this time was ready to trade before such a show of force but refused da Gama's unreasonable request that all Muslims depart the city. The admiral brought his ships in close and let loose a fierce bombardment. Many people were killed and fires started. On his exit from the harbor, da Gama ordered the crews to fire on fishing boats, sinking many and killing their crews. What was on da Gama's mind? Here one can only speculate that he intended to inspire fear along the Malabar Coast and force the Hindus to expel the Muslims from the trading ports. Filling his ships with spices at Cochin and Cannanor, he sailed home. Profits from the cargo were enormous. Cochin, meanwhile, was taken over by the Portuguese in 1503 and became the site of the first European colonial settlement in India.

CASA DA INDIA

The Portuguese cornered most of the European spice market in the sixteenth century, and cities and towns that cooperated with Portugal prospered on trade; those that did not were shelled and burned. The center of Portuguese overseas commerce was the Casa da India (India House), which was situated on the ground floor of the Royal Palace on Lisbon's waterfront. All transactions were in the king's name, and the commodities most traded were gold, silver, spices, slaves, silk, copper, and coral. The most profitable item, however, seems to have been slaves, especially later as Brazil became the primary importer. The Casa da India managed all Portuguese trade overseas during the fifteenth and sixteenth centuries, and maintained a royal monopoly on the trade in cinnamon, cloves, and pepper, levying a 30 percent tax on the profits of other articles.

INDIA

When Francisco de Almeida was appointed to his post of viceroy to India in 1505, he demanded that all ships trading in the East have a license authorized by him; without it, they were subject to arrest. This caused a furor in the non-Portuguese trading community and threatened immediate ruin to all Portuguese rivals. Resistance was eliminated by Portuguese firepower. Muslim merchants shifted their trade further east and collected spices in Malacca at the southern tip of the Malay Peninsula and the Sunda Islands, and they shipped the goods to Ceylon and the Maldives for transshipment directly to the Red Sea and the Persian Gulf, outflanking the Portuguese, who lacked the resources to patrol the entire Indian Ocean.

Almeida, meanwhile, amassed 19 ships and 1,600 men to meet the threat. The two naval forces met on February 2, 1509 at Diu, resulting in the total destruction of the Muslim fleet and its Indian allies. The Portuguese naval guns and gunnery were far superior to those of the enemy, and Portuguese sea power in the Indian Ocean was guaranteed for a while. Fifteen more ships arrived from Portugal in October 1509, and an attack was launched on Calicut, though it resulted in failure.

Under the new viceroy, Albuquerque (who replaced Almeida), an attack was launched on Calicut in January 1510 whereby the Portuguese forces underwent heavy losses. As a result, it was decided that the port of Goa would make a better Portuguese capital because it could be well defended due to its island location. The first assault failed, but the city soon fell to the Portuguese and served thereafter as the eastern trade empire's primary entrepôt. Fortifications were constructed, administrative offices set up, and intermarriage with Indian women was encouraged. Many Portuguese went out to Goa to work in the factories, and many died of disease. For better or worse, Goa also became a center of evangelization by Jesuits and Franciscans, whose proselytizing gained some converts but antagonized many Hindus and Muslims.

ADEN AND HORMUZ

To close the Indian Ocean to Arabs and their commerce, the busy port city of Aden, which guarded the entrance to the Red Sea, was a target for the Portuguese navy An attempt to attack and capture Aden failed in 1513, as the citadel there proved too strong.

Situated on the Strait of Hormuz, the city of the same name commanded the entry to the Persian Gulf. The Portuguese, under Albuquerque, finally secured it in 1515. A fort was built and a strong garrison manned it, closing off Muslim entry to the Indian Ocean.

BATTLE FOR MALACCA

Skirmishes and major sea battles were conducted in the Arabian Sea and Indian Ocean, and coastal cities were fought over by the Portuguese and their adversaries—Indians, Muslim Arabs, Persians, and Turks. The Portuguese completed the conquest of the Malabar Coast and maintained a firm hold of the sea. Malay boats were small, sailing vessels steered by two oars mounted in the stern. By and large, most Muslim merchants had large ocean-faring ships, complemented by smaller coastal ships, but even these were not outfitted to carry artillery and no iron was used in their hull construction. Consequently, the merchants' vessels were highly susceptible to damage, much more than were the Portuguese ships, allowing them to gain control of the Indian Ocean with comparative ease.

With 17 ships, flags flying and cannons roaring in salute, Albuquerque sailed into the harbor of Malacca in 1511, demanding the surrender of the city. The sultan hastily set his men to work building defenses, but after some ferocious fighting, the city was eventually taken. The sultan fled and a massive fortune in precious metal, jewels, silks, and spices fell to the victors, but most of the treasure sent back to Goa was lost at sea. A fort was built using stone from the mosques and tombs of former sultans, enraging the inhabitants.

THE MOLUCCAS

Meanwhile, three ships of the fleet were ordered to the east to find the Moluccas, the source of cloves and nutmeg. The Moluccas, a group of islands just west of New Guinea, were the only place on earth where Europeans believed cloves could grow. Highly prized for their medicinal uses, they were worth their weight in gold. Meanwhile, Albuquerque back in India made peace with the sultan of Calicut, built a fort there, and set out to destroy the remainder of the Muslim trade in the Indian Ocean.

On the principal island, Ternate, at the chain's northern end, the Portuguese constructed a stone fort in 1522 and called it São João Bautista. Only Aden, at the entrance to the Red Sea, was left to capture in order to sever Muslim trade in that quarter, but Albuquerque died without attaining his ultimate goal of controlling the entire spice trade and its sources, destroying all Muslim commerce, and seizing the body of Mohammad, the Prophet, from Mecca, destroying that city, and holding the body for ransom in exchange for the city of Jerusalem.[10] A series of weak and corrupt governors, intent on enriching themselves, followed Albuquerque to India, and their policies ultimately ended in disaster. Others, later, such as Vasco da Gama, taken out of retirement and sent to India, corrected many of the abuses and cleaned up much of the corruption, but in the end, Portugal was too small and too far away to control such a large part of the globe. Portuguese arrogance, cruelty, bigotry, and disrespect for foreign customs and traditions did not help their cause, and proselytizing by religious orders that accompanied expeditions to the East alienated many people of different faiths who might have done business with them. Conversion was usually achieved overtly or covertly by means of cunning seduction, fraud, and manipulation by ruthlessly repressing the indigenous religions such as Buddhism and Hinduism.[11] When the Portuguese controlled a large section of the Island of Ceylon (Sri Lanka), a sacred relic for a large part of the population was a reputed tooth of the Buddha. It was ordered burned by the archbishop of Goa as an object of heathenism. Padre Alexandre Valignano, a Jesuit priest who worked in Asia, observed that

the striking success of the missionary work of Francis Xavier on the Fishery Coast [southern India] was primarily due to the deliberate mixture of threats and blandishments. The Portuguese fleet lying off shore had the capacity to deprive people of their fishing and sea borne trade and using this power Xavier influenced a large number of people living in coastal areas to embrace Christianity.[12]

At the time the Portuguese arrived in Ceylon, the country and its people were fairly prosperous; by the time they left, temples were devastated, the country depopulated—those who survived lived in misery, having suffered inhuman barbarities and atrocities. Contentment and well-being had been replaced by total chaos as a result of Portuguese trade policy and religious fanaticism. Much later, measurements indicated that the antimeridian of the Treaty of Tordesillas placed both the Molucca Islands and the Philippines in the Portuguese commercial hemisphere.[13]

Determined to maintain its trade routes and prevent usurpers from encroachment on its commercial profits, the Portuguese crown built forts to supply its ships and guard the sealanes. Besides the coasts of Africa, the Portuguese built forts at Socotra, Hormuz, Malacca, Macão, and Timor, but Portugal could not muster the finances and manpower to govern such a large, seaborne empire. The forts were always undermanned and ill equipped. They were unable to defend their possessions and trade against larger powers that were anxious to take charge of the lucrative commerce and who took no interest in the pope's division of the world. The English, Dutch, and French shattered Portuguese illusions of a trade monopoly in the East.

CHINA

Portuguese traders reached China about 1516 and attempts to establish trading posts along the coast were thwarted by the Chinese. Trying to do business with the easily offended Chinese but failing to know their customs only led to problems. When Fernão Pires de Andrade arrived in Canton in 1517, he fired the ships' cannons as a salute. The Chinese, believing that guns should be fired only in anger, were highly offended. His brother, Simão, arriving in 1519, set about constructing a fort at the mouth of the Pearl River without authority, and was said to buy Chinese children as slaves, or have them for dinner. The Chinese had already heard news of Portuguese behavior from Malacca, which paid tribute to the Ming Chinese. After many delays, Andrade was allowed a Portuguese embassy to proceed to Beijing. Relations were soon in turmoil, however, as negative reports reached the royal court about their conduct, especially the actions of Simão, that infuriated the

Chinese. Upon Pires' arrival in Beijing, instead of an audience with the emperor, he faced charges of misconduct. Even the letter he carried from the king of Portugal that addressed the emperor as an equal and not as a superior, was insulting. He returned to Canton where he was arrested based on a royal edict that all Portuguese were to be expelled from China. Pires died in prison. Nevertheless, a good deal of smuggling went on between Chinese port officials while the Portuguese employed Malays or other nationals to crew their ships and trade on the shore. The Portuguese stayed out of sight but continued to press the Chinese for a trading base that was finally granted in 1557 when Macão was established.

PORTUGUESE TRADE FROM MACÃO TO JAPAN

Macão's existence depended on the Portuguese carracks that sailed annually there from Goa and on to Japan. Those in command of the ships were assured of great profits, provided they made safe crossings. In China, scarce silver was highly prized, used for currency, and in demand; in Japan, silver was mined, but not much of it was used for currency, since as much as 60 percent profit was to be made from taking the silver to China and exchanging it for silk that then returned to Japan.[14] The silk was bought at the biennial trade fair up river at Canton. The Jesuits took care of the trade, sending their priests to Canton to purchase silk for 90 ducats a bale, that they subsequently sold in Japan for 140 ducats. To be certain no losses were incurred (if all the silk was not sold), the priests managed to convince the Council of Macão that their bales were always included in the transaction.[15]

For many centuries, Japanese pirates raided China's coasts, and the Ming Dynasty had prohibited trade with Japan, a country that Portuguese ships made contact with in 1543,[16] when they repeated their previous mistakes. Christian missionaries, Jesuits, Franciscans, and others were allowed to enter Japan and proselytize, but eventually they were considered a threat, as were the local people who had converted to Christianity. Loyalty to the pope above their Japanese leaders was unacceptable. All Christian priests were ordered out of Japan, and converts were forced to return to Buddhism. Those that did neither were executed. By 1640, nearly all vestiges of Christianity in the country were eradicated, and for the following two centuries, all Japanese were forced to register every year at a Buddhist temple and then trample on pictures of Christ or the Virgin Mary as proof they were not secret Christians.[17] It was not long before Portuguese traders associated with missionaries were expelled. Still, much clandestine trade continued as the Portuguese brought spices to China, exchanged them for silk and porcelain, sold the Chinese products to the Japanese for silver from their mines, carried it back to Macão (which lacked silver), and traded it for gold. Chinese trade with Japan was officially forbidden, and the emperor's navy attacked Portuguese ships carrying the contraband goods, but Portuguese firepower usually triumphed. Traders from Macão became wealthy through illicit exchanges.

From their offices and warehouses established in Antwerp, the Portuguese distributed their Eastern products, especially spices, throughout Europe, and the crown made a substantial income from this trade. The king, Manuel I, was referred to as the *roi épicier*, or "grocer king," by the French.

ACEH

When the Portuguese seized the strategic port of Malacca, many Asian and Arabic traders moved to the developing port city-state of Aceh, located on the northern end of the island of Sumatra. It became a booming and wealthy international trade center and a thorn in the side of Portuguese commerce in the East. Aceh handled much precious cargo that traders would have liked to absorb and was Portugal's main rival in the Indian Ocean, trading with Venice and the Ottoman Empire. It was already a pepper-producing region from which ships carried cargo to the south of Ceylon, generally beyond the Portuguese blockade, to Aden and from there to Alexandria and Venice for distribution in Europe. From Aceh and other sources as much as 7 million tons of pepper reached the West annually.[18] Aceh's command over trade in the entire region reached its high point about 1630. The attempt of Portugal to maintain a monopoly was challenged by the traders of North Sumatra, as well as by others in the region.

In areas where the traders were subject to Portuguese control, merchants found themselves eliminated from the inter-Asian trade, and those who did survive did so by acceding to Portuguese demands for payment for safe passage. Eventually, many of the local traders began arming their own ships and using smaller ports to avoid the larger, more important ones controlled by the Portuguese.

DECLINE IN EASTERN TRADE

Due to the costs of maintaining the empire, and the penchant of the Portuguese for bullying their way into commercial enterprises, their particular disposition to create enemies (in part due to their Christian fervor and support of missionaries), their quick and indiscriminate use of firearms, their ignorance of foreign customs, and lack of tactful approaches to trade, and last, if not least, their general state of disorganization and corruption of high officials, the trade repository at Antwerp fell into bankruptcy and closed down as the Casa da India was unable to meet its expenses. The monarchy, too, was hard pressed to meet financial obligations.

BRAZIL

Intent on the Eastern trade, the Portuguese made little effort to colonize Brazil and its population of about 1 million people of scattered seminomadic Indian tribes. Brazilian wood and exotic animals were at first about all that were considered to be of any trade value. Gold lay still undiscovered in the vast land, but a rumor of silver mines in the interior caught the attention of King João III, who began a program of colonization in 1530. As the Eastern empire disintegrated, new commercial opportunities for the country opened up in Brazil. The territory went to 12 captaincies, called donatories, from the royal court, and each was given a district to colonize and organize trade. A governor-general, Tomé de Sousa, was appointed, who established a government in Brazil with the capital at Salvador (Bahia) in 1549. As usual, forts were built all along the coast. Sugar and tobacco plantations were created whose products were exported, with tobacco reaching Lisbon in 1550, and France about 10 years later.[19] In addition, sugar, brandy, rice, animals, and hides, as well as gold were exported to Angola in exchange for wax, ivory, and slaves—the latter in demand on the plantations in Brazil.

SLAVES

From the interior of Africa, slaves were brought to the coast after seemingly endless weeks of walking chained together. It could be said that the fortunate ones died on the trail. On the African coast at places such as São Jorge da Mina, they were baptized and branded. It has been estimated that some 50 percent died before they embarked on the ships. The voyage across the Atlantic to

Brazil might take as long as 50 days that often involved many more deaths. The human cargo that reached Brazil were then sold and sent on their way, often another long trek, to the plantations or mines, where life expectancy was between seven and 10 years.[20]

The transportation of high-value, fragile goods was carried out by slaves instead of mules. Slaves often carried items on their heads in containers. Sometimes, teamwork was required for the transportation of heavy loads such as casks.[21] When rivers were available, the Portuguese used the boats of their own design, either of fragile construction and using three or four paddlers for shallow waters, or larger types of canoes hollowed out from tree trunks, that included sails of cotton and rigging of vines for negotiating larger rivers or coastal waters. Portuguese missionaries for subduing the local population, especially along the Amazon, also used these stronger boats.[22]

COMPETITION

The French founded a trading colony at Rio de Janeiro, but the Portuguese destroyed it in 1560 and soon established their own site there

Much of the native population of Brazil succumbed to enslavement and disease such as malaria, plague, tuberculosis, influenza, and smallpox (which was lethal), brought in by the Europeans and against which the local people had no immunity.

The Portuguese could not compete with stronger nations that encroached on their empire. Dutch, English, and French traders and trading companies had no scruples about infringing on routes and acquiring products that the Portuguese claimed and tried to protect.

In 1580, Felipe II of Spain, as rightful heir to the crown, added Portugal to his domains. The amalgamated empires—Spanish in the New World and Portuguese in Africa and the Indian Ocean—continued to be administered by their respective mother countries, but both were challenged by other European powers. In the East where Portuguese entrenchment was strong—in Macão, East Timor, Goa, Angola, and Mozambique—they held on to their possessions.

NOTES

1. Saraiva, 105; Livermore 1966, 170.
2. Livermore (1966), 186.
3. Livermore (1966), 170.

4. Livermore (1966), 190–192.

5. Abbot, 19.

6. Boxer, 132.

7. Livermore (1966), 218.

8. Mather, 34.

9. Livermore (1966), 231.

10. Livermore (1947), 236.

11. http://www.vgweb.org/unethicalconversion/port_rep.htm.

12. Boxer, 76.

13. Borschberg, 36.

14. Spence (1984), 174.

15. Spence (1984), 176.

16. Perez, 41.

17. Perez, 56.

18. Bernstein, 190; Curtin, 148.

19. Tobacco was imported into France by Jean Nicot.

20. Boxer, 114–115.

21. Russell-Wood, 51–52.

22. Russell-Wood, 56–57.

12

PRECOLONIAL AFRICA

Local trade has been carried on in Africa since the Stone Age, but long-distance trade became more important when camel caravans began to cross the desert a little before 800.[1] The Roman army may have introduced the camel to western parts of North Africa in order to patrol the fringes of the empire, but the Berbers soon adopted it for their own trading and raiding purposes. Even then, the central interior remained dark and mysterious to Europeans until the nineteenth century. Local Africans traded goods that had to be carried on their backs in the tropical regions, or by river canoes, rather than pack animals that were subject to the deadly tsetse fly.

NORTH AFRICA AND THE SAHARA

The tribal communities of North Africa and the great desert were largely self-sustaining. Their social hierarchy included an upper class, their vassals, and slaves. Artisans and blacksmiths furnished the community with most household utensils, weapons, jewelry, and leather accessories. The peoples of the Sahara tended goats and sheep along with camels for milk, meat, and cheese. Donkeys provided local transport. Up until the mid-twentieth century, Tuaregs raided neighboring settlements and used slave labor for many tasks.

Camels in a caravan loaded with goods. (North Wind Picture Archives.)

With the Muslim conquest of North Africa in the seventh century, Berbers converted to Islam. Today, about 40 percent of them work in flourmills, artisanal woodcarving, quarrying stone, and producing pottery or jewelry. Women employ their skills in weaving and pottery. Most Berbers, no longer nomadic, live in rural areas where housing usually consists of clay huts or tents made of goatskin. In larger villages, they may be made of stone. Many Berbers are currently engaged as migrant workers in Spain or France.

Gold from west Sudan (throughout the Middle Ages, the swath of land across Africa, just south of the desert, was known as the Sudan—Arabic for "land of the blacks," not to be confused with present-day Sudan) was the major attraction of the trans-Saharan trade, stimulated by the demand for gold for coinage and also for the Catholic church's decoration and ostentation.

In the eighth and ninth centuries, Arab merchants operating in southern Moroccan towns such as Sijilmasa, located near the

African slave caravans on the march. (North Wind Picture Archives.)

present-day Moroccan-Algerian border, exchanged salt for gold and financed the caravans that transported the goods across the desert. The gold and other products, after reaching the Mediterranean, were then shipped to Europe and the Levant. After the subjugation of North Africa by Arab Muslims, Europeans were deprived of direct trade on the African continent.

Besides gold, slaves traveling north were an important commodity along the Saharan trade route and were often exchanged for salt. Hundreds of thousands crossed the desert to supply Muslim countries with servants, concubines, and soldiers. The demand was continuous and lucrative until the twentieth century.

RELIGION AND TRANS-SAHARAN TRADE

Merchants transported more than valuable commodities along the trans-Saharan routes. Just as Buddhism reached the Chinese Empire via the Silk Road, so Islam reached black Africa through Arab merchants on Saharan caravan routes who brought the Koran and written Arabic to the traditionally oral cultures of Africa. Although it seems the average local people usually felt no pressure to convert from their ancient religions, royal families and merchants took up Islam in order to curry favor with Arab traders. The civilizations that arose and flourished in West Africa were based on trade, since West African kings and nobles were more interested in wealth than in pursuing warrior aspirations. From the north over the desert wasteland came luxury goods that included oil lamps, fine pottery, glass, and cowry shells, which were sometimes used as money in the exchange process. In return, Africans traded mostly gold and slaves

The region of the western Sudan saw the rise and fall of the four most important empires of medieval Africa: Ghana, Mali, Songhai, and Bornu-Kanem. Other, smaller kingdoms, often subservient to these empires, were of lesser consequence. Arabs crossing the Sahara encountered these civilizations that had had only very limited contact with the outside world.

GHANAIAN EMPIRE (200–1235)

Ancient Ghana was an influential trading entity for cattle, grain, and metals within African society, but by around 700, Arab camel caravans transported commodities such as salt, textiles, tools, and books across the Sahara to Ghanaian trading centers, where they were exchanged for gold, slaves, and ivory. Ghana also served as a depot for other items, many having come from further south, including foodstuffs, cotton, cloth, ornaments, and leather goods. The ruins of Koumbi Saleh in southeast Mauritania seem to have been the medieval capital of the Ghanaian Empire. Arab merchants described it as consisting of two towns set apart from each other, one for the king, the other, Islamic with a number of mosques, established for Arab merchants. The people lived in stone or wooden houses between the two towns. The geographer al-Bakri described the eleventh-century court at Koumbi Saleh, where he saw gold-embroidered caps, golden saddles, shields and swords mounted with gold, and dogs' collars adorned with gold and silver.[2]

Much of the gold that found its way across the Sahara came from a little south of Ghana, passed through the kingdom, crossed the desert, and was turned into coins and jewelry when it reached the Mediterranean shores. The empire of Ghana thrived on, and was sustained by, the gold trade. It should be kept in mind that Ghana at this time was situated hundreds of kilometers to the north and west of its present location. The gold-for-salt route began in the city of Sidjilmassa and passed through the salt-rich village of Taghaza, then on through the Sahara and finally to the gold region, known as Wangara, on the southwest border of Ghana.

The kings of Ghana maintained tight control over the realm's gold production in order to keep prices high. Only the king, for example, could possess nuggets; other residents could own only gold dust. The king also profited by taxing traders who used routes that passed through the empire, presumably from Wangara. Nuggets, illegal to trade in the empire, were given over to the imperial treasury in exchange for an equal value of dust. The king kept the locations of the mines secret, to prevent direct access by commercial traders.

MALI EMPIRE (1235–1400)

A change in the political control of West Africa occurred when the Islamic Mali Empire arose about 1235 and, replacing Ghana as the major gold supplier, took control of the trade, still the life's blood of West Africa. The Mali Empire extended over much of the previous Ghanaian Empire, an area larger than Western Europe, and consisted of numerous vassal kingdoms and provinces. Merchants established a second major gold-salt trade route northeast across the Sahara that passed through Tunis to Cairo, usurping some trade from the traditional western Sudan-to-Morocco-to-Europe trade route. While Ghana's kings restricted gold's availability during their reigns, the rulers of Mali did not.

A detrimental effect of gold imports into Europe was felt in 1324 when Mansa Musa, the tenth emperor of Mali, on a pilgrimage to Mecca, appeared in Egypt with an enormous amount of gold. He was thought to have had some 80,000 people in his entourage, all carrying sacks of the precious metal that he freely distributed along the way. So much gold so suddenly on the market depressed the price and caused inflation that led to economic difficulties for many merchants for years to come. In the fourteenth century, cowry shells were introduced as local currency, but gold and salt remained the principal items of long-distance trade.[3]

By the beginning of the fourteenth century, Mali, located in the far north of the modern state of that name, produced about half of the world's gold. The Saharan towns of the Mali Empire carried on trade as staging posts in the long-distance caravan commerce, and as trading centers for various West African products.

Ibn Battutah in Mali

In 1352, Ibn Battutah set out from Fez (Morocco) with a caravan of traders, reaching the city of Sijilmasa and from there moving south to visit the "land of the blacks." They travelled 25 days before arriving at Taghaza, where he stated,

its houses and mosque are built of blocks of salt and roofed with camel skins. The village had neither attractions, nor trees, and was surrounded by sand. The only inhabitants, miserable slaves of a Berber tribe, the Massufa, dug the salt, loaded the slabs on camels, and lived on dates and camel meat. Black people came from their country [to the south] and took it away. In the city of Mali it sold for three to four times the price paid at its source in Taghaza, traded and sold in the same manner as other people did with gold or silver.[4]

Ibn Battutah goes on to describe the undrinkable water, with flies all about. Lice, too, were so abundant that people wore vials of mercury around their necks to kill them. To lag behind or go on ahead of the caravan could be dangerous, as it was easy to be lost in the desert, the wind stirring up the sand and erasing all tracks. At Tasarahla Oasis, along the 500-mile route to Walata, the caravan halted for three days to rest, repair gear, and fill the bags with fresh water from the spring. (Walata was the southern terminus of the trans-Saharan trade, later replaced by Timbuktu.) A local guide from the Musafa tribe performed the duties of scout, going ahead of the caravan to Walata to inform the merchants there that a caravan would soon arrive. The merchants would prepare a company of water-bearers to travel four days into the desert to meet the caravan. According to Ibn Battutah, there were many dangers in the desert such as devils, poisonous snakes, and mirages, and if the scout died or failed to find water, the entire caravan might become lost and perish. Mountains of sand appeared in one place and then in another after a windstorm—there were no tracks or roads. Much travelling was done at night when the air was cooler. The caravan reached Walata after a two-month journey from Sijilmasa Not knowing the customs of the black African people, Ibn Battutah often found them bad mannered and was astonished that as Muslims, the women went about unveiled and shamelessly had male friends. A man might find his wife in the house conversing with a male and not be offended. Once when Ibn Battutah entered a room to find a man sitting on a rug and another sitting on a couch, both talking to the former's wife, Ibn Battutah asked the husband if he were not ashamed. The response was that it was good to have male and female friends. Ibn Battutah reported, "I was astonished at his silliness." Although invited to the house many more times, he never accepted.[5]

The town of Mali (which no longer exists) was about 24 days travel from Walata, and Ibn Battutah went on to visit it. He described the wealth of the sultan whose guards displayed quivers of gold and silver, maces of crystal, and his entourage who were dripping with precious metals. He had his four wives with him and about 100 concubines, all elaborately dressed.

A feature of the people that much impressed Ibn Battutah was the peace and lawfulness he found strictly enforced in the Malian Empire. The people were meticulous in their prayers; dressed in clean white clothes on Fridays, even the poorest; and spent a good deal of time memorizing the Koran. Those who were slow to learn it were shackled until they did. Ibn Battutah did not like the fact that servants and slave girls went around naked and unveiled, as did the young daughters of the sultan. He also found it distasteful that people ate carrion as well as monkeys and donkeys. His remarks on cannibalism among the infidels of the surrounding country were hearsay when he reported that they did not eat white people because they were unripe and that the parts of women they liked best were the palm of the hand and the breasts. They lived in gold-bearing country and sometimes sent a delegation to the sultan, who once gave them a slave woman whom they promptly ate. Following Mansa Musa's death, Mali underwent a long decline.

SONGHAI EMPIRE (1468–1591)

Under their leader Sunni Ali Kolon, the Songhai challenged the Mali Empire in the early fifteenth century and captured Jenné (Djenné–Jéno) in 1491 and then Timbuktu—both wealthy and important commercial and educational centers that controlled most trans-Saharan trade in gold, salt, kola nuts, and slaves. Gao, on the eastern route, a city that began to grow in importance during the Mali Empire, became capital of the Songhai and a significant market center.

In addition, the copper mining town of Takedda on the eastern trans-Saharan trading route contributed to the Songhai Empire's commercial growth. Finally, during Sunni Ali's reign, trade along the eastern trans-Saharan route reached a peak. Not until the sixteenth century did such matters begin to change with the Portuguese voyages of discovery along the west coast of Africa and the establishment of trading posts, bypassing the Muslim land trade over the desert.

The learned and well-traveled Leo Africanus, a Christian convert born in Granada, Spain, about 1493, made several trips to Timbuktu, where he was impressed with the palace and the mosque, and recorded finding many erudite men retained at the king's expense. He also found books and manuscripts sold for higher prices than any other merchandise. The coin of the city was made of gold, and the king possessed vast amounts of it.

The Songhai Empire was even richer than those of Ghana and Mali, primarily because of the gold trade. However, the great empires did not actually control the source of gold, since it was mined by communities further south and west. In 1591, the Songhai were defeated by an army from Morocco. By the time the empire fell, Europeans were already well acquainted with the western coast of Africa.

BATTLE OF TONDIBI (1591)

Desirous of seizing control of the trans-Saharan gold trade and revitalizing its importance, the sultan of Morocco, Ahmad al-Mansur, sent 4,000 troops across the Sahara with up-to-date European guns, including some cannons, and 10,000 supply camels—all bought with West African gold. The two-month journey found the Songhai surprised and unprepared. At the Battle of Tondibi on the Niger River near Gao, Moroccan firearms were decisive. Next to fall were Timbuktu and Jenne. The Songhai warriors regrouped at Dendi to the south and began a campaign of guerilla warfare as the Moroccan army failed to capture the entire area, and maintaining an army south of the Sahara drained the Moroccan treasury without any real lasting benefit to the sultan. Not enough gold was sent to Morocco to make the enterprise worthwhile. The Songhai Empire broke up, and Morocco withdrew from the region at the end of the seventeenth century, leaving a group of small kingdoms.[6] This military action disrupted and dramatically reduced trade to a fraction of its former activity.

BORNU-KANEM (1220–1600)

The Islamic kingdom of Bornu-Kanem, today Niger, Chad, and Nigeria, arose in north central Africa in the region of Lake Chad, the wealth of the kingdom derived from the ability of its rulers to control trade. Their main exports were ostrich feathers, slaves, and ivory. By virtue of its central location, Kanem was a natural connecting point in the vast network of Saharan and Sudanic trade routes. Kanem was a kind of confederation of nomadic tribes banded together under one dynasty called Saifawa about 900, but not until the eleventh century did they establish a permanent capital at Njimi (its exact site remains obscure) and gain wealth through trade across the desert to Egypt and Tripoli. Kanem reached the height of its power in the first half of the thirteenth century. Captives taken in raids were traded in the North African states for horses. The tributary state of Bornu, to the southwest, was established in the thirteenth century, but by the following century, it refused to pay tribute and conducted its own trade across the Sahara. As a result, the situation reversed itself, and Kanem became a tributary state of Bornu. In the sixteenth century, Turkish Ottoman advisors, mercenaries, and firearms paid for by taxes and trade—much of the latter taken away from the Songhai and the western routes—trained Bornu's army. In the following centuries, slave-raiding to the south remained a priority income for the noble class.[7]

EAST AFRICA

The large area of East Africa encompassed the modern countries of Egypt, the Sudan, Ethiopia, Kenya, Tanzania, and Uganda, and to the south, Mozambique. The region once contained a plethora of kingdoms and trade networks; one of the earliest known was Nubia (also known as Karmah or Kush). Others included Aksum, the Buganda kingdom, and Rwanda along with the Muslim Swahili coastal city-states such as Mogadishu, Mombasa, Malindi, Zanzibar, Kilwa, Sofala, and others.

Meroë, Berenike, and Axum

Iron smelting furnaces have been excavated at Meroë, revealing an important trading city on the Nile, well before the common era.[8] Due to plentiful iron ore in the area and an abundance of hardwood trees for making charcoal, the region of Meroë flourished and became one of the important states of the southern Sudan. From the sixth century BCE until the fourth century CE, Meroitic ironworkers were renowned for their craftsmanship, but the region also exported cotton textiles and jewelry. Cotton reached its highest output in Nubia around 400 BCE. Trade in gold and animals obtained further south also helped the economy.

The city of Berenike, on the Red Sea, was a primary center for trade with India from the third century BCE to the fourth century CE.

All along the African coast were market towns trading goods both with each other and over long distances. Further down the gulf and inland from the port of Adulis lay Coloe, a market for ivory coming from beyond the Nile River.[9] From Egypt, goods such as cloth and sheets of copper for cooking utensils, cups and decoration, brass to be made into ornaments, iron for spears and axes, swords, and even wine from Italy were brought to these Red Sea communities and traded inland for ivory, rhinoceros horn, and turtle shells. Arab merchants spread Islam among the villages on the coast and further inland. Berenike was conquered by the Romans, became a Roman province, and was one of several Roman ports that traded with India. It was abandoned in the sixth century as the harbor silted up and the city became buried under drifting sand.

By the eighth century, Muslim Arabs controlled the Red Sea. Manda, an early trading center, exported mangrove wood, and possibly also ivory and iron, in exchange for luxury goods that included fine pottery. After the eleventh century, its commercial role passed to Kilwa and other towns. Kilwa exported raw materials and traded glass beads, Islamic pottery, and cloth inland.

Axum, once a great mercantile Christian kingdom, controlled an important trade route in pre-Islamic times. Located near the Red Sea in the Ethiopian highlands, the kingdom and cities of Axum, Matara, and the port city of Adulis (now in Eritrea) rose to prominence in the world of commerce in about 100 CE. Axum conquered neighboring lands and parts of Yemen across the Red Sea. Its position transformed the kingdom into a wealthy realm that participated in commerce from the Mediterranean to India, the Levant, and Alexandria. The rulers of Axum renounced their polytheistic beliefs for Christianity in the fourth century. The kingdom went into decline in the sixth century and eventually, as Muslims took over the trade routes, faded away into a backwater. Although surrounded by Muslims, Christianity continued.

Great Zimbabwe (present-day Zimbabwe)

The most advanced civilization in Central Africa was that of Great Zimbabwe, where the nobles constructed immense stone palaces between the eleventh and thirteenth centuries. Great Zimbabwe grew into the largest inland settlement. It covered 40 hectares and was made up of stone wall enclosures dating back to the tenth century. Found here were Chinese and Islamic pottery, cowry shells, and glass beads from Kilwa and other coastal towns. Great Zimbabwe provided gold, copper, tin, and iron in return. Copper was mined some 300 kilometers to the south. Both Kilwa and Great Zimbabwe, now archaeological sites, declined about the same time, around 1450. Great Zimbabwe appears to have served as a religious center for the surrounding regions and as the home of kings and their elite. The rise of upper-class groups in the interior seems to have coincided with an increase in production and trade.[10] Great Zimbabwe traded with western India, as attested by glass beads and Indian cotton cloth found there. Arabs, both in East Africa and coastal India, became intermediaries in this trade, dominating the Arabian Sea and Indian Ocean.

SOUTH AFRICA

Various tribes occupied the lands of South Africa before the coming of Europeans. The first, Khoikhoi, were herders. Then came the San, who were hunter-gatherers. Both were Stone Age cultures. The San hunted and herded for the Khoikhoi in exchange for food. Also occupying the southern land were the Nguni and Sotho, which were split up into numerous tribes. Out of the Nguni arose the Zulu kingdom and the dominant language. To the north developed the Swazi kingdom out of the Nguni and Sotho peoples, along with other small South African states. South Africans were primarily subsistence farmers or hunter-gatherers, and similarities and intermarriage between tribes indicate some degree of interaction.[11]

Bantu people from the north with iron tools and weapons moved south before 400, displacing the Khoikhoi and San. The first appearance of sheep in South Africa about this time suggests they were imported by the invaders, a pastoral people, who measured their wealth in the number of cattle the family possessed. Trade among these earlier inhabitants can only be assumed.

NOTES

1. Curtin, 15.
2. Shillington, 83–84.
3. Harris, 56–58. See also http://library.thinkquest.org/13406/sh/?tqskip1=1.
4. Mackintosh-Smith, 281.
5. Mackintosh-Smith, 285.
6. Shillington, 180.

7. Shillington, 182–183.
8. Shinnie, passim.
9. Schoff, 23.
10. *Past Worlds*, 252.
11. Harris, 153–54.

13

COLONIAL AND MODERN AFRICA

In 1884, a conference was held in Berlin under the directorship of Otto von Bismarck and attended by 14 European powers and the United States. Its goal was to agree on the dividing of Africa among them. They established rules for the exploitation of the continent. Africans were not invited, nor were they made aware of how their territory was to be partitioned and turned to the advantage of Europeans.

Major countries had already staked out claims in Africa, and the conference clarified some and delineated others. A major aspect of the gathering was to eliminate slavery by the native population and Muslim merchants, and the various European states signed pledges to abolish it in their spheres of interest. The Congo Free State was validated as the private property of Leopold II of Belgium, but it was to remain open to European traders and missionaries. Free trade areas were designated, including the Congo and Niger River waterways, and each European nation could obtain the legal right to land in its possession if it was effectively occupied and administered. Days after the conference, the wily Bismarck used the "effectively occupied" clause against the British, whose claims in East Africa were vague and informal. He proclaimed a German protectorate in the middle of the British sphere of influence on the grounds that Peters, a German representative, had recently been in the region and made treaties with local chiefs. Germany thus claimed what would eventually become Tanzania.[1]

European dominion in Africa was primarily based on securing trade routes, with control over the areas and means of production. Since the sixteenth century, trade had been the primary factor in colonization and an important aspect of a developing global economy. African European empires were the result of Europe's need for new markets for its industrial goods and its need for raw materials. Africans sold the raw materials for cash and used the money to buy imported European manufactured products. It often happened that European governments, settlers, and merchants seized land and raw materials, giving little or no compensation to the native people.[2]

Portuguese, Spanish, British, Belgians, Dutch, French, Germans and Italians were all involved in the colonization of Africa to various degrees and at various times. Each had networks of traders and missionaries there, and they set up formal colonial governments to administrate their individual regions.

PORTUGUESE COLONIZATION

The first European attempt to establish a colony in Africa was the 1415 Portuguese conquest of Ceuta. Various European nations followed by establishing trading posts along African coasts, mostly for slaves, but the scramble for African land and colonial administrations over the indigenous African people began in the early nineteenth century. In 1575, a colony was created at Luanda in Angola when 100 Portuguese families arrived, accompanied by soldiers. Thirty years later, Luanda was granted city status and became a major slave-exporting center. Also of interest to the Portuguese and others was the diamond trade. In 1752, Mozambique was established as a colony, and a governor-general was installed. Ivory was an important export item, but slaves were the principle trade commodity. Attracted by the slave trade and African resources, other nations set up trading stations that soon became colonies, and in Senegal (in West Africa), the French began to establish trading posts along the coast in 1624. Besides Portugal, England and France claimed large regions of Africa.

The European powers came to be in competition with one another for control of resources and by the end of the nineteenth century, there was little left of Africa that was not claimed as a colony. In the barren zones of North Africa, and in the tropical climate of the west, Europeans extracted mineral and agricultural wealth but built little in the way of infrastructure. They were not inclined to settle in the arid or sultry territories, but East and South Africa, with temperate climates, except on the coasts of East Africa, beckoned to many Europeans, who took up residence and built plantations and mining industries to send the products to their home countries.

GREAT BRITAIN AND EXPLORATION

In the early nineteenth century, the interior of Africa was largely unknown. The British African Association materialized in 1788 and began exploration of the continent with a view to enhancing European knowledge of the geography, peoples, and trade. Many explorers were sent out to Africa, and the reports sent back stimulated great interest in merchants and missionaries alike, the former for trade, the latter hungry for converts and concerned about the slave trade. Both often came to stay. The discovery that quinine could alleviate the worst of the malarial fever that killed many earlier adventurers induced more Europeans to come to Africa. The discovery of gold mines also brought many thousands of English people to South Africa.

In 1875, England established a base in Egypt when Benjamin Disraeli bought a large block of stock in the Suez Canal, a project already aided by France under the direction of Ferdinand de Lesseps between 1859 and 1869. Heavily in debt to both England and France, and unable to pay, the ruler of Egypt, Ismail Pasha, was forced to submit the Egyptian treasury to those two countries. He was subsequently deposed, and England and France took over the rule of Egypt. Complete military occupation followed as an anti-imperialist uprising began. France then withdrew, and England created an Egyptian protectorate with a view to further expansion into the Sudan.

During the early 1870s, Britain bought out Danish and Dutch trading posts. This eliminated competition, and soon there was a British trade monopoly along the Gold Coast. This in turn led to a British protectorate over what is today modern Ghana. Further expansion into Nigeria, where there was already an English coastal colony at Lagos, gave the British a monopoly on palm oil exports from the lower Niger River region. The National African Company was formed to control the exports.[3] Resistance to this control of trade was put down by gunboat diplomacy. The remainder of Nigeria was taken by force using recruited African soldiers with modern weapons, including artillery and machine guns. Cities that fell to British troops were looted and burned.

FRENCH COLONIZATION

In 1879, the French initiated a concerted effort to colonize West Africa and began to buy up large tracts of land in what was to become the French Congo, including Dahomey, Senegal, and the Ivory Coast. French possessions there were handed over to concessionary companies, and agents combed the jungles, kidnapping natives and forcing them into labor camps. Villagers were obliged to hand over a certain amount of rubber and ivory, or suffer brutal consequences. Local people were used as pack animals to transport goods, and some 16,000 died building a railroad from the coast to Brazzaville to move goods more quickly and efficiently.[4]

Meanwhile, the French expanded into Tunisia and south into the Sahara Desert. By 1898, their possessions in West and North Africa were linked. Moving further east into the Sudan, they came up against the British and, on the brink of war, the problem was solved peacefully by dividing the area into spheres of influence.

While European colonization often met with resistance and some terrible battles were fought, European superior arms generally won out. France took over Algeria and most of Morocco, except for a small Spanish enclave on the Mediterranean coast opposite Spain. The French came to control an enormous part of West Africa along with equatorial Africa, Madagascar, and a few small territories. The British claimed domination over Egypt, Sudan, Kenya, Tanzania, South Africa, Rhodesia, the Gold Coast, Nigeria, and a few minor enclaves. Portugal ruled in Angola and Mozambique, and Italy took over Libya.

Sent from the French African possessions to France were palm oil, timber, diamonds, gold, jewels, rubber, ivory, and minerals along with exotic fruit, vegetables, and animals—all in exchange for small manufactured articles.

BELGIAN CONGO FREE STATE

Belgium controlled the Congo, where the native peoples appear to have suffered the most by foreign rule. In 1878, King Leopold II persuaded Belgian banks to underwrite the International Congo Association, a private enterprise organized to purchase land for the acquisition of rubber resources. Leopold declared that all land not actively occupied belonged to him and his Congo Free State government. For local people, this was a travesty, since most of the land fell under this category. Leopold kept some for himself and leased the rest to individual companies that employed private armies to force the local people into the forest to collect rubber from the trees. A report in the *London Times* on November 18, 1895 described the conditions: each town in the district had to supply a certain amount of rubber to the headquarters of the company every Sunday. Those who refused to collect it were shot, even women and children. People deserted their villages, preferring homelessness, hunger, and a nomadic existence rather than endure the cruelty of their exploitation.[5] Congo chieftains with no knowledge of private property exchanged large tracts of land for beads and other trifles. The Congo was under the control of the private corporations until 1908, when the Belgian government took it over as a territorial possession. The Belgian Congo Free State was anything but free for the Congolese.[6]

ITALIAN AND GERMAN COLONIZATION

Although somewhat late in colonial ventures, Italy and Germany were not to be left out. Italy attacked Ethiopia but was defeated at Adowa in 1896. It nevertheless secured control over the territories of Eritrea on the Red Sea, and Somalia on the Indian Ocean. Italy forcefully annexed the North African state of Libya in 1912. Imperialism and competition for trade drove the major European nations toward World War I.

Germany cut out a stretch of land in what came to be called German East Africa, lying between British Uganda and Rhodesia. It also claimed German Southwest Africa south of the Congo (Cameroon). Here, control over the locals was brutal. They were deprived of their best lands, which were given to settlers, forcing the native people to work for the white man and to carry passes in their own country.[7] By 1900, Germany challenged France in a failed bid to control Morocco. In 1904, France and England signed an anti-German *Entente Cordiale* that, amongst other things, granted France a free hand in Morocco, and England the same in Egypt and the Sudan. Germany had a large hand in African exports of coconuts, sesame, and dyes.

AMERICAN INTERESTS

After about 1820, the United States entered into direct trade with East Africa, centered mostly on ivory—high in demand for piano keys, billiard balls, and even combs. A resident agent was assigned to Zanzibar and by mid-century, became the major trading partner with the East African city. American commerce with Zanzibar fell away sharply with the outbreak of the American Civil War.

Southern planters in the United States formed the American Colonization Society in 1816. Its purpose was to resettle free, black Africans in Africa. The reasons were not altruistic, but based on fear that free blacks would generate unrest among slaves. With government support,[8] the first free blacks were sent to Liberia in 1821, followed by 20,000 more.[9] The new Liberians developed trade in palm oil, sugar, coffee, and molasses but were prohibited to trade with their neighbors under colonial rule by the European powers. Although the country had become independent, it remained at the mercy of European states' economic policies.[10]

In 1927, the Liberian government and the Firestone Rubber Company of Ohio entered into a contract for a loan of $5 million from the company in exchange for the right to lease 1 million acres of land and extract rubber. The United States, or at least one of its companies, now had a vested interest in colonial Africa.[11]

SOUTH AFRICA

A European settlement was founded in Cape Town in 1652 as a stopover for ships of the Dutch East India Company (VOC) en route to India and the Dutch East Indies. The VOC traded tools, metals, and trinkets for cattle and fresh vegetables to supply its ships. As settlers arrived in larger numbers, and contention for land began, the Khoikhoi and the San were pushed north into the Kalahari Desert, or became farm laborers. The settlers and the Bantu, who arrived long before the Europeans, engaged in brutal wars for farmland in which the settlers with modern weapons ruled the day. In 1806, the British seized the Cape Colony from the Dutch.[12] As the English moved into the region, wars were fought with the Zulus that ended Zulu independence.

In 1870, with the discovery of diamonds and then gold, many thousands came to South Africa from England. One of these, Cecil Rhodes, premier of the Cape Colony and founder of De Beer's,[13] proposed building a railroad from Cape Colony to Cairo, and the British began to move northward along the east coast to link up the Egyptian and Cape possessions.

Around the turn of the twentieth century, the English and Dutch came to blows in the Boer War (1899–1902), which was fought over land and resources. The Dutch concentrated in the Transvaal were also concerned about being cut off from the sea and seaborne commerce.

ZANZIBAR

A few miles off the east coast of Africa, the island of Zanzibar was ideal for traders. The Portuguese arrival at the island in the sixteenth century established relations with the Muslim population, and set up a trading station and a mission of friars. In the seventeenth century, Portuguese presence on the island ceased, and Oman Arabs moving down the east coast took Mombasa from the Portuguese and found the defensible island of Zanzibar to their liking. The island became a base for trade along the African coast from Somalia to Mozambique. From Zanzibar, traders moved inland to establish a base at Tabora in Tanzania, allowing more ready access to the African interior. By the nineteenth century, thousands of slaves from the interior were sold every year on the Zanzibar slave blocks. Commerce in the African interior was hampered by yellow fever and malaria—diseases that were often fatal, especially for unaccustomed foreigners. Omanis introduced to the island sugar, indigo, and palm plantations worked by slaves. A British Council was established there in 1870, with orders to bring an end to the slave trade, a matter it concluded in 1873 by treaty with the Islamic ruler, Bargash. The economic loss by the abolition of the slave trade was made up when John Kirk of the British Council suggested that the island trade in rubber and ivory collected at Tabora from the interior be sent to Zanzibar. As a result, the sultan became extremely wealthy. In summer of 1885, German warships arrived in the harbor of Zanzibar. With guns leveled at the palace, the commander demanded that Sultan Bargash turn over to Bismarck, the Prussian leader, the sultan's mainland territorial holdings. The British diffused the dangerous situation by suggesting the two countries—Germany and England—cut out spheres of interest on the mainland, and the crisis was resolved. The sultan received a 10-mile-wide strip of land along the coast, while England took charge of what is today Kenya. Germany received Tanzania. Zanzibar and the coastal strip were proclaimed a British protectorate in 1890, and Zanzibar achieved independence in 1963.

WORLD WAR I (1914–1918)

World War I, while a European conflict, had repercussions in Africa due to European countries' commercial interests there. Allied nations with interests in Africa endeavored to prevent Germany from utilizing its African colonial resources to aid its war effort. England joined forces with France and Belgium in attempts to invade the German colonies, and South Africa, on the side of the allies, took over German territory in southwest Africa. The struggle in East Africa continued throughout the war. Armies requisitioning food, burning villages, recruiting labor to carry supplies, and pressing natives into the army as soldiers, subjected the African people to severe hardship. Famine and disease took their toll among the black population. At the end of the war, Germany lost its African possessions to the allies. The havoc created in Africa brought the little international trade there was to a standstill, and trade with Europe, the African nations' primary source of commerce, was severely disrupted. African commodities also rose in price, hurting African sellers, as they were more difficult to obtain during the war.

WORLD WAR II AND THE POSTWAR PERIOD

As the Japanese Empire expanded in Southeast Asia in 1941, taking over European possessions and cutting off trade with the allies, colonial Africa assumed much more importance for vital wartime food and minerals. African palm oil, now the only source, rubber, sisal, cotton, peanuts, tea, coffee, and cocoa brought high prices in Europe, although African producers received no benefit because prices remained at a fixed rate. Colonial governments reaped the profits, however, and African farmers paid higher amounts for imported European manufactured goods as inflation rose in wartime Europe, and they were forced to grow more, export more, and work harder just to keep up. The overall result of the war on African farmers was negative.[14] Cut off from European-made products needed at home for the war effort, South Africa underwent major changes by manufacturing its own foods, chemicals, and steel. Black people in the south flooded to the cities to find work in industry, and when World War II came to a close, ideas of independence were in the wind and would soon become a reality for many African nations that were tired of seeing their natural resources disappearing and being forced to buy them back in the form of European manufactured products. Africans received low wages for their work and had to pay high prices for the imported products. Independence did come, in the 1950s and 1960s, but not without bloodshed in many regions. Commerce between African states themselves has been hindered by the inclination to trade within the currency zones previously established by the colonial powers. Poor or nonexistent roads, transport, and communications also presented problems along with insufficient industrial development. Intra-African trade consisted of such items as food, drinks, tobacco, sugar, cattle, and meat. Since the beginning of World War II, external foreign trade had risen significantly relative to the need for primary commodities during and after the war, but imports surpassed exports, leading to trade imbalances for many African countries. In the 1960s, however, independence fueled exports in order to achieve economic development. The discovery of oil, especially in North and sub-Saharan Africa, was a major factor in the export business, coupled with the opening of new diamond and mineral mines, including uranium.

THE IMPACT OF COLONIALISM AND THE EFFECTS OF FOREIGN TRADE

With some exceptions, the French denied human rights to their African subjects, who could be sent to prison indefinitely without a chance of due process.[15] Likewise, the British employed local chiefs to carry out their mandates, collect taxes, and gather a labor force, but they did allow minor cases to be tried by local indigenous magistrates as long as Europeans were not involved. This was, of course, cheaper. British indirect rule also emphasized tribal differences to divide and rule, inhibiting unified opposition.

The Portuguese ruled their domains in a similar manner to the French. A very small minority of the local people, those who learned Portuguese and became educated, gained some exemptions from taxation and forced labor. Belgium adopted a system of colonial rule that allowed a minority of educated Africans from the missionary schools to live better lives but, like the Portuguese, with no input into politics. Education above the primary level was not encouraged.[16] Under such circumstances, the vast majority of native people remained ignorant and subject to forced labor for the benefit of the colonial powers.

European countries left behind 80 years of misrule and faltering economies.[17] At the expense of the Africans, they controlled all the conditions of trade. Africa exported wealth to Europe and America; poverty was their legacy.

In remote times Africa had a number of stable states that offered security for their people. Two major developments retarded continental growth: the slave trade and colonization. The results of the slave trade in which some 50 million Africans were enslaved considerably reduced the population of the young and able, the generation the slavers coveted, for over four centuries. Tribal wars to capture and sell prisoners increased, and in some places, laws were passed to punish criminals by sending them into bondage. Insecurity was rampant among black people, and mistrust prevailed as some tribes even sold their own members. Under the circumstances, there was little incentive for development. Towns were deserted as the inhabitants fled to escape the slave trade, and other types of commerce dried up, as the dealers in human life were only intent on one thing—healthy bodies. As a source of free labor, Africans were looked upon as mentally inferior, as subhuman, by many white traders. Black African civilization was virtually obliterated. Across the Sahara, from the east coast and Red Sea, and from the west coast across the Atlantic to the New World, Africans traveled in chains.

Colonial impact on Africa varied across the continent, but there were many similarities. Colonial powers acquired land for plantations and mines, and forced labor to work them. Commercial crops for export were cultivated at the expense of local food, while the traditional trade networks between villages disappeared. The extraction of minerals, work done by low-paid laborers, fed European industry. In their wake, they left little in the way of local industry but plenty of poverty-stricken, uneducated people easily controlled by dictators, and rife with corruption.

The majority of Africans are Muslims (the result of trade contacts) followed by Christians, primarily the work of missionaries. Only small minorities are of other faiths. Apart from abandoning old beliefs and adopting new ones prompted by exchange of goods and ideas in most African colonies, other factors were at work that profoundly changed society. European extraction of minerals, and farming and building of infrastructure such as railroads to facilitate commerce, required workers and people to go to the places where the jobs were available. Migrations of entire villages to new rural environments or to urban areas separated families and broke up tribal unity. Men enlisted to labor in the mines or on plantations generally had to leave their families, and women and children left behind were forced to adapt to new situations. The extended family before colonialism was common throughout Africa; but by the end of the period, it was no longer the case.

INDEPENDENT AFRICA

African nations began breaking away from colonial rule in the 1950s and 1960s, achieving independence and developing their own commercial policies. It was not an easy task, as the infrastructure, such as roads, railroads, and communications, was not in place, or had been neglected and was in need of repair. Under the supervision of European advisors, African leaders copied the industrial models of Western Europe and North America, hoping to rapidly industrialize their countries to gain economic independence by manufacturing their own products and consumer goods that were previously imported from Europe. Such measures shifted the adverse terms of trade in Africa's favor, thereby stopping the flow of African wealth to developed nations. African nations, however, found it necessary to import from these very nations the machinery, building materials, technology, transport facilities, and expertise for their projects. These imports ran up huge debts, resulting in increasing exports of cash crops and minerals to pay them off. The trade arrangements remained much the same as in the colonial period and in fact became worse as the terms suited the suppliers of needed machinery and technology rather than the Africans, and marketing and prices of African exports remained under the control of the exporting nations.[18] One after another, African nations succumbed to dictatorships. The poor became poorer, and the politicians became richer.

AFRICAN IMPORTS AND EXPORTS: MODERN PERIOD

Items imported by many African countries, and their rising costs, have outweighed export earnings as these states have imposed import restrictions or subsidized essential export items. Most imports today come from the European Economic Community (EEC) and those countries with colonial ties with Africa. More and more imports are, nevertheless, coming from the United States, China, and Japan in the form of machinery, industrial products, transport equipment, durable consumer goods, and so on. A shortage of skilled African workers to organize and manage transport networks on either local or multinational levels is a result of colonial times when most blacks were shut out of educational and technological development. Also up to the time between the World Wars, all trade unions were illegal.

Semblances of democracy started to appear in the 1990s, and multiple political parties began to appear as the Cold War ended and dictators could no longer rely on aid from the United States or Russia by declaring they were pro-West or pro–Soviet Union. Parliaments became more than simply rubber stamps, and voting for leaders took hold in many places. Democratic movements in nations south of the Sahara were not repeated in North Africa, however, where Muslim clerics and brotherhoods rejected Western capitalism, democracy, and globalization. Over half of the mercantile African exports are to Europe, and most of these are minerals. The leading exporters today are South Africa, Nigeria, and Algeria.[19] African petroleum exports come mostly from Nigeria and Angola. A grim page in African modern times is the sale of blood diamonds from regions such as Sierra Leone and Liberia, sold illegally to buy arms that fuel civil wars and other bloody conflicts.

ACCESS TO ORGANIZATIONS

African nations can take their complaints to the World Trade Organization (WTO) and try to right any injustices they think are warranted. The African Growth and Opportunity Act (AGOA), signed into law on May 18, 2000, offers opportunities to African countries to open their economies and construct free markets. Since its inception, AGOA has promoted investments, generated jobs and trade, and aided the integration of sub-Saharan Africa into international commerce. The free-trade Common Market of Eastern and Southern Africa (COMESA) also provides an organization for both internal and global trade.

NOTES

1. Shillington, 304.
2. Shillington, 332.
3. Shillington, 309.
4. Shillington, 336.
5. For more detail, see Shillington, 334–335.
6. Harris, 216–218.
7. Harris, 218–220.
8. Thomas, 617.
9. Harris, 111.
10. Harris, 114.
11. Franklin, 430.
12. Findlay and O'Rourke, 390.
13. Braudel (1993), 515.
14. Shillington, 372.
15. Shillington, 355.
16. Shillington, 357.
17. Shillington, 419.
18. Shillington, 421–422.
19. *EWT*, 10.

14

INDIA

From ancient times until the modern age, in spite of being home to millions of poor people, India has nevertheless been renowned for its wealth. Much of the early trade was with Rome and its empire, and Romans such as Pliny, in his *Histories* of the first century, list a great number of gems found in India, including diamonds, emeralds, opals, and beryl. A visitor to India, the unknown author of the *Periplus*, which was written in the first century, recorded details of commerce in a number of places, one of which, Barigaza (now Bharuch, a thriving port city), situated on the banks of a river on the west coast of India, was prominent at this early time. Imported into this market town were wine, lead, copper, tin, coral, and topaz from Arabia and Asia Minor. Gold and silver also made up imports along with many mundane items, including flint and clothes. For the king, expensive silver vessels, costly ointments, and slave girls were brought, and according to the *Periplus*, singing boys. Exports were of a large variety and included aromatic gums, pearls, hardwoods, ivory, carnelian, lyceum, bdellium, cotton cloth, silk, yarn, pepper, and other items from the region.[1] Among other writers, at a later period, Hazrat Amir Khusrau, a poet, accompanied a military expedition to south India in the years 1310 to 1312 and wrote of the great wealth he saw paraded on the backs of elephants, riches that dazzled the minds of observers. The Muslim jurist and traveler Ibn Battutah, from Morocco, also visited India in the fourteenth century and described its prodigious wealth in gold, silver, and gems, as well as the flourishing markets and magnificent mosques. People were dressed in rich silk embedded with diamonds and wore turbans studded with precious stones. Even elephants and horses were brightly caparisoned in silks and gems for special occasions.[2]

It should be kept in mind, of course, that such visitors were the guests of sultans and emirs, and lodged in royal style in grand palaces. They attended sumptuous feasts and were looked after by slaves and servants. There is much less information on the lives of the people who worked in the rice paddies, gathered the fruit, grew the cotton, built the palaces, and labored in the mines.

The millions of Hindus, locked into their caste system, administered to the well-off upper classes, but the vast numbers of so-called untouchables of the lowest caste, those who did the unpleasant jobs of slaughtering animals, attending the dead, cleaning the rubbish from the streets, and living in slums, have left little trace of their existence. After the arrival of the Aryans and before Islam came to the subcontinent, the land was deeply divided among Vedic kingdoms and nomadic peoples. Rearing cattle was a major activity and milk an important ingredient of the diet. Cows were a component of exchange as were agricultural products such as grain, vegetables, and fruit. Beef was phased out of the diet, however, and by the sixth century, with the ascendency of Buddhism and Jainism, a vegetarian diet became widespread. Cows were sacred to the Hindu from early times.

Muslims distinguished between the Sind, the Indus River region, and the Hind, the rest of India that they began to conquer in the eleventh century. From the province of Sind to Delhi was a journey of 55 days, and when Ibn Battutah and his companions reached the Sind, the sultan's officials wrote reports about them that would reach the sultan in five days by relay runners stationed about every half kilometer. There was no delay, as the relay runners sounded a bell on approaching the next runner, who grasped the message and immediately set out. Letters about the new arrivals were meticulous in detail, including appearance, behavior, number of persons in the party including slaves and retainers. On his journey, Ibn Battutah encountered some strange customs. For instance, in one village the Muslim inhabitants, the Samirah, who married only within the clan, allowed no one to observe them eating. In another town, Siwasitan, a rebellion had recently occurred, and the inhabitants were slaughtered by the sultan's guards after the guards promised not to hurt them if they surrendered. They were flayed alive, their skins filled with straw and hung up on the city walls fixed on crosses. Others were beheaded or cut in half and piled up in the middle of the city. Ibn Battutah could not bear to look at the walls outside his rooms and changed residence.[3]

EARLY EMPIRES

Well before the advent of the Middle Ages and 1,000 years after the Indus Valley civilization, the Mauryan Empire (about 321–185 BCE) arose, encompassing nearly the entire Indian subcontinent. Oriented toward economic progress, the state encouraged commerce. Foreign trade burgeoned through trade with China, the Near East, and Mesopotamia, although agriculture remained the major base of the economy. The Mauryans faded away rather suddenly, replaced centuries later by the Gupta Empire (about 320–550 CE), which reunited much of the northern and central subcontinent. Commerce continued, much of it with Rome, whereby India exported more to the Roman Empire than it imported. Some Romans complained about the balance of payments, but Roman gold coins continued to fill Indian coffers.

TAMIL CHOLA EMPIRE (985–1279)

During the Middle Ages, the Chola Dynasty in southern India reached the apex of its influence. By the eleventh century, the Chola people—who were knowledgeable in the way of the sea—carried on trade with China and Southeast Asia.

One of the Tamil-speaking kingdoms of southern India, it gained hegemony over other southern tribes and reached its height under Rajaraja, who conquered Kerala, northern Ceylon (Sri Lanka), and the Maldives during his reign from 985 to 1014. The Chola also controlled trade along both the eastern and western coasts of southern India. Subject villages sent tribute that was used to support the king's large retinue of dancers, servants, singers, craftsmen, goldsmiths, and numerous others at the court. Chola rulers allowed considerable autonomy for local institutions as long as they maintained order and paid taxes.

Near the end of the ninth century, the inhabitants of southern India had developed widespread marine commercial activity. The Cholas were well situated for trading enterprises with the T'ang Dynasty in China, and the Abbasid Caliphate focused on

Baghdad, while the Srivyijava Empire spread over much of modern-day Indonesia. Rajaraja's son, Rajendra I (1014–1044), continued to increase Chola power overcoming rivals in southern India and expanding his territory northward. Eager to exploit their opportunities, the Cholas sent several trade missions to China. One of them reached the Chinese court in 1077 and appears to have been very profitable, returning home with a fortune in copper coins in exchange for some glass articles and spices as tribute to the emperor. The empire lasted for four centuries, after which it lost its territory in Ceylon, and its power was reduced to the status of one regional kingdom among many.

THE MUSLIM SULTANATE OF DELHI (1206–1526)

Of Turkish provenance, the Muslim Delhi Sultanate conquered the north, and later sultans included much of central India under their hegemony. The Indo-Muslim amalgamation of cultures brought about new modes in dress, building construction, and crafts. Ibn Battutah, who received an audience with the sultan, was given a high post in the royal court and remained there for some time. He gave his gifts to the sultan and eventually received in return money from the sultan's treasury to pay off his creditors. As elsewhere in the Orient, visitors often borrowed the money to buy presents for the king and high officials, expecting to receive more valuable gifts in return that they could then sell and use the money to pay off the original debt. This gift trade often took care of the expenses of the journey. Ibn Battutah described Delhi as a major center of commerce and exchange. The most superior quality rice and sugar from Kannauj, wheat from the Punjab, and betel leaves from Dhar in Mutter Pradesh found their way to the markets there. He also described the bustling markets of other cities, and the well-maintained roads linking various parts of the country to facilitate domestic trade. The threat from bandits did not in any way affect the flow of goods as merchants travelled in well-armed groups to ensure their security. The sultans of Delhi took a great interest in trade even to the extent that the fourteenth-century sultan Alauddin Khilji administered the marketplaces. Shopkeepers who were caught cheating were punished, and a price list, set out by the government, forced traders to adhere to the prices, often to their detriment.[4] India exported raw silk, indigo, opium, rice, wheat, sugar, pepper and other spices, precious stones, and drugs; however, the country was self-sufficient in agricultural products and craftsmanship. Farmers supplied their own needs and shared any excess with the village artisans in exchange for tools or other needed implements for household use. Some agricultural products, for example, grain, were stored by farmers as insurance against a bad year. Irrigation systems were a major factor in farming and the more canals, dams, and reservoirs that were built, the more agricultural production grew; more available food then led to increases in population. Delhi, for example, rose to a population of some 400,000 in the fourteenth century, second in the Muslim world after Cairo. Between the seventh and eleventh centuries, the entire country grew from about 5 million to about 80 million. In the south, public activity organized around Hindu temples that took a share of the agricultural output, coordinated labor, stored grain for difficult times, and gave rudimentary education. The authorities (Brahmins) also functioned as bankers, administered loans, and encouraged trade. Exports to Persia, Arabia, and Syria included all manner of objects from coconuts, scissors, and knives to decorated pottery and luxuries such as cloth embroidered with gold. The list of significant exports also included sugar, indigo, oils, ivory, sandalwood, spices, diamonds, and other precious gems.

The Red Sea served as the conduit for Indian goods reaching the southern Mediterranean under the auspices of Arab traders. The goods were then loaded onto European vessels for delivery to northern Mediterranean ports in Italy, France, and Spain. Some goods were also traded in East Africa. Other destinations for Indian traders included Southeast Asia and China. Goods sent by overland routes through the Khyber Pass were destined for Persia and Central Asia.

Rivalries with other southern tribes led to the dynasty's fall in 1279 with the last Chola ruler, Rajendra IV.

HINDU EMPIRE OF VIJAYANAGAR (1336–1565)

Hindu kings and princes in southern India held sway over small states where regional rivalries were fairly benign, and compared to the north of the country, they were relatively free from incursions from northern peoples. The Vijayanagar kingdom arose when two brothers, Harihara and Bukka, were sent by the sultans of Delhi to instill court customs among the southern Hindus. Once there, they saw an opportunity to administer and rule for themselves and, renouncing Islam, they returned to their original faith, Hinduism. Muslim merchants continued to do business with the "infidels," and the sultans in Delhi let the matter stand—perhaps it was too far away to worry about. The city of Vijayanagar and its first dynasty founded in 1336 under Harihara I (1336–1356) expanded to become the largest empire of southern India and flourished between the fourteenth and sixteenth centuries. The empire was often in conflict with the Muslim sultanates that were established in the northern Deccan, the vast plateau encompassing much of central and southern India.

The city was a teeming marketplace for both exports and imports, and the fabulous wealth left foreigners astonished. Domingos Pães, a Portuguese traveller who visited the area around the year 1520, described the citizens as being heavily bejewelled. Abdur Razzak, the Khurasani ambassador to the court of Vijayanagar, referred to the treasury that had chambers filled with gold.[5] As the wealthiest and largest state in the fifteenth and sixteenth centuries, it profited from maritime trade with Persia, Arabia, Africa, Southeast Asia, China, and the islands in the Indian Ocean. Shipbuilding was a major occupation in the many port towns, as was the movement of trade goods.

Trade Products

India had all three of the materials that produce textiles: wool, silk, and cotton. Cotton plants were widespread, silkworms were cultivated, and goat hair was spun into wool such as cashmere. Dyes of beautiful colors and hues were extracted from various plants, and the bright and vivid textiles, along with Indian embroidered fabrics, were in great demand.

Over many centuries, diamonds—formed when carbon modules crystallize under intense pressure and heat—were thought to come only from southern India where geological conditions were right and kingdoms were not averse to going to war over a diamond mine. Greatly valued in India and the Middle East, diamonds were scarce and less sought after in Europe compared to emeralds, rubies, and gold.

In addition to manufactured items, farmed products for trade included sorghum, cotton, rice, sugarcane, wheat, and spices such as pepper, turmeric, cardamom, and ginger.

In 1565, the empire's armies suffered a catastrophic defeat at the hands of an army formed from an alliance of the sultanates of the Deccan. The capital city was depopulated and destroyed, and it was never reoccupied. It is said that Tirumala Raya, a surviving military commander, left Vijayanagar with an enormous treasure loaded onto the backs of 550 elephants.

MUGHAL EMPIRE (1556–1857)

In 1526, Babur, a descendant of Genghis Khan from the Fergana Valley in modern Uzbekistan, invaded India through the Khyber Pass and installed the Mughal Empire. Mughals were Muslim descendants of earlier Mongols. After numerous battles, the empire was firmly established under Akbar (1556–1605), and the Mughal dynasty ruled most of India by 1600. During the late medieval and early modern periods, the country remained reasonably prosperous with growing towns and cities, a consequence of economic management by Mughal rulers. They administered the country for about three centuries, and much of their wealth was based on trade that stimulated substantial development in agriculture and textiles. They also supported the flourishing caravan routes from India to Kabul in Afghanistan and the markets in Lahore (now the capital of the Pakistani province of the Punjab). This trade route brought to India horses from Central Asia, fine porcelain and silk from China, and gold and silver from Europe. When merchant ships unloaded at the many Mughal Indian ports, the goods were tallied by official customs officers and taxes levied. Secure storage was available. Traders of numerous nationalities resided in Calicut, attracted by the burgeoning commercial opportunities.

During the time of Akbar, control of the country was secure and expanding, roads were made safe for merchants, and annoying tariffs were dispensed with. As it stretched south to nearly the tip of India, east to the Burmese border, and north to Afghanistan, the empire encompassed over 100 million people. Merchants and traders were recognized as valuable members of society, and many became wealthy and politically influential. Nobles, understanding the value of trade, invested in ships for overseas commerce in goods, in marketplaces, and in royal workshops that contributed to the rise of new northern Indian towns[6] that grew into trade and industrial centers, which in turn led to general prosperity due to the establishment of a sound currency system based on silver and copper *dirhams*. The centuries of Mughal rule, from the sixteenth to the eighteenth, was a time of peace in which trade flourished and artisanship escalated in number and variety in order to meet foreign demand.

The Portuguese officer and writer Duarte Barbosa, residing at Cannanore in India, wrote in 1516 that the roads facilitated the exchange of goods between the different parts of the country.[7]

The eighteenth century brought significant changes in India as the Mughal Empire declined along with the rise of Maratha peoples, embodying a renewal of the power of the Hindus. After the great Mughal emperor Aurangzeb (1658–1707), the state was unable to ensure the safety of traders, and imperial disintegration went hand in hand with diminishing commerce.

The Arrival of the British East India Company

The appearance of the British East India Company (EIC) in the mid-eighteenth century sounded the death knell of the waning kingdom. In 1757, the Battle of Plassey, an English victory over the Mughal governor of Bengal, signaled the culmination of Indian prosperity. The EIC consolidated its grip on Bengal, imposed onerous duties on imports and exports, and prohibited trade with Asian countries and export of Indian textiles to England except those in the hands of the company.

The last of the Mughal emperors, Bahadur Shah II, took part in the revolt of 1857 against the English. After the failure of this revolt, he was imprisoned and deported to Rangoon, where he died in 1862. This marked the end of the Mughal dynasty.

Products and Manufactures

Indian textiles were a major export, especially from Gujarat, a leading cotton commercial center in the west. Indian materials were shipped to retailers in Southeast Asia, throughout the Arab countries, and to Europe. Bengal in the east was also important for textiles, especially muslin and manufactured silk. In the south, the Malabar Coast in Kerala was known for colored and printed fabrics, all of which were prized for design, vivid colors, and textures. Inlayed and carved furniture made from Indian hardwood was a sought-after trade item along with handmade carpets woven in floral patterns. Southern India exported pearls, ivory, cut and polished stones, tortoise shells, diamonds obtained from the Deccan region, and rubies from Sri Lanka.

Foreign Trade

Limbodar, in Gujarat, now a village, was once a major export center in which commercial life was in the hands of local and foreign traders, while further south on the west coast, Goa was a major importing city, especially for horses from Arabia. From Goa, they were dispersed to the southern kingdoms. Most of the imports—including iron, bronze, gold, and wool—were channeled through the cities of the Malabar coast and Gujarat. Ships from China and Southeast Asia traded at Quilon and Calicut, but their primary port of call was on the east coast at Sonargaon (now in Bangladesh).

The bulk of foreign trade in the west went to Khambat (Cambay), where the harbor was filled with vessels of many nations. Merchants from many places took up residence under Mughal authority. The trade was in the hands of Hindus.[8]

From Afghanistan and Arabia, horses were big business and imports on a somewhat smaller scale were glassware, wines, perfumes, and coral for noble households. Raw silk and porcelain came from China.

The Gujarati and Marwari businessmen who controlled the trade between the coastal towns and northern India were extremely wealthy and spent large sums for the construction of temples. Many Hindu and Muslim traders who grew wealthy through control of commerce with West and Central Asia, and many from Gujarat, settled in Delhi and built grandiose mansions and temples. The ports on the gulf linked central India with the seaborne trade of the Indian Ocean. Khambat was the leading port at first but was replaced in this role by Surat when the port silted up. Surat became the harbor of choice for the Mughal Empire, and a good deal of foreign trade passed through its streets.[9]

MARATHA (HINDU) EMPIRE (1674–1818)

An independent Hindu kingdom developed by Shivaji Maharaj (who died in 1680) emerged in the Deccan and expanded near the end of the seventeenth century as the Maratha Empire, a formidable foe of the Mughals. The empire reached its height in the eighteenth century. But British commercial policies snuffed out the Maratha trade and the last holdings of the empire were incorporated into the British Empire in 1818.

The EIC set about monopolizing Indian foreign trade and often bankrupted local commerce and industries, in part due to importing into India horses, cloth, and utensils for farms and households—all items produced in England. While the English manufacturers became better off, the Indians were compelled to take up other employment or go hungry. The great market that was India and that flourished during the Mughal period, benefiting so many local people, faded away by the beginning of the nineteenth century.

A hindrance to the advancement of local trade may be seen in the structure of Indian society, that is, the caste system.[10] The higher caste residents in rural villages found it beneath their dignity, and thus distasteful, to trade with members of the lower caste. In those villages with mixed-caste residents, the lower groups were worse off than they were in villages where all the residents were of the same social level. This situation was and is due to the fact that although the high caste controlled the water rights, they did not readily share with their so-called inferiors. Thus, the low caste, with little access to water, were not able to produce the crops needed for a surplus to sell in the market for income. In villages where everyone was socially equal, trade was commonplace and the residents were better off.

Indian Merchants

The variegated group of Indian merchants did business together but were socially distant. The Jain traders of Gujarat, in Surat or Khambhat (Cambay), for example, could not eat nor drink with the Chettiar traders on the Coromandel coast, let alone intermarry. Before the arrival of the Portuguese in the sixteenth century, commerce on both east and west coasts of India was oriented eastward to the Indonesian archipelago, and traders relied on their own ships and financing. There were few Indian ships that could be found in Aden, since generally trade in the Red Sea and Persian Gulf was conducted by Arabs, Jews, Persians, and Armenians. After the Portuguese commercial intrusions into the Indian Ocean, the trade became reoriented toward the West, and Indian merchants could be found throughout the Middle East in the following centuries.[11] In India, the port of Surat achieved its lofty position in seaborne trade after the province of Gujarat succumbed to Akbar and his Mughals in 1573. When European trading companies came to the regions, Surat was the major trade and financial center in the western Indian Ocean and remained so for several more centuries.[12]

JEWISH TRADERS

For a minority group of people such as the Jews to achieve standing in maritime trade in medieval times, the Indian Ocean proved more compatible than the Mediterranean. The Mediterranean was a hostile sea as Christians and Muslims were at each others' throats to gain mastery of the shipping lanes. The maritime trade routes to India, however, were sailed by peoples of numerous nationalities and beliefs who, until the arrival of the Portuguese at the beginning of the sixteenth century, seem to have shown little animosity toward one another. The multinational men of commerce and of various religions—Hindus, Jews, Muslims, and Christian Abyssinians—were interested in making money, not war. Before the intrusion of Europeans, the Indian interreligious ocean trade was generally peaceful. The Jewish trustee of the merchants of Aden, a man who looked after the estates of foreign traders who perished at sea, collaborated with esteemed Muslim merchants in the city.[13] Jews and Muslims sometimes formed trading partnerships to facilitate their activities. Such was the case of a Jewish trader who built a ship in Aden and sent goods to Ceylon in partnership with Sheikh Bilal.[14]

NOTES

1. Schoff, 27, 42.
2. Mackintosh-Smith, 170.
3. Mackintosh-Smith, 152–153.
4. http://www.gatewayforindia.com/articles/tradeyore.htm.
5. http://www.historydoctor.net/Advanced%20Placement%20World%20History/Islamic_and_Hindu_Kingdoms_In-India.htm.
6. *EWT*, 679.
7. http://www.gatewayforindia.com/articles/tradeyore.htm.
8. See Bernstein, 104.
9. www.gatewayforindia.com/articles/tradeyore.htm.
10. Anderson (2011).
11. Chaudhuri, 100–101.
12. Chaudhuri, 117–118.
13. Goitein, 181.
14. Goitein, 183. See also Saumitra Jha, passim.

15

SOUTHEAST ASIA

Around the second century BCE, China and India were in contact with one another through trade over difficult overland routes. Jungles, raging rivers, heavy rain, and mud were hard on men and animals. Both East and West trade once crossed the Isthmus of Kra (Malay Peninsula) from the Gulf of Thailand to the Bay of Bengal, a distance of about 60 kilometers at the narrowest point that was easily controlled by local headmen or dynasties. A change in the route became more economical when sealanes through the Strait of Malacca and the Sunda Strait were opened up and control of the waterways from the seventh to the eleventh centuries was managed by Srivijaya, who commanded a partial monopoly on trade on the southeast coast of Sumatra. As middlemen between China and the Arabs after the rise of Islam, Srivijaya commerce was very lucrative.[1]

SRIVIJAYA EMPIRE (650–1280)

Extensive Chinese trade with Southeast Asia in the eighth and ninth centuries helped bring about the rise of the Srivijaya Empire.[2] Muslim traders carried Southeast Asian products that were destined for Europe across the Indian Ocean to the Red Sea or Persian Gulf. This seaborne trade dropped off in the fourteenth century due to Muslim and Christian conflict in the eastern

Mediterranean resulting from the crusades, from the plague that considerably reduced the European populations and thus lessened demand for exotic goods, and from the Mongol peace that again made the Silk Route across Central Asia safe for commerce.

An important center for Buddhist expansion in Southeast Asia, Srivijaya was also a great commercial empire and the overseer of two major waterways between India and China. Its territory took in part of the island of Java and extended west to the Malay Peninsula, with its base on the island of Sumatra. From Palembang, the emperors controlled the Sunda Strait, and from the Malay Peninsula, the Strait of Malacca. The empire's territory produced camphor, aloes, cloves, sandalwood, nutmeg, cardamom, pepper, ivory, gold, and tin.[3]

At the apex of its power in the eleventh and twelfth centuries, the empire provided security along the seaborne routes, keeping pirates at bay. This profitable commerce attracted the attention of neighboring kingdoms, especially the Tamil Chola in southern India. In 1025, Rajendra, the Chola ruler, launched a naval attack on Srivijaya from which the city never recovered. The attack appeared to have been motivated by trade, at least in part, to give Tamil merchants more access to it in the region, not to mention the plunder for Rajendra.[4] The Chola peoples weakened Srivijaya power through raids and conquests of parts of Sumatra and the Malay Peninsula.[5]

Decline of Srivijaya

The absence of safeguards for private property suppressed the role of financial institutions and development of fixed capital investments. The greed of rulers was always present, and they were ready to take what they wanted from those who gained wealth to prevent the rise of a middle class that could own private property in its own right. Absolute rulers, nobles, and states could confiscate anything of value; as a result, people preferred to invest in mobile wealth such as precious stones, coins, fine cloth, and jewelry, all of which were easily movable or could be hidden from the eyes of royal authority. Wealth was not for show; it was concealed. Southeast Asians shunned putting their money into ships, houses, and trade goods, as it could all disappear in an instant. Common people lived in wooden houses of light construction that were easily destroyed and easily rebuilt.[6] Rulers and ministers participated in trade, and the successful merchants were the elite of the court.

Expanding from the eastern part of the island of Java between about 1300 to 1500, the Majapahit kingdom replaced the Srivijaya Empire. The Majapahit wanted a larger stake in the commercial wealth of Southeast Asia and the trade to pass through its waterways.

Major centers of Southeastern Asian seaborne trade were laid waste or seized by foreign forces in the sixteenth and seventeenth centuries. Much of the devastation was at the hands of first the Portuguese, followed by the Dutch, English, and Spanish—all with a crucial advantage in military maritime power, that was used for commercial purposes. They also altered the balance of power by establishing nearly impregnable forts and trade centers on foreign shores, and patrolling the sea lanes where possible. From the start, the European interlopers fought among themselves for the spoils.

The region of Southeast Asia is today made up of Burma (Myanmar), Cambodia, Laos, Thailand, Vietnam, Indonesia, Brunei, the Philippines, Singapore, and Malaysia. Rice is the major export of these countries, but other products include spices, wood, rubber, tea, coconuts, oil, and tin. In the Middle Ages, when city-states were prominent and vied for trade, some of the most important were Malacca, Pegu, Pnompenh, Hoi An, Brunei, and Aceh. They lost their preeminent commercial status to Portuguese Malacca after 1511, Spanish Manila after 1571 when the sultan was deposed by the Spanish, and Dutch Batavia after 1619.[7]

FLUCTUATIONS IN TRADE

Before the seventeenth century, China was the major market for Southeast Asian products, with numerous spice-carrying ships frequenting Chinese ports. India was a close second. Commerce with the southeast picked up dramatically in 1405 when the Chinese Ming emperor sent a trade mission. Pepper and sappanwood flooded into China in such quantities in the fifteenth century that warehouses were full, and the products were used to pay officials and soldiers.[8] Southeast Asian cities involved in this trade such as Malacca and Brunei prospered enormously. Cloves and nutmeg from the Spice Islands were in great demand everywhere, and many merchants became rich.[9] Ten pounds of nutmeg could be purchased in the Spice Islands for one penny and sold in London for 50 shillings—an enormous markup.[10]

Burgeoning trade was severely disrupted when the Portuguese appeared in the Indian Ocean and sank or ransacked every

Muslim spice ship they encountered. Few spices reached Europe via the Middle East in the first three decades of the sixteenth century; those that did had to be procured through Lisbon. Trade with Southeast Asia took on a new dimension between 1570 and 1630 when Japanese ships in significant numbers brought silver from Japanese mines. Between 1604 and 1616, there were 173 Japanese vessels that visited Southeast Asia.[11] The trade stopped in 1635 when the Japanese government forbade their subjects to leave the country.

The Ming ban on private trade to the south was lifted in 1567, and licensed junks left China by the score, setting sail for Indo-China and the southern islands, including the Philippines, bringing prosperity to China and its trading partners. Southeast Asian sugar, spices, and deerskin were important items exchanged for Chinese silk at Manila and Hoi An on the coast of what today is Vietnam. About 1620, political and economic disturbances began in China, and trade with the southeast went into a downturn. Europe, on the other hand, developed a growing appetite for Southeast Asian products, and demand grew rapidly for spices from the Moluccas, which were shipped around the Horn of Africa in European ships.

Muslim merchants endeavored to avoid Portuguese strongholds on the coasts of East Africa and India by sailing across the Indian Ocean to the Maldives from Aceh, and up the Red Sea and Persian Gulf to send the goods overland to the Mediterranean. The Portuguese could not patrol the entire Indian Ocean, and Aceh thus became, for a time, one of the most important commercial cities in the region, attracting merchants from all quarters. It began to decline when the English and Dutch East India Companies (EIC and VOC, respectively) appeared on the scene in fierce competition with each other.

Manufactured goods in Southeast Asia found local markets for products but took little part in exports. Neighbors China and India, as manufacturing states themselves, had little use for such items. Southeast Asian exports, however, were somewhat unique in that no other place could produce cloves, nutmeg, benzoin, sugar, and tropical forest products that included lac, camphor, and various kinds of wood. The Ternate and Tidore islands first brought clove trees into cultivation, an enterprise that then spread to other islands.[12] Cane sugar also spread vigorously in Vietnam, Thailand, Cambodia, and Java and was exported to China and Japan. Benzoin, a resin used for incense, was found in Cambodia, Sumatra, and Laos; it was exported all over Asia.

Village headmen who had access to merchants and labor took a portion of the sales and controlled these cash crops. Between the ruler's taxes and the merchant's conveyances, which took the lion's share of profits, farmers were left with little. Capital loaned to the farmer by the chief to tide the farmer over until the crop was ready bonded the farmer to him; but in return, the farmer had to sell his crop to the chief. In some places, cash-cropping was done by slaves on the lands of wealthy merchants.

TRANSPORT

Trade vessels of Southeast Asia, junks, were often large. The biggest, sometimes with three or four masts, carried a great deal of cargo but were slow and unwieldy, and thus subject to enemy ships that were smaller, faster, and carried more firepower. Discipline on the large junks was severe. Misbehavior or neglect was punished with lashes. The highest authority on board was the ship's owner or his representative, and rebellion could mean death. Unlike most voyages in other parts of the world, women were often passengers on commercial vessels and, unlike European ships, junks were constructed with a great many small, private cabins. Seamen were forbidden to look at the stern of the ship, where the man in charge had his quarters, along with perhaps his wife or a concubine.[13]

Rivers and overland trails served to move goods to inland cities in Burma, Thailand, and Laos that had no direct access to the sea. The capital of Laos, Vientiane, for example, was 600 kilometers from the sea. Indian cloth was in demand in Vientiane, and the Mekong River system was used to transport it. Carrying goods inland was many times more expensive than rates on seagoing ships; in addition, state borders had to be crossed and taxes paid. Highwaymen were just as much a problem on land as pirates were at sea. Even along the waterways, tolls were exacted. Although rivers helped to carry bamboo rafts and canoes, the trip to Vientiane from the sea still took some three months.[14]

In some places, for example, in Java or across the Malay Peninsula, carts pulled by oxen or buffalo were used to transport goods as well as passengers over land routes. Tigers and bandits were a constant threat, and travel in carts with no springs was anything but pleasant. Traders moved in convoys and in the mornings when it was cooler. By afternoon, the animals were allowed to graze and the wagons were circled. At night, men and animals slept in the center of the ring of wagons. Sometimes, in dangerous places, the camp was fortified with thorn bushes, guards were posted, fires burned all night, and shots were periodically fired as a reminder to dangerous animals to stay clear.[15]

TRADE DISPUTES

Traders formed ethnic communities in which the headman was charged with maintaining order. If traders from different ethnic groups—for example, a Chinese and a Javanese—had a quarrel, the headman of each community would take up the matter and try to set it right. Anything was better than taking the dispute to the king's court, where witnesses might be subject to torture to discern the truth, and opposing claims might be settled by ordeal. In Aceh, it was not uncommon for the court to order the defendants to reach into a pot of molten lead to recover a piece of pottery inscribed with sacred writings. The man of truth, with heavenly guidance on his side, would be able to endure the pain longer.[16]

WOMEN TRADERS

Before Europeans arrived in Southeast Asia, some of the long-distance traders were women. Southeast Asians were more tolerant toward them in business circles than were many other societies the world over. Women could control their own property and choose husbands for themselves. They found ways to abort unwanted children. Such women running businesses, controlling their own fertility, and operating on a level with men—according to the Muslim, and later Christian, missionaries—needed to be controlled. The Dutch East India Company tried at first to send women from the Netherlands out to the company employees, but few wanted to go, with the exception of some prostitutes. Often, local women gained advantages by marrying a company man to protect their interests in the multifarious and often brutal world of trade. Some of the businesswomen were wealthy, having come from upper-class families, and others had money gained from widows' endowments from one or more husbands. They were used to their native climate and immune from local diseases, but their foreign spouses were apt to die young, leaving their inheritance to their wives. This might happen several times. These widows were sought by the next batch of the Dutch East India Company men for their knowledge of local affairs, capital assets, and business acumen. Missionaries and moralists were intent on domesticating these women and making them into passive, obedient homemakers for their often "bland and stodgy husbands."[17]

In the market city of Aceh, in Malacca and elsewhere, women traded goods and also worked as moneychangers in and outside the marketplace. The local domestic markets were almost completely run by women,[18] and in the international markets, women not only traded, but some became financiers on a grand scale.[19]

Sea trade with China picked up in the fifteenth century as Southeast Asian cities became trading stations for the Chinese, and spices began to flow again into Europe after the devastation of the Black Death.[20] The ports of Alexandria and Beirut shipped large quantities of goods from Southeast Asia to the European port cities of Venice, Genoa, and Barcelona.[21] Cloves, nutmeg, mace, and pepper made up the bulk of the cargos. With the Portuguese conquest of Malacca in 1511, European demand for spices that had been but a fraction of Southeast Asian trade rose considerably in the sixteenth and seventeenth centuries.

An interesting cultural difference between Europe and Southeast Asia in this period of extensive commerce appeared to have been "the security of person and property against the whim of an arbitrary sovereign."[22] The Banten Sultanate created in the sixteenth century, whose capital was the city of the same name, a port on the northwest coast of Java, had an embassy at the court of King Charles II of England in 1682. The Banten officials found it difficult to comprehend that under English laws, property could be privately owned; nor could they understand how English subjects could possess anything or have any property rights that were not sanctioned by the prince.[23]

VIETNAM

Out of sync with the growing prosperity of Southeast Asia, North Vietnam, with its capital city Thang-Tong (now Hanoi), disavowed the benefits of trade. In accordance with Confucian philosophy that taught agriculture was the only solid foundation of a state, and traders were parasites that should be despised, the ruling classes of North Vietnam were against commerce, and foreign merchants were unwelcome. When the English protested this attitude in 1672, they were told by an official that his country had no need of anything foreign.

The southern kingdom, however, was more amenable and welcomed foreigners who flocked there, including Europeans,

Japanese, and Chinese, and helped establish the commercial city of Hoi An. Fighting between the North and South opened a great rift between the two by 1600.[24]

Known to the French as Indo-China, Vietnam became a part of its colonial empire, begun in 1887, that included Vietnam, Cambodia, and later Laos. France had a history in Vietnam dating back to the seventeenth century when French missionary settlements were established. For France, Vietnam with its good harbors was a stepping off point for trade with inland China. They also afforded the French naval bases from which they could protect their trade. The country was a good source of rubber and other forest products. In the eighteenth century, a good deal of trade between the two countries benefited both, but France became involved in military disputes and during the frequent nineteenth-century wars, it took over Vietnam by force. There was little resistance. The French were instrumental in developing communications and irrigation networks, as well as roads and railroads to move resources out of the country, but little was done to improve the welfare of the local people.

The Vietnamese feared and hated the Jesuit missionaries, who were the cause of much trouble. In 1930, Vietnamese troops rebelled in a fruitless attempt to shake off French colonial rule. French occupation ended with another form of colonial rule by the Japanese in 1942 that continued until the end of World War II. After the war, France tried to regain control of Vietnam and other Southeast Asian territories but was defeated in May 1954 by a Communist army under Ho Chi Minh, as were the Americans in the Vietnam War of the 1960s.

THE DUTCH

With the subjugation of Java and Sumatra in the nineteenth century, the Dutch went on to extend colonial rule throughout the Indonesian islands, whose exploitation fueled industry at home in the Netherlands. Subject farmers were required under the Dutch to harvest certain amounts of coffee and sugar, along with other crops, to supply the Dutch homeland. A good part of Java consisted of large Dutch plantations where workers were practically slaves. Quotas of forced exports included not just sugar and coffee, but also tin, rubber, copra, tobacco, tea, and oil. Protests in Holland over the treatment of workers on the plantations forced the government to put an end to the quota system.

THE ENGLISH

Spices cultivated in Burma were shipped to India on East India Company ships and then on to England, but the British were interested in the source and annexed southern Burma in 1852 as an adjunct to India. Burmese kings ruled in the north and controlled foreign trade, mostly in silk, cotton, and teak. Commerce with the south, even under British rule, continued as treaties with the northern kings and the English were negotiated and ratified. Not satisfied, the British conquered upper Burma in 1886, and all of the country came under their colonial rule. Trade grew immensely as the British siphoned off rice, timber, and oils in exchange for manufactured goods and textiles. Overrun by the Japanese in 1942, severing Western trade for the duration of the war, Burma gained its independence from Great Britain in 1948.

Besides India and Burma, the British Empire in the East included the Malay Peninsula (whose EIC settlements incorporated Malacca, nearby Singapore, Dinding, and Penang), which came under British government control in 1867 which terminated in 1946 after a short Japanese occupation from 1942 to 1945.

The surrender of the "impregnable" fortified city of Singapore to numerically inferior numbers of Japanese forces left the British Empire stunned, and Australia and New Zealand more vulnerable to Japanese aggression. Both countries formed closer ties with the United States and became less dependant on the mother country, a situation that also altered trade patterns as the United States helped arm the threatened countries. After the disruption of World War II in the South Pacific and Southeast Asia, trade patterns and networks were never again the same. Singapore, a free port, supplanted Malacca as a major hub of commerce, mostly importing and reexporting goods, and attracting merchants from Malaysia and China. Singapore today is one of the world's major ports where container ships unload their cargos that are then placed on smaller ships for distribution to lesser ports in Southeast Asia. It is the world's largest depot for general cargo.[25] Indonesia became a major hardwood exporter, Thailand became known for its metals (tin, tungsten, and lead), Brunei for oil, and Cambodia for rubber.

UNITED STATES

At the end of the short Spanish-American War in 1898, the United States took over the Philippines, usurping Spanish control. Cheap labor in the Philippine islands benefited the United States and its imports of sugar, rice, coconuts, bananas, pineapples, mangos, and many electronic manufactured products. The country gained its independence after World War II in 1946, and vigorous trade has continued.

Now, in the third millennium, the independent nations of Southeast Asia belong to the Association of Southeast Asian Nations (ASEAN), designed to promote trade throughout the region.

NOTES

1. Findlay and O'Rourke, 36.
2. Reid, 10.
3. *EWT*, 861.
4. Findley and O'Rourke, 71.
5. Chaudhuri, 37.
6. Reid, 269.
7. Reid, 2.
8. Reid, 12.
9. For facts, figures, and sources of Southeast Asian commerce, see Reid, Chapter 1.
10. Milton, 267.
11. Reid, 18.
12. Reid, 32.
13. Reid, 49.
14. Reid, 55.
15. Reid, 58.
16. Pomeranz and Topik, 31.
17. Pomeranz and Topik, 28–30.
18. Reid, 93.
19. Reid, 124.
20. Reid, 13.
21. Reid, 13.
22. Reid, 130 for quote and source.
23. Reid, 130.
24. Reid, 63–64.
25. Levinson, 211.

16

EAST INDIA COMPANIES

English ships of the sixteenth century were thought to be inadequate for the long voyage to the East, unlike the larger Portuguese carracks. The English government requested that the Portuguese allow some English merchants to accompany them to Calicut in India and bring back spices for the home market. The Portuguese response to this request was negative.

Francis Drake's circumnavigation of the globe in 1577 through 1580 in an English light galleon proved the assumption wrong. In 1582, an expedition of four ships left the English shores with the primary purpose of rounding the Cape of Good Hope and trading in the East. The voyage failed because the officers could not get along, and it was abandoned. Nine years later, in 1591, London merchants tried again, but once more, the voyage was doomed to failure, with only one ship reaching the East and returning to England with a starving and mutinous crew.

Having seen the results of captured Portuguese carracks with their fabulous wealth, and their navigational charts, London merchants were even more determined to have a share in the richest trade route yet known. One of the captured ships, the *Madre de Deus*, was brought to the port of Dartmouth in 1592. At 165 feet in length with a beam of 45 feet, and some 1,600 tons, she was the largest ship Elizabethan England had ever seen. Beneath her

hatches was a cargo of jewels, cloth, ebony, and spices with an estimated value of half a million pounds sterling, or about half the total
holdings of the Crown's Exchequer at the time. This fabulous haul
not only created a sensation, it gave England's merchants a firsthand glimpse of the wealthy trade they were missing out on.
Another expedition of three ships was outfitted and sent eastward
around the Cape. Sickness decimated the crews, and the last
remaining ship was lost off the coast of Burma, with the captain's
fate unknown. One survivor was picked up by a Dutch ship in
1601 off an uninhabited island.

ENGLISH EAST INDIA COMPANY (EIC, 1600–1874)

By the beginning of 1595, the Dutch had already sent 15 expeditions to the Eastern world. By 1599, they had cornered the pepper
trade, usurping the Portuguese, and tripled the price.[1] London
merchants were not to be left out, however. They set up a joint-
stock company financed by wealthy aristocrats and merchants
who bought the shares and received a charter from Queen
Elizabeth in the year 1600 when the East India Company (EIC)
was born. The directors set about purchasing ships and in the
spring of 1601, under the command of James Lancaster, a fleet of
four vessels set sail for the East.[2]

The first voyages of the EIC proved financially successful and
within a few years, the company possessed 24 ships and entered
into the pepper trade, competing with the Dutch. Competition
engendered violence and atrocities, especially around the Spice
Islands. Fierce encounters between the rivals there seem to have
been a factor in the British decision to concentrate its Eastern commercial activities on India in the form of cotton, silk, indigo, spices,
and saltpeter.

Surat

During the Mughal epoch, Surat on the Gulf of Cambay in the
northwest was the major port of India. The English established a
trading post there in 1609 and by mid-century, it was a thriving
metropolis with a population of some 700,000 to 800,000. Wealthy
Indian merchants and bankers with a reputation for honesty controlled the trade in Surat where, as the gateway to the Orient, merchants—Muslim, Christian, Hindu, and others from nearly every
continent—rubbed shoulders.[3]

For the collection of textiles and spices, warehouses had already been constructed at Surat. It was from these warehouses that English ships, loaded with cargo, began sailing in 1615. The city continued as British headquarters in India until it was replaced by Bombay (now Mumbai) in the 1670 to 1680s. In 1690, Calcutta (Kolkata) on the Hugli River in West Bengal, became British headquarters for Indian inland trade. The river formed an important artery to the Sea of Bengal. Thus, following in the wake of the colonial ambitions of Portugal and Spain in the sixteenth century, the British, in the seventeenth, began to expand exploration and trade networks throughout the world that would, over the next several centuries, create the largest empire ever known. America, Africa, India, and the Far East were all, or in part, subject to British rule. Dominions, colonies, or protectorates that were established on a global basis formed a colossal trade network. Colonies provided raw materials for England's manufacturing output that was resold in the form of finished goods at home or back in the colonies. By the time of the empire's collapse after World War II, it had become the most powerful trading empire on the planet.

In 1612, the British soundly defeated the Portuguese in a sea battle off the coast of Surat, so the Mughal emperor of India, Jehangir, thought it best to do business with the English. With the British presence in India in the early seventeenth century, EIC executives investigated the possibility of a foothold in India with official consent of the Indian government. King James I of England charged Tomas Roe in 1612 to call upon the reigning Mughal emperor, Nuruddin Salim, and try to arrange a commercial treaty. The visit was resoundingly successful. The EIC acquired the exclusive rights to construct offices and warehouses, and to reside in Surat (among other places) with the obligation to send the emperor interesting and unique merchandise from Europe to embellish his residence. The EIC wasted little time in broadening its operations under royal patronage.[4]

About 1670, the EIC became more than just a company. A series of royal decrees promulgated under Charles II (1660–1685) allowed it the right to govern new territories, mint money, hire and command military troops, and build fortresses where needed. It could undertake alliances, declare war on its own account, and sign peace treaties. Its autonomy even extended to include jurisdiction over civil and criminal law in its territories

British Influence on Trade

The decline and fall of the Mughal Empire in the mid eighteenth century contributed to the East India Company's accumulation of power. In 1757, the Company defeated and killed the Mughal governor of Bengal, Sirajud-Dawla, after he had captured Calcutta in an attempt to prevent the Company from depriving Indian merchants of their trade and the government of revenue. By 1765, the Company had acquired control of the revenue systems of Bengal, Orissa, and Bihar, on India's east coast, and became the largest territorial power in India.

The EIC was a corporation that held a legal monopoly on imported goods from Asia to England, and it had the freedom to develop monopolies in any other market, by force if required. It maintained its own military to protect its interests, built forts in strategic areas, and established colonies. To extract trade concessions, it spent money on grand residences and lavish gifts to foreign rulers to show itself powerful and worthy of a ruler's attention. Prestige was important, as was involving the employees in local cultural affairs to show unbiased goodwill. Over the life of the EIC, these practices changed as budgetary considerations cut down on expenses, and moral attitudes hindered the carefree mixing of cultures. The company's accountants eventually found it too extravagant when bills came in for meat to feed the tiger on the estate of the chief representative in Madras, and expenses of other employees having a good time with local elites. Rules for expenses were tightened up as were the those for what might be considered immoral behavior such as taking a local wife when an employee already had one at home in England. Coming to an end was the practice of "going native," and a kind of apartheid with its sense of racial superiority became the norm. Local wives were now considered simply whores.[5] When the EIC set up a factory in Bombay, Surat went into decline, and the population fell to about 80,000. The company proceeded to establish trading posts in many other places, and by the middle of the seventeenth century had 23 factories.

The Mughal emperor allowed the English to extend their trade into Bengal and later waived all customs duties. The EIC was now heavily into trade in silk, cotton, indigo dye, tea, and saltpeter. After about 1650, it began making incursions into the monopoly of the spice trade that the Dutch had taken over by defeating the Portuguese in 1640. In 1694, the British government, perhaps looking for ways to bring in more money from commerce, passed a bill that accorded the right to trade in India to any English company that wished to do so. The grip of the EIC on the subcontinent was so tight, however, that competition was not a great concern. The Battle of Seringapatam in 1799, in which the British defeated the Muslim ruler of the kingdom of Mysore, Tipu Sultan, culminated in British control of much of southern India.

The EIC hired armies of Indians as soldiers and supplied them with up-to-date European weaponry to increase the company's might over its Western competitors. This army was even used to control the courts of Indian princes, and thus English policies and interests penetrated all facets of life in India. Colonial rule lasted for centuries and profoundly affected society there.

In the Battle of Assaye in 1803, with forces under the command of the duke of Wellington the British took charge of all of southern India except for the small French enclaves. The remainder of the country was slowly consolidated by diplomacy, threats, and military expansion. The EIC suffered many problems, one of the worst of which was a cholera pandemic that spread throughout India in 1820, decimating thousands of British troops and an untold number of Indians. Periodic famines also reduced the Indian workforce.

East India Company Act (1773)

Despite strong resistance from the EIC and its shareholders, the British Parliament imposed administrative and economic reforms by which it projected its control over the company. It placed EIC land under the authority of the Crown but leased it for two years to the EIC. Under the new terms, the first governor of Bengal, Warren Hastings, was given administrative power over the whole of British India. Hastings was also given power to decide on peace or war, a heavy responsibility for a civil servant.

The EIC maintained its trade monopoly for a price paid to the government and was obligated to export a minimum quantity of goods yearly to Britain. The costs of administration were to be met by the company, but with these financial burdens, its income steadily declined.

India was a particularly good source of saltpeter, a commodity in demand for making gunpowder, and thousands of tons arrived in England as ballast in company ships. It was needed to supply the army and navy in European wars. Saltpeter from Bengal was of a particularly good quality, and the English developed a monopoly on it for a period of time—a matter that antagonized France and other European countries.

Tea Act (1773)

The complaint of American colonists that they wanted no taxation without representation in the English Parliament was a direct challenge to England but was ignored by the British government.

The passing of the Tea Act in 1773 gave the EIC greater autonomy in organizing its trade in America, and allowed it an exemption from the tea tax that its colonial competitors were required to pay. When the American colonists, who included tea merchants, were told of the act, they tried to boycott it, claiming that although the price had gone down on the tea, it was a tax all the same. The arrival of tax-exempt company tea, which undercut the local merchants, triggered the Boston Tea Party in December 1773, a major event that led to the American Revolution in 1776.

East India Company Act (1784)

The Parliamentary Act of 1784 separated the EIC's political and commercial functions. In all political affairs, it fell under the jurisdiction of the government, entrusted to a board of control made up of government officials. In spite of Crown interference, however, the EIC expanded its influence to nearby territories by threats and intimidation. By mid-nineteenth century, its authority had spread throughout most of India as well as Burma and Malaya, including Singapore. Its commercial enterprises encompassed about one-fifth of the global population.

BRITISH RULE (1750–1947)

India was the jewel of the empire, and British coffers overflowed with wealth extracted from the subcontinent. The initial acquisition of India under the EIC, and the ongoing domination under the British Raj of a population many times the size of the occupying force, proved to be a remarkable feat. Beyond the economic justification, the British believed the Indians constituted one of the many inferior races around the world and that a strong European influence would enlighten the people there. By 1922, the British Empire held sway over about half a billion people, or one-fifth of the world's population at the time, and covered nearly a quarter of the earth's land mass.

Free Trade Decree and Corn Laws

Published in 1776, Adam Smith's *Wealth of Nations* profoundly affected commerce. Smith warned that monopolies were not good, and he advocated free trade and its concomitant competition. For economic prosperity, governments should eschew tariffs and subsidized exports, allowing prices to be set by supply and demand. Several decades later, the English Parliament passed a Statement of Principle in support of the concepts advocated by Smith.

A Corn Law, meanwhile, was introduced into Britain in 1804, when landowners, who dominated Parliament, imposed a duty on cheaper imported corn (i.e., grain) to protect their profits. This, of course, benefited the landed aristocracy. The English working poor responded in riots and in 1815, demanded free trade as they marched through the streets of London. Parliament gave no ground and prohibited imports of all grain when the price fell to less than 80 shillings. This law protected the wealthy and powerful to the detriment of the poor and weak. The workers found an ally in the growing manufacturing magnates, however, who wanted cheaper grain to feed the hungry laborers and feared that if they were starving, they would demand higher wages. Industrial workers considered the Corn Laws a good example of how parliamentarians passed legislation that advantaged the elite. By 1840, the tide was turning in favor of free trade.[6]

By the 1820s, increased population and food demands led to regulations that gave lower import duties to colonial over foreign imports. Lower rates helped offset transatlantic transport expenses for British North American grain and built up a colonial interest in wheat exports. In 1843, the English Parliament passed the Canada Corn Act, which allowed wheat to be sold in England with a minimal import duty. Flour, too, could be imported from Canada at low rates. The St. Lawrence River began to bear more freight and was seen as an important waterway for commerce. The act stimulated Canadian grain production and investment in the development and enlargement of farms and flourmills. Nonetheless, British-Canadian investors were soon disillusioned. The Corn Laws were repealed in 1846 as England prepared for the advent of free trade.

Great Britain stuck to its agricultural free trade policies for another century, only departing from them in 1932 at the Ottawa conference that convened the colonies and dominions to discuss the Great Depression. The idea of imperial preference was born to allow for lower tariffs within the British Empire and higher tariffs for the rest of the world.

DUTCH EAST INDIA COMPANY (VOC, 1602–1799)

There was a good deal of money to be made in the spice market, as the Portuguese had already demonstrated, and there was room for others to compete with the small Portuguese nation. The Dutch East India Company (*Vereenigde Oost-Indische Compagnie*, or VOC) also wanted a piece of the pie if not the entire bakery, and nine merchants who gathered in an Amsterdam wine house in 1594 considered ways to circumnavigate the Portuguese monopoly on Eastern spices and make their own fortunes. Capital for the enterprise to build, buy, and outfit ships was not difficult to raise in the cities of the northern Netherlands where much wealth had accumulated through Baltic Sea trade in wood, fish, and grain and the export of cloth and dairy products.[7] The nine merchant administrators formed a company and sold shares in it.

In April 1595, four ships sailed for the East. The expedition was a failure: crews died of scurvy during the 15-month voyage to Java, the men in charge did not get along with each other, the Javanese were hostile to the surly Dutch, and one ship was abandoned in Asia for lack of crew. Of the original 240 crewmen, only 87 returned alive, and the cargo of pepper only just covered expenses. During the following seven or so years, other marine companies dispatched ships to the East in search of spices. Some returned with cargos that made the owners wealthy, others failed to reach their destination or were lost at sea. In the East, competition drove up the price of commodities while prices dropped in Holland as the market became satiated. Competition also came from Portugal, Spain, and England, deflating the European spice market. Encouraged by the government, the Dutch overseas companies finally merged their resources into a United Dutch East India Company (VOC) in 1602, and were awarded a monopoly on all Asian trade. Seven directors at Hoorn were responsible for its operations.

The VOC not only received the unique right to trade east of the Cape of Good Hope, but it was authorized to make war and treaties with Asian governments, to recruit soldiers, and build forts for its own security—exceptional circumstances for a private company. In previous times when an expedition returned, the crews were laid off, the shareholders paid off, and the ships sold. This time, the company became a permanent fixture with a long-term renewable charter.

The Dutch East India Company grew into the largest trading company in the world until its dissolution in 1799. With thousands of employees, over 100 ships, 30 settlements in Asia, and six

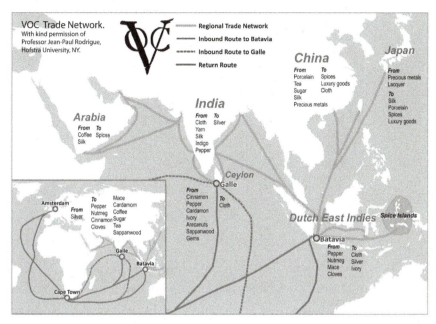

VOC Trade Network. (With kind permission of Professor Jean-Paul Rodrigue, Hofstra University, NY.)

different offices, warehouses, and shipyards in Holland, its global influence was unrivaled.[8]

Life aboard Ship

Mortality was high at sea with men crammed together on a vessel where, besides scurvy, diseases such as typhus or flu could spread rapidly, decimating the crew in short order. Friction on board might arise between sailors and soldiers, or between different nationalities, on the crowded upper deck where the men slept and maneuvered for space for their sea chests in which were a few personal belongings—a comb, extra clothes, a knife, soap, a mirror, tobacco, a plate and mug, a mattress and pillow, maybe a Bible, and various permitted games such as a checker board. Cards and gambling were forbidden. Abridgment of the rules was punished and ranged from fines or confinement on bread and water, to death. Tying the guilty man to the body of the victim and throwing both over board was a redress for murder. On average, two out of three sailors working for the VOC never returned to Holland, many having died at sea, others in foreign tropical lands. Water stowed aboard the ship became repugnant in tropical

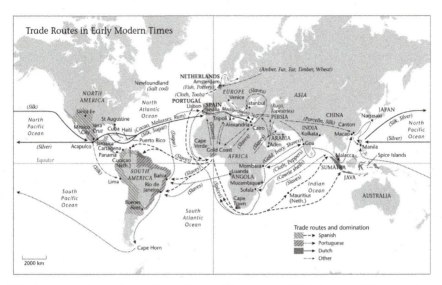

Trade routes in early modern times. (Courtesy of Leinberger Mapping.)

climates and sailors drank it holding their noses, allowing it to filter slowly between clenched teeth to filter out the myriad of worms that had made their way into the barrels.[9]

Cargos, Routes, and the Cape of Good Hope

From Europe to Asia, the VOC transported gold ingots, coins, and silver bars, much of it originating from Spanish mines in South America. Other merchandise included linen and flax, wine and beer, trinkets, lead, mercury, and red dyes.

Ships embarked from the Netherlands for the East in December and January, and in April and May. The winter departure could be treacherous in the North Sea with brutal weather conditions, but they reached and crossed the equator with the northeastern trade wind filling the sails from astern. The Christmas fleet arrived at Batavia, its Asian headquarters, at the right time to distribute the European merchandise to the company settlements there. Leaving soon after the slaughtering season, the fleet could carry freshly salted meat to the settlements.[10]

The spring, or Easter, fleet left port under better weather conditions but reached the equator and Asia under less pleasant circumstances. As commerce picked up, departures from the homeland increased, as did the sailing times that were spread throughout the year. Departures from the Netherlands were also governed by the European political climate.

Dutch East India House in Amsterdam, showing warehouses and ship-yard. (North Wind Picture Archives.)

The outbreak of war was always a threat to the VOC and the men who sailed the ships. War with England or France, for example, made a longer voyage necessary; instead of sailing from the Netherlands through the English Channel to the Cape of Good Hope, VOC ships had to skirt north around Scotland to avoid enemy warships and pirates. It was sometimes due to war that the ships sailed in convoys to protect each other. Dutch naval ships came out to escort the transporters when they neared their home ports in the Netherlands.

The ocean offered challenges for the square rigged sailing ships of the period, whose ability to tack against the wind was nil. As the fleet proceeded past the Canary Islands, the current carried it along the coast of Africa, but reaching the Gulf of Guinea, shifting currents could easily take them into the gulf if they were too close to the shore. If they sailed too far out to sea, the Equatorial Current could carry them toward the Caribbean and the feared doldrums. In 1627, the company set out a course for all its ships to follow that took them, once beyond the Cape Verde Islands, along the coast of South America to latitude 30 south (about as far as southern Brazil), and then they were to sail eastward. The eastward route took them to the vicinity of the Cape of Good Hope and an obligatory stopover at the company's supply station established in the mid-seventeenth century. Here the fleet took on vegetables, water, and meat for the several months' voyage ahead to Asia. There were other ports of call along the sea route where ships could resupply such as the Cape Verde Islands and Saint Helena in the Atlantic, and Madagascar and Mauritius in the Indian Ocean, but where only limited provisions could be found. The South African supply depot was owned and administered by the VOC and comprised a fort, warehouses, a hospital, and a ship repair works. An aqueduct was constructed to bring fresh water from the nearby mountains, vegetable gardens were laid out, and meat was solicited from cattle herders among the local people, the Khoikhoi. The relationship between the natives and the Dutch was not friendly. A shortage of manpower was manifest, and the company allowed Dutch settlers to establish farms and businesses to stock their ships. Before long, a small city developed at Table Bay (present-day Cape Town).

From the Cape of Good Hope India merchantmen set a course due south to pick up the westerly winds at about 35 degrees, 40 minutes south latitude and then turned eastward. The faster route avoided the hostility of the Portuguese settlements on the coasts of East Africa and the Strait of Malacca, as well as the adverse winds. Discovered in 1611 by Hendrick Brouwar, a VOC master, the route became the obligatory sea route for VOC ships a few years later. Besides being quicker, another virtue of the new sealane was the cooler climate that was more conducive to the well-being of crews and cargos. After a voyage of about 1,600 kilometers eastward, the VOC captains had to steer north and reach Java. A drawback was that it was not easy to determine when the ship had reached the 1,600-kilometer turning point. Longitude determinations were still a difficult problem at the time. Two small islands—easily missed—some 1,100 kilometers east of the cape helped served as a guide, but the turning point was crucial and if missed could lead to shipwreck on the west coast of Australia. The VOC lost four ships this way.[11] One of them, the *Batavia*, wound up on the coral reefs of western Australia in 1629 carrying some 322 crew and passengers. The master, along with a few officers and merchants, reached Java on a small boat, but many of the remainder perished due to systematic murder by a few over food. When discovered, the killers were tried in Batavia, and those proven guilty were hanged.[12]

Nor was the return voyage in heavily laden vessels easy, and the Indian Ocean was the most dangerous part. Crews were sometimes inadequate, members having contracted diseases and died in the tropical climate, and while they might be replaced with Asians, the latter were frequently inexperienced. The wooden ships were often in need of an overhaul, having suffered in the tropical seas from rotting timbers infused with sea worms. Due to the company directors' concern for the safety of its fleets and the enormous losses that could accrue from the sinking of even one vessel, the VOC spared no effort to ensure a successful voyage. The selection of captains was meticulous and involved rigorous examinations, both written and oral, and a good deal of experience was required for Eastern voyages. The captain received in his sailing orders the best charts available and all navigational equipment he might need. The charts were produced by the company in its two hydrographic offices in Amsterdam and Batavia. The highly secret information on the charts was drawn by hand, not printed, in order to keep production to a minimum. By determining the angle of the sun at noon, and stars at night, with an astrolabe, sailors were able to fix their latitude. The master of the ship made corrections to them if required. Not until the 1750s were the problems of longitude at sea solved when John Harrisson, after many years labor, perfected the chronometer, which was reliable on ships. After this discovery, along with the care taken by the company, few ships were lost on the eight-month, 24,000-kilometer voyage from the Netherlands to Batavia. Between 1595 and 1795, with about 4,800 sailings, only 4 percent of the vessels succumbed to shipwreck.[13]

The VOC drove the English out of the Indonesian islands, the last 10 English merchants and their Japanese servants remaining at Ambon were seized in 1623, and after confessions extracted by torture, they were executed on a charge of conspiracy against the Dutch colony. Protests from London were ineffective. The EIC was finished in the Moluccas and abandoned further endeavors there, pulling back to trade in India. The Dutch acquired more and more land in the East Indies, built forts, and hoped to close the western entrances to the eastern sea to all European shipping other than the Dutch. For this, armed ships were necessary and were supplied. Batavia commanded the Sunda Strait and had designs on the Strait of Malacca, the city still held by the Portuguese as their last stronghold. The Dutch took it in 1641.

Batavia

Situated in West Java, Batavia was the hub of VOC trade in Asia. Using military force, diplomacy, and commercial pressure, the

VOC maintained its major goal of a monopoly on spices. Its tactics could be seen in the Banda Islands, the only place where nutmeg and mace (originating from the same tree) were grown. In 1602, the local population agreed to sell only to the Dutch who were unwilling to provide clothing and food to the Bandanese—the things they needed from VOC in exchange for spices The Bandanese also carried on trade with the Portuguese, Spanish, English, and other Asian merchants, much to the chagrin of the Dutch.

Cloves, of great interest to the VOC, grew wild at first on the island of Makian in the northern Moluccas. From there, small plants were taken to be grown on other islands to the south such as Ambon, Seram, and Ternate, whose inhabitants promised to sell cloves only to the Dutch. They, too, did not keep their promise, however, and the VOC took action attempting to concentrate all cloves on the Island of Ambon, which was most firmly under its control. Each family was forced to maintain 10 clove trees and local men, overseen by company servants, were ordered to go to other islands and destroy the clove trees they found there.[14] The aggressive company soon drove other nations out of the region. Portuguese forts were taken over by the Dutch, Spanish initiatives in the area were switched to the Philippine Islands, and the summary execution of 10 men of the EIC prompted the English also to withdraw from the Moluccas. The VOC's hand in the clove trade, a near monopoly, was enough to supply most of Europe by 1650 and by 1667, the major Asian spice port of Macassar on the island of Celebes succumbed to the VOC's grasp.

Cinnamon and Pepper

The VOC initiated military operations against the Portuguese in Ceylon to acquire its cinnamon trade and took over the Portuguese possessions. In 1658, the last Portuguese were forced from the island. Similar actions on the Malabar Coast and on the Malay Peninsula resulted in Dutch acquisition. With a firm grip on the important waterway of the Strait of Malacca wrapped up, the VOC made trade contacts for pepper with local rulers on Sumatra but was unable to monopolize the trade due to the fact that, unlike mace, cloves, cinnamon, and nutmeg, pepper grew in so many other locations in Asia.

The VOC's Council of the Indies had its headquarters at Batavia, a city of around 70,000 in 1700 that grew to about 180,000 by the end of the century, and answered only to the directors of the company. Due to the long distance, and the many months required to convey messages from Holland to the Indies, the Council of the Indies controlled all facets of business in the East and sent an annual report to the Gentlemen Seventeen (the directors). The council also supervised trade among the 30 settlements. The number of civil servants and soldiers in the Asian branch of the company rose from 2,500 in 1625 to some 20,000 by 1750.[15] Expenses increased to protect the commercial empire, while profits decreased since cloves and other spices were no longer in such great demand as Europeans now desired Chinese tea and Indian textiles, and English merchants were making strong inroads in Indian trade where the VOC lost much influence. In compensation, the company established large coffee and sugar plantations in Java, near Batavia. Ultimately, it pulled back to the Indonesian islands that became the Dutch East Indies.

Trade Goods

In the seventeenth century, spices were the most important trade items, making up some 60 percent of freight shipped to Europe from the East. Risks were inevitable, but profits were high. The VOC traded over 100 different Asian products, shipping about 6 million pounds to Europe annually. In Japan, copper and precious metals were traded and exported, as the demand for copper in India for making coins was high. Japanese silver was converted into *rupees* in India so that the company could buy Indian textiles for shipment to Europe and other parts of Asia. Raw silk from China, Persia, and India (Bengal) was shipped to Japan in exchange for copper, gold, and silver. When Japan limited the export of metals in the latter half of the seventeenth century, the VOC suffered a blow. At the conclusion of the seventeenth century, the VOC's share in the spice trade had diminished greatly, and less profitable Indian cottons were shipped in large quantities. Indian textiles were used in the Netherlands for making curtains, tablecloths, clothes, and bedspreads among other things.

The VOC continued its practice of shipping dried tea leaves in Chinese junks to Batavia for distribution, as the demand for tea in Europe increased; competitors sailed directly to China. The company was uncharacteristically slow to respond to the dangers from English and other merchants who bought better quality tea at cheaper rates there. By the time the VOC opened a direct route to

China in about 1728, the European tea market was already under the control of others. On the other hand, coffee from VOC plantations in Java was much cheaper than Arabian coffee imported into Europe in the seventeenth century. As a result, the European coffee market expanded to the benefit of the Dutch.

Profitable also for them, especially in Asia—much of it from Bengal—was opium, on which they held a monopoly and sold to Asian merchants. The VOC pretty much controlled this trade well into the eighteenth century. A ballast cargo on the voyages to Europe, saltpeter, also acquired in Bengal, was much in demand for the production of gunpowder. Tin, another valuable item in the eighteenth century, was exported from mines in Southeast Asia and transported to China, where demand was great for a kind of tin foil burned at religious offerings. The metal was also used to line tea chests to maintain the freshness of the leaves throughout long voyages. The sugar plantations of the VOC supplied inexpensive sugar throughout Asia but not so much in Europe, where it competed with sugar from the West Indies. VOC trade also included horses from Persia, elephants from Ceylon, dyes, trinkets, Indian diamonds, Japanese lacquer ware, and porcelain from China.

Competition

From 1609, the Dutch laid claim to the Moluccas and sent out the first governor-general in 1611 to Bantam in Java.[16] An attempt was soon underway to quash English trade on the islands. The Dutch made every effort to instill hatred among the natives toward the British, whose ships were seized, cargos confiscated, and Englishmen imprisoned under any pretext. The only redress was to the Dutch courts established there. Protests from London were useless, as was an English fleet sent out in 1618. The Dutch were too well entrenched and outgunned the British.

Appointed governor-general in 1618, the ambitious Jan Coen embodied the ruthless aspirations of a company bent on profits over all else. "Coen was to the Dutch what Albuquerque had been to the Portuguese."[17] He based his policies on force (without the Portuguese religious component) and established the administrative capital at Batavia, constructing forts as strategic trading ports. He expelled the Portuguese from the East Indies and although the Spanish held the small islands of Tidore, their days were numbered. Coen took the Banda group of islands, the most valuable producers of spice, in 1621 and either slaughtered the inhabitants or enslaved them. Their land was distributed among the VOC's employees, who were directed to sell all their products to the company at company prices.

Fate of the Sultanates

The Dutch played off the native princes of the islands, one against the other, and sooner or later, by force or intimidation, the rulers submitted to Dutch demands. They were in part responsible, as they sometimes called on the Dutch to aid them in one war or another with their neighbors, or to settle some dynastic problem. Dutch services were naturally rewarded with favorable commercial concessions. A typical example of VOC duplicity was to pick a quarrel with Bantam, a trading town at the western end of Java on the Sunda Strait, and then defeat the sultan of Bantam in a resounding naval victory. He was then forced to abandon his territorial possessions, grant a monopoly on pepper to the company, and close his ports to all other foreigners. By the end of the seventeenth century, the Dutch controlled all Java's ports.[18]

Demise of the VOC

From the largest shipping and trading company in the world in the seventeenth and eighteenth centuries, the VOC descended into bankruptcy by the end of the eighteenth. The reasons were many: in spite of government support, the company could not withstand the expenses brought on by declining trade in spices, its mainstay, the costs of protecting its monopolies from interlopers, fraudulent activities by its servants, declining investments in the trade, and perhaps the *coup de grace*, the Fourth Anglo-Dutch War. The English captured a number of homeward-bound ships with their cargos and ousted the Dutch from several of their settlements in Asia. The VOC failed to bring in revenues for a few years, while debt continued to accumulate. A shortage of personnel and ships existed in spite of government subsidies, and the French invasions of the Netherlands did not auger well for commerce. The gargantuan company was nationalized in 1799, and the Dutch government took over its debts and possessions. By 1803, it had disappeared as a commercial entity. During its time in business, the VOC's aggression, and policy of profit at any cost, was sometimes little better than that of the Portuguese that so often alienated the local dignitaries. Unlike the Portuguese, however, missionaries did not accompany the Dutch traders.

FRENCH EAST INDIA COMPANY (*COMPAGNIE DES INDES ORIENTALES* 1664–1794)

The French East India Company was founded in 1664 for the purpose of commercial activity in India, in competition with the English and Dutch. Chartered by King Louis XIV, stock in the company sold readily, and the company was offered a 50-year monopoly on French trade in the Pacific and Indian Oceans. The first French mariners to round the Cape of Good Hope and enter the Red Sea in 1708 came to buy coffee at its source at Mocha in Yeman. The French, as was the case with other European East India companies, wanted to eliminate Arab and Indian middlemen in the purchase of the valuable commodity.

Jean de la Roque signed a trade treaty with the king of Yeman to trade, then waited six months for the coffee to be harvested and another six months to gather in the 600 tons.[19] Ordinarily, the coffee beans were sent along the route from Yeman growers to the port by camel. They were then shipped to Jiddah on the Red Sea. There the cargo was placed on Turkish ships for Suez, where camels again took over for transport to Cairo or Alexandria. From there, the goods went by ship to Istanbul or Marseilles. Much to the consternation of middlemen, de la Roque bypassed this arduous and expensive route, and the Arab monopoly on coffee was broken. Cheaper coffee grown in Martinique later displaced Mokha coffee, even in Cairo. By 1900, Yeman produced next to none. After 300 years of coffee trade, the city disintegrated into ruin.[20]

French ambitions for empire in India were abandoned in the wake of the Seven Years' War (1756–1763), in which Major-General Robert Clive, Commander-in-Chief of India, defeated the French forces in India under Joseph Dupleix. In the Treaty of Paris in 1763, the French were allocated only a few small unmilitarized trading posts. For the EIC, a major competitor for trade in India had been eliminated.

NOTES

1. Bernstein, 219.
2. Williamson, 121–123.
3. Braudel (1985), 583–585.

4. By this time, the EIC was called the HEIC or Honorable East India Company.

5. Pomeranz and Topik, 36–37.

6. Bernstein, 307.

7. Jacobs, 8.

8. Jacobs, 12.

9. Jacobs, 41–48.

10. Jacobs, 55ff.

11. Jacobs, 63.

12. Bernstein, 210–211.

13. Jacobs, 63–64.

14. Jacobs, 73–74.

15. Jacobs, 77.

16. Jacobs, 83–86.

17. Parry, 90–91.

18. Parry, 136–137.

19. Pomeranz and Topik, 82.

20. Pomeranz and Topik, 83.

17

CHINA

Topographically varied and rich in mineral wealth, China supports the largest population in the world, the most prevalent group of which are the Han. Large minorities include the Manchu, Mongolians, Koreans, Tibetans, and Turkish Uighurs. The country has had a long history of trade and in the third millennium, is a major participant in world commerce.

HAN DYNASTY (AROUND 206 BCE–220 CE)

In the chaotic conditions that followed dynastic change, a prince of the Han secured the throne. Under his rule, literature and music were encouraged, beautiful murals were produced, and craftsmen made exquisite jade and gold jewelry, as well as glazed, brightly colored pottery. Paper was invented, and in medicine, acupuncture was successfully tried.

The elite were buried with numerous material objects that included gold, jade, lacquerware, bronze, and silk. Grave murals might include depictions of farming and mining operations—matters of everyday life.[1] Miniature clay models of houses, stoves, carts, boats, servants, furniture, lamps, and other belongings accompanying them suggest such things considered to be needed in an afterlife. While ironwork was perhaps the most important manufacturing industry in Han China, silk was the most significant trade item. Chinese silk was known in India as early as the fourth century BCE, and by the first century of the Common Era, trade between the two countries was well established. Foreign merchants who arrived by sea were confined to certain ports by the xenophobic Han government, which made certain they were segregated from the Chinese people.[2]

In the first century BCE, as the Han increased its lands to the west, and the Roman Empire expanded eastward, the two great civilizations came into contact, resulting in the opening of the Silk Road.[3] Caravans carried jade, silk, spices, and lacquerware to Byzantium that were then shipped to Rome in exchange for gold, silver, slaves, coral, textiles, pearls, glass, and amber—the latter from the Baltic Sea coasts.

FIRST RISE AND DECLINE OF THE SILK ROUTE

Settlements were established along the Silk Route to accommodate merchants and allow for participation in the exchange of commodities. Merchants did not, generally speaking, traverse the entire distance across Central Asia, but at certain junctures turned their merchandise over to others, who would then transport it to the next point of exchange. Profits were made at each stage as the goods changed hands. Policing the routes was always a problem in the rugged and wild lands of Central Asia, as small caravans faced danger from marauding bandits, and added costs were required to hire guards. Merchants who worked the Silk Route endured a long and grueling journey even if they did not go the full distance. The road followed the Great Wall of China westward onto the fringes of the Taklamakan Desert in the Tarim Basin that, enclosed by mountains on three sides, stretched some 1,000 kilometers east and west, and over 400 kilometers across. The approximately 4,500-kilometer journey from China to the Mediterranean was a challenge for man and beast across high barren mountains and waterless stretches of parched land. Unbearably hot in summer, icy cold in winter, the road climbed to great elevations in the rugged Pamir Mountains in present-day Tajikistan and Kyrgystan, where caravans were subject to fierce blizzards and deep snow, bringing travel to a halt. Small stone-built villages where rest stops might be found were sometimes few and far apart, and after leaving the mountains, the road entered the dry, treeless steppes of Afghanistan and Persia.

Best suited of any animal for the long distances over high mountain passes and the waterless stretches of Central Asia, the camel was the preferred beast of burden. A single animal could carry about 200 kilograms of merchandise, and large caravans might include thousands of camels and many hundreds of men (including guides, guards, and drivers). The time of year was important: when the winter snows had gone, muddy trails had dried, and edible plants were appearing upon which the animals could graze, the time was right for the long trek. In the desolate terrain with numerous branch roads feeding into the Silk Route from remote areas, it was easy to lose one's bearings; a wrong turn could lead to delays, upset the calculations for the time of arrival at the destination, and the amounts of food and water required for the passage. The merchant investors of the caravan and its goods might lose money through delays or some mishap along the trail.

Trade caravans on the Silk Road, the great highway of Central Asia. (North Wind Picture Archives.)

The primary commodity exported from China, silk, was in high demand throughout the Roman Empire but was not the only important item. Also traded were porcelain dishes and vases of exquisite workmanship and designs—items that carried a substantial price in European markets. There were also metal objects such as bronze mirrors and weapons, along with medicinal herbs, perfumes, and much sought after Chinese paper.

China imported horses, camels, grape seeds, woolen goods, carpets, curtains, tapestries and blankets, semiprecious stones, and glass products from Central Asia and the eastern Mediterranean. The finest glass came from Samarkand. Exotic animals— including peacocks, leopards, lions and elephants, hunting dogs—and even food items such as watermelon and peaches, as well as utensils and arms found their way there also. From India came spices, fabrics, stones, dyes, and ivory. From Persia came silver. Europeans traded wool, skins, furs, cattle, honey, and slaves for Chinese rice, cotton, and silk garments. Camels carried heavy loads of rhino horns, originally from Africa, turtle shells, and coral. Spices such as cinnamon and ginger were transported over the routes along with tea, asbestos, and iron. The majority of traders during antiquity were Indian and Bactrian. The decline of the Han diminished commerce and travel along the east-west trade routes. Collapse of Han power was due in part to royal feuds, high taxes, government corruption, and peasant revolts. Northern nomadic tribes continued to ravage the land, and Tibetans began to emerge as a military threat. Finally, revolts in the army led to a state of anarchy. The chaotic centuries between the fall of the Han and rise of the Sui Dynasty have been considered China's dark ages.[4]

SUI DYNASTY (589–618)

After the fall of the Han, unity was reestablished in China under the Sui, and reforms were introduced that reduced taxes on peasants and merchants, overhauled the bureaucracy, and promoted religious tolerance. Nevertheless, an ambitious son, incited by dissatisfied nobility, had his father killed and became emperor under the name Sui Yangdi. He engaged in major works that facilitated trade and food supply between the north and south by extending the Grand Canal, and improving the transportation network. Wars with Turks, Tibetans, and Koreans bankrupted the government, however, and he was assassinated.

THE T'ANG DYNASTY (618–907)

With its capital at Chang'an in northcentral China, the eastern terminus of the Silk Road, the T'ang Dynasty enlarged its territory into Central Asia by military conquest. Excavations of the T'ang capital have brought to light walls, streets, public buildings and markets, royal palaces, and richly decorated royal tombs. It may have been one of the richest cities in the world at the time. Massive walls enclosed about 78 square kilometers in which, by about 700, lived 1 million people. The streets were wide and laid out on a grid plan with a central avenue running north and south that it was believed channeled cosmic forces in such a manner as to benefit the inhabitants.

Merchandise from the West and from Central Asia reached Chang'an. Over 200 guilds occupied the area of the vast market-place wherein some 3,000 stalls displayed their diverse wares. On some of the narrow streets printers, brothels, teahouses, restaurants, and moneylenders proliferated.[5] Dozens of ethnic groups such as Indians, Japanese, Turks, Sogdians, Iranians, and Koreans worked, mainly as merchants, jostling and bartering in the confines of the lanes. Many of the goods arriving at Chang'an via the Silk Road found a temporary home in the warehouses adjacent to the walls surrounding the market, where they were stored and registered by agents who would find buyers. Chang'an became one of the most international cities of the time as the population rose to close to 2 million by the middle of the eighth century; a 754 census of the city listed about 5,000 foreign residents.

T'ang prosperity brought about an upswing in traffic along the Silk Road from the seventh well into the ninth century that also coincided with the expansion of Islam from Arabia through Persia and into Central Asia. Chinese merchants transported silk and other wares into Central Asia, where they were exchanged by Muslim middlemen for Western goods. These were then carried to the Levant, exchanged again, and shipped to clients in Europe. After about the middle of the eighth century, the Silk Route again underwent a decline.[6] The reasons were many: the fall of the T'ang, growing turmoil in Central Asia (especially in Tibet), the loss of the Chinese monopoly on silk, and perhaps the most compelling reason that did not auger well for the land route was the increasing and cheaper use of trading ships to and from the coasts of China via the South China Sea, the Indian Ocean, the Red Sea, and the Persian Gulf to Europe.

Merchants

Merchants were not aristocrats, nor did they work the land. In the Chinese view, they were parasites taking advantage of the labor of others and thus were generally considered as beneath contempt. Successful merchants invoked the ire and resentment of officials and peasants when they paraded their wealth by riding in chariots or built luxurious houses with pools and gardens. Some were sufficiently well off to purchase a title from the emperor; the vast majority, however, lived in humble circumstances and performed the job of small-scale middlemen between farmers and urbanites, or short-haul trade between towns and villages. Usually the ones who garnered the wealth were long-distance traders who invested in ships and caravans, and transported precious goods. The risks were high, as were the profits.

SONG DYNASTY (960–1279)

By the time of the Song Dynasty, the population of China had reached about 100 million, mostly living in the Yangtze River Valley and further south. In this period, manufacturing increased, as did agricultural production. The compass was invented, and ocean-going ships (junks) of great size were constructed with a capacity that allowed large quantities of merchandise to sail to the East Indies, Southeast Asia, Ceylon, and the Malabar Coast of India.

Foreign trade under the southern Song (1127–1279) became a major enterprise. In return for spices, they traded porcelain, silk, and copper. Their first capital at Kaifeng at the confluence of the Yellow River and the Grand Canal became a major ironworking industrial city. With a new and growing mercantile class, ordinary Chinese could make money in commerce, and landholdings ceased to be the only way to become wealthy. Foreigners were encouraged to trade in China and even to settle.

The lower classes were not so fortunate, however, as the benefits of trade seldom filtered down to them. The middle class moved into larger houses, while the laborers lived in tenements where bathrooms were only buckets whose contents fertilized the surrounding fields. At the bottom of the scale, laborers, prostitutes, and peddlers lived a precarious life, and farmers in bad years might find it necessary to sell their land or their children, turn to banditry, or commit suicide.[7]

The Song Dynasty faltered at the end of the twelfth century. It had adhered to the peaceful principles of Confucius, had neglected its army, and was unprepared for what was coming. By about 1280, the Mongols conquered the greater part of China.

Family, Farming, and Food

The fundamental unit of Chinese society was the family, and Confucians maintained that the state should model its organization on the family, with the emperor as the father who had absolute authority, even to the point of taking the lives of his children (with the emperor's permission). The mother had total management of daughters as well as daughters-in-law. Parents arranged marriages, and offspring had no say in the matter. Male heirs were highly valued because they carried on the family line, while baby girls were sometimes drowned or left outside to die. Families had numerous children, but there was a high mortality rate. The great majority of men and young children worked in the fields tending crops, while the wives worked in their homes preparing meals, looking after the younger children, and weaving cotton. At about age four or five, to enhance their beauty in the eyes of men, girls had their toes broken and their feet bound to keep them small and dainty, resulting in painful feet and difficulty walking. The bonds between family members were exceedingly strong and led to collective responsibility for a wrongful act committed by any one of them. Monogamy was usual, but a husband could legally have concubines. Maternal authority, however, was always in the hands of the first wife.[8]

A farm might have a few pigs, a mule, some chickens, and, if they were a little better off, an ox for plowing. Life was hard and often short. Until the sixteenth century, when sweet potatoes, corn, and peanuts were introduced, crops could include tea, sugar, and cotton besides rice.

Farmers went to bed at sundown and rose before dawn. Dressed in simple clothes, men and women wore shirts and pants made of poor-grade cloth, and straw sandals on their feet. They stuffed their clothes with paper for warmth in winter.

The rich, of course, ate very well. They consumed grains like rice, wheat, and millet and ate plenty of meat, including pork, chicken, duck, goose, pheasant, and dog along with vegetables such as yams, soya beans, broad beans, turnips, onions, and garlic. They also ate quantities of seafood from the coast and rivers. Soup was made with shark fins, birds' nests, bear paws, and sea slugs. People drank wine made from rice or millet; they also drank tea.

Poor people ate a monotonous diet. In the south, it was rice; in the north, it was wheat in the form of noodles, dumplings, or pancakes. Famines occurred periodically, and the poor were fortunate if they did not starve to death.

Houses belonging to the wealthy were arranged around a central courtyard, imitating the imperial style of living. Large, elaborate homes were decorated with drapery, plush carpets, and fireplaces for the rooms, many of which displayed intricately carved furniture and walls painted with floral designs, or were hung with pictures and mirrors. High, earthen walls often surrounded the house, which would have had a single entry, inside of which might be another, short wall to conceal the door of the house and garden from curious passersby. Gardens were beautiful and highly decorated, and tiled roofs were typically built with an upward curve at the corners.

Throughout Chinese history, little changed for the poor. Common people lived in one-room bamboo or mud brick houses with thatched roofs, often built partly underground. An open fire pit in the center was used for cooking and provided warmth. Some better-off farmers might have had two-story houses with tiled or thatched roofs, windows covered with curtains, and a barn or two nearby. Several families often shared one home and worked the fields together. They did not own the farms, but in good years, a larger number of workers could often produce more food than required for their needs, allowing a surplus to trade for other necessary items.

Furniture, basic and sparse, usually comprised a few wooden benches. Poor people living in or near urban sites occupied shanties without sanitation, packed tightly together. With little to eat, begging was often the only alternative. These makeshift hovels were breeding grounds for crime where adolescent males formed street gangs and terrorized the occupants of the city. Not unlike today, they had particular clothing styles and weapons that gave them their identity.

MONGOL INVASIONS, YUAN DYNASTY (1279–1368)

Genghis Kahn united Turkish and Mongol tribes under his leadership and upon his death in 1227, his sons greatly expanded his empire, conquered China, and ruled far to the west over Persia (that included Baghdad), Afghanistan, and much of Russia for two centuries.

A grandson of Genghis Khan, Kublai Khan, established the Yuan dynasty in China in 1279, and Mongol suzerainty endured until 1368 with Peking (now Beijing) as the capital. Under the Mongols, China came to know a period of peace, and trade increased both locally and over long distances. Muslim and Italian merchants were welcomed. Mongol control of the caravan trade routes across Central Asia ensured more security, and foreign merchants were allowed to do business throughout the empire. The Silk Road again prospered in the thirteenth and fourteenth centuries under the Mongol Empire, whose leaders facilitated trade and travel. The disintegration of the Mongol khanates, together with more use of sea routes from Europe to Asia in the late fifteenth century, disrupted the Silk Route trade leading, to decline in parts of Central Asia.

Ibn Battutah

The Moroccan Koran scholar and jurist Ibn Battutah traveled to China, partly by sea, and described aspects of the country. His journey in this case took him from Sumatra through the South China Sea to Quanzhou and further north, possibly to Peking, before he retraced his voyage to Sumatra.

With regard to men of commerce, he reported that even a merchant of incalculable wealth cared little about clothing and might wear a coarse cotton tunic. Cotton was more expensive than silk, the latter common apparel among the poor. The people bought and sold with paper money about the size of the palm of the hand and stamped by the office of the emperor.[9] In all cities, there was a Muslim quarter with a mosque where the followers of Islam lived and worshipped, and they were treated with respect by the Chinese. Ibn Battutah was surprised that after a visit to the palace, he passed through the bazaar and discovered hanging on the walls perfect paper paintings of him and his companions. These had been done secretly at the palace for the purpose of identification if one of them committed a crime and was sought after by the authorities. A Muslim merchant had two choices upon arrival in a Chinese city: he could lodge with another Muslim trader or find quarters in a caravanserai. In either case, his money was taken from him and spent on his needs. This might include an inexpensive concubine. According to Ibn Battutah, all Chinese sold their sons and daughters, and to do so was not considered shameful.

It was felt that by turning his money over to another removed any temptation for a merchant to engage in a degenerate life style that might reflect back on China as a land of "debauchery and fleeting pleasures."[10]

On the Road

Ibn Battutah found the roads safe in China, saying, "A man may travel for nine months alone with great wealth and have nothing to fear."[11] This was due to the fact that all caravanserais were *funduqs* (hotels) with a live-in director and a company of soldiers. The director wrote down the name of everyone who stayed there and locked the doors at night. In the morning, he sent someone to take the guests to the next station. The courier would then return with confirmation from that director that all arrived safely. In each stopping place, all the provisions a traveler needed were provided; compared to the dangers of travel in medieval Europe, the watchful eye of the state must have been welcomed.

When Ibn Battutah visited a shop where plates were made for export, he was delighted with the skill of the artisans who made them of such strength that they were almost unbreakable.

In general, he did not like China, however. Although the great orchards, cultivated fields, and beautiful palaces appealed to him, he stated in his writings:

> China, for all its magnificence, did not please me. I was deeply depressed by the prevalence of infidelity, and whenever I left my lodgings I saw many offensive things ... I tended to stay at home as much as possible.[12]

Some of these things may have been the manner in which animals were slaughtered in a non-Muslim way and perhaps the extensive use of pork and pork fat in cooking, idol worship, and incineration of the dead.

MING DYNASTY (1368–1644)

As Mongol power weakened, the Ming dynasty arose to rule for nearly three centuries. The first Ming emperor, Yong-le, extended China's influence beyond its borders by demanding other rulers send ambassadors to China to present tribute. A large navy was built, including four-masted ships, and a standing army of 1 million men (some estimate nearly 2 million) was created. The Chinese fleet sailed the South China Sea and the Indian Ocean. Several maritime Asian nations sent envoys with gifts to the Chinese emperor.

During the first century of the Ming dynasty, China became a powerful seafaring nation with a fleet of over 100 ships that were built to prodigious specifications, much larger than anything known in the West, ranging in length up to more than 122 meters.[13]

Chinese maritime records show that during the 28 years from 1405 to 1433, at least seven voyages were made to the West carrying silk, porcelain, and *objets d'art* to exchange for ivory, jewels, pearls, and rhinoceros horn.[14] It has been claimed, however, that these voyages were not for trade, but rather an endeavor to demonstrate Chinese strength throughout the world.

The government was able to finance costly projects partly from the proceeds of silver that poured into the country via Japanese merchants and Western traders purchasing tea, silk, and porcelain. The silver that arrived through Spanish Manila in the Philippines originated in Japan and later in Mexico or Peru. Such trade was restricted to a few Chinese ports over which officials kept a sharp eye so that Chinese society would not be contaminated by foreign influence.

After 1433, Chinese seafaring adventures ceased as followers of Confucius, including the emperor, objected to commerce and foreign contacts. Ships were expensive to build and operate, threats from northern nomads had to be dealt with, the Great Wall of China required expensive extensions and repairs, and pirates took a large share of the commercial proceeds. Japanese and Chinese pirates raided the largely undefended coasts of China and Korea, plundering and taking slaves and hostages for ransom.

In 1549 in an attempt to curb piracy in the South China Sea, the Ming imperial court banned the Japanese from China and Chinese merchants from trading overseas. China's activities on the high seas were stopped, and the death penalty awaited anyone who disobeyed. As a result, Chinese merchants became trading partners with Korean and Japanese pirates, and black market trade began to be extremely lucrative. China's inward turn took place about the time that Western countries were on the verge of exploration and trade in far-off lands.[15] The abandonment of China's Grand Fleet, the government's lack of interest in exploration and trade, and its focus on the threat of northern barbarian nomads increased acts of piracy in the unguarded South China and Yellow Seas. The Ming navy was abandoned, and laws were passed that foreign trade was to be conducted only by the government, and this through the tribute method.

Out of control piracy influenced the decision to reverse the ban on commerce, however. The restrictive measures were lifted in 1567, and the Ming court started collecting large sums in custom duties. The demand in China for Japanese silver, and Japan's interest in silk and gold from China, remained strong.

New crops were cultivated and industries, such as porcelain and textiles, flourished. Iron was produced in vast quantities. Many books were printed using movable type (a Chinese invention), and the imperial palace in Beijing's Forbidden City reached its highest splendor. However, it was also during this period that China fell substantially behind Europe in technological and military power—an event known as the Great Divergence.

A number of innovations were also permitted: the ruling classes, as before, were exceedingly rich, as grave goods confirm, but the Ming revitalized agriculture after the Mongol period and engaged in public works. Beijing, around 1500, was one of the largest cities in the world with the largest population. Much more of the city's confines were given over to commercial enterprises than ever before. The stability resulting from strong government led to industrial expansion in ceramics, textiles, cotton, and silk; commerce grew by leaps and bounds.

Workers and Wages

Unskilled workers in China earned such small wages that supporting a family was nearly impossible. Hard work all day might bring in enough money to buy only a handful of rice. Craftsmen were little better off. They hurried through the streets displaying their tools and crying out for work, as clients did not seek them out. In coastal regions and on canals and rivers, thousands of poor people lived on small boats and tried to supplement their diet with fish. Dead animals such as cats and dogs floating in the water might be scooped up and eaten.

Education and Superstition

While most young people worked in the fields receiving the rudiments of education if their parents could give it, only boys from well-off families ever saw the inside of a classroom or were tutored at home. At school, they studied and memorized the teachings of Confucius along with the art of calligraphy. These upper-class boys would become government officials and scribes. Besides religion, they also learned math and science, art and music. Examinations were required to become a high government civil service worker (a Mandarin).

Foreign traders to China encountered a society in which it was easy to find oneself in trouble if proper observances were not adhered to, most of which were alien to the Western mind. The trader who wished to learn the language had to be especially careful because Chinese is a tone language, and a difference in tone on a particular syllable could change the meaning and upset or offend the host. Colors were also important: red and gold brought good luck, while black was associated with evil tidings. A foreign merchant might do well to learn some of the Chinese superstitions such as the most favorable phase of the moon for a successful transaction to take place.

Foreign Traders

Following the attempt to set up trade relations with China, the British established trade routes there in 1596. Captain Weddell was given command of a squadron in 1637 and arrived at Portuguese Macão where, on hearing of the great wealth at Canton, he sailed up the Pearl River toward the city, intending to trade there. Making his way as far as the castle-fort on the riverbank, he sent a note to the Chinese commander asking permission to go on to Canton. Due, it is thought, to Portuguese interference and their slandering of the British, the Chinese fort opened fire. Weddell landed sailors on shore, captured the fort, stripped it of its guns, and then burned it. Not a good beginning. The governor of Canton agreed to allow the English free trade at Canton if Weddell would return the cannon taken from the fort along with some junks he had captured. Weddell concurred, and his ships loaded sugar and ginger. The Chinese then accused Weddell of forcing trade upon them, and the British ships had to fight their way back along the river. Meanwhile, the Chinese put the blame for the hostilities at the feet of the Portuguese, who were heavily fined. Weddell was baffled and discouraged by the Chinese officials and their resistance to trade.

In 1613, the Dutch East India Company (VOC) decided to trade directly with China, although in the decade before, Dutch merchants had been rebuffed there. In 1623, in search of an Asian base, the Dutch arrived at Taiwan (Formosa) intending to use the island as a station for commerce with Japan and the coastal areas of China. They built a fort and traded for Chinese silk and Japanese silver, among other items. At the time, Taiwan had prodigious herds of deer whose leathery skins were desired by the Japanese samurai for armor; Chinese merchants, already established on the island, shipped them to Japan. The Dutch were soon in on this trade.

Americans joined the Canton trading arrangements in 1784, after which they no longer had to rely on the English East India Company (EIC) with their goods routed through England. The first U.S. trading vessel carried in her cargo the medicinal plant ginseng, which was thought to be an aphrodisiac, found in the forests of New England, and sought after by the Chinese. Within a few years, some 15 U.S. ships were sailing to China and making profits of 100 to 200 percent.[16]

Clippers from the United States carried otter and seal pelts from the Northwest, traded them for Chinese luxuries, and greatly inflated the pockets of some New England families. Opium, too, was taken to China by U.S. ships, purchased from Turkish dealers at Smyrna in the Mediterranean and traded at a substantial profit.

Chinese officials treated the Americans, as they did all foreigners, as ill-bred barbarians. At the same time, merchants' reports reaching London and the United States deemed the masses of ordinary Chinese illiterate, devoid of human rights, and immersed in superstition, poverty, and filth.

QING DYNASTY (1644–1912)

The last of the imperial dynasties, the Qing, was founded by Manchus from Manchuria that expanded their territory throughout China, tripling the size of the preceding Ming Dynasty. A national economy developed that included all minorities. People of Mongolian stock, they established their capital at Beijing, and ruled China for over two and a half centuries. Preferring to keep the Manchu people "pure," they forbade intermarriage with the Chinese and prevented Chinese immigration into their homelands. The Qing were, however, open to Western science and trade.

From the beginning of the eighteenth century, foreign traders for the most part were confined to Canton under rigid commercial conditions. The Hong, a Chinese guild, was the only agency allowed to deal with foreigners. They concluded all business deals, and were accountable for foreigners' debts and comportment, while the Hong themselves were liable to the governor and customs officials. The government also heavily taxed foreign ships, but fees paid to customs through the Hong for limited port facilities did not sit well with the British East India Company, whose directors decided to send a royal representative to the Imperial Court at Beijing to negotiate a treaty.

In 1793, accompanied by a large entourage, George Macartney arrived in Beijing to become Britain's first envoy to China. The mission to open commerce with China failed, however, since Emperor Qian Long was not interested. A second mission, conducted by William Amherst in 1816, was also a failure, and he returned without having seen the emperor. Although attempts were made by the British government to remove restrictions, clandestine trade continued as the EIC supplied Indian cottons and British wool in exchange for silk, porcelain, and tea. The latter subsequently became the greatest item in British-Chinese commerce.

The Chinese manufactured porcelain for the imperial family long before it was produced for export and traded in Korea, Japan, India, and the Middle East. Porcelain trade reached its highest stage in the seventeenth and eighteenth centuries when first the Portuguese, followed by the Dutch, traded directly with China. Chinese porcelain was expensive in Europe and only the affluent could afford it. By the mid-eighteenth century, some 150,000 pieces of porcelain entered Europe in one day.[17] By the late eighteenth century, fine china was being made in England.

Opium Trade and First Opium War (1839)

As the Qing Dynasty took on increasing importance in the field of commerce, Westerners flocked to do business with China. The Qing court restricted contacts with the outside world to only one port (the Canton system) to minimize foreign contamination of its society. Irritated by the high customs duties they were forced to pay, the British hoped to open up all of China.

Chinese authorities attempted to stop the growing import trade in opium. The drug had long been used as medicine, but in the seventeenth century, people in all classes began to use it for pleasure.

In 1796, the Chinese imperial government forbade opium import and usage; nonetheless, it flourished. Privately owned vessels from many countries, including England and the United States, made gigantic profits from the increasing number of Chinese addicts by selling it to smugglers and on the black market. To the Beijing government, foreigners seemed intent on the ruination of the Chinese people through drug addiction. Disputes over trade and the fact that China would not accept Western governments as equals broke out in hostilities between the Manchu and the British Empire. In 1838, a Cantonese government official arranged the seizure of about 20,000 chests of British opium from their ships, refusing to compensate English traders for the loss. This inflamed the British and sparked the first Opium War of 1839.

Since the Chinese government had repeatedly banned the smoking of opium, the EIC sold its product at auctions in Calcutta to private business so that its legal trade in tea would not be endangered. The drug was then shipped in heavily militarized clippers to armed receiving vessels positioned off the coast of southern China. From these storage boats, the illicit drugs were placed in fast rowing boats manned by Chinese pirates who took the opium to coastal depots where bribed officials allowed it to be unloaded and distributed along a maze of smuggling corridors mostly operated by the Triads.

The EIC's monopoly on trade in China ended in 1834, and commercial activities fell into the clutches of private British, Indian, and American companies, for example, Jardine Matheson, founded as a trading company in China in 1832, switched its tea trade to the more profitable imports of opium into China from India.

Treaty of Nanking (Nanjing)

The Chinese were roundly defeated by British forces in the first Opium War, and the Treaty of Nanking, signed two years later in 1842, ceded Hong Kong to the British and opened five ports to foreign commerce—Canton, Amoy, Foochow, Ningpo, and Shanghai. It also allowed foreign extraterritorial rights and most favored nation status. The unequal Treaty of Nanking forced the Chinese to pay an indemnity of 21 million silver dollars.[18]

The Chinese government was not interested in maintaining the Treaty of Nanking and attempted to keep foreign merchants to a minimum while persecuting any Chinese who did business with them at the treaty ports. It also persisted in refusing to see foreign ambassadors at the court in Beijing. By flagging friendly Chinese merchant ships with the Union Jack and British registration, the English expected to safeguard their Chinese contacts.

Second Opium War (1856)

Chinese officials at Canton appropriated the *Arrow,* a pirate ship under a British flag but with expired registration. Taking this as an insult to Britain, the governor of Hong Kong sent warships to bombard Canton, and wanting more trade with China, the British government supported this act of war. The French, also with complaints in Canton, joined the British.

A strong Anglo-French force occupied Canton in December 1857 and five months later captured the forts near Tientsin, resulting in arbitration between China, Britain, France, the United States, and Russia. The Tientsin Treaties in the summer of 1858 maintained a fitful peace. China was coerced into opening more ports to foreign trade and to consent to opium imports. Foreign inspectors were given authority to watch over Chinese customs, and foreign legations were allowed in Beijing. Even missionaries were given a free hand in the interior. China reneged on the treaties and refused foreign access to the capital, however, and French and British forces closed in on Beijing, forcing the Chinese to ask for an armistice. The allied negotiators sent to arrange matters were taken prisoner, and the French and British continued the assault, looting and burning the royal summer palace. Again, the Chinese requested peace and this time gave in to all demands, including opening more ports for commerce. Foreign delegations were again allowed to lodge in Beijing, and another large indemnity, 5 million ounces of silver, was paid by the Chinese. Indignation in England over the drug trade in China, and England's role in it, was not a major factor. Opium (laudanum) was accepted by the majority of the population in England and was openly sold for self-medication. Most people ingested it, and sometimes working mothers used it to tranquilize their babies. Medical opinion at the time was that the drug produced no ill effects, and addiction was not physically damaging. Few were aware that traders gave away samples of opium to foster addiction.

Shanghai: Rise of a Trade City

From a fishing village, Shanghai grew rapidly to become a crowded metropolitan commercial city following the opium wars. Well located near the mouth of the Yangtze River, foreigners flocked there from all parts of the world as it became one of the leading ports for the opium trade. In 1843, the British formed their first colony there, followed by the French three years later. With the Americans in 1862, an international settlement was established, each group maintaining its own police, customs, and justice system. In short, they formed local governments on Chinese soil, controlling trade and tariffs. Shanghai, with the bulk of the trade in silk, opium, and tea, saw its growth increase enormously as

Chinese business moved to the city to set up shop in the foreign enclaves. Gangs moved in, such as the Triad, to take over the distribution of opium to the hinterlands.

Fearful that the other foreign powers might close their lucrative ports in China to U.S. trade, stifling its growing commerce in cotton textiles to China, the administration under President McKinley achieved the Open Door policy that demanded noninterference with U.S. goods at any Chinese treaty port city. By the 1920s, Shanghai was one of the most corrupt and vice-filled cities on earth.[19]

Boxer Rebellion (1898–1901)

Beginning in 1898, groups of peasants in northern China secretly banded together into a society called the Boxers by the Western press. Among their rituals, members practiced boxing (hence the nickname), which they believed would make them impervious to bullets.

At first, the Boxers wanted to destroy the Qing Dynasty and to eliminate all foreign influence, including foreigners themselves. When the dowager empress backed the Boxers, they turned their attention solely to driving out the foreigners. In 1899, gangs of Boxers began murdering Christian missionaries and Chinese Christians, and by 1900 they converged on Beijing and carried out ferocious acts of killing. To counter the threat to their China interests, an international force of Russians, Americans, British, French, Italian, and Japanese was sent to destroy the Boxers.

The sympathetic dowager empress of the Qing, Cixi, commanded the death of all foreigners whose establishments in Beijing were besieged. The escalating violence continued for several months, but the foreign enclave, protected by strong walls, held out. The foreign nations brought to bear a 19,000-man army with superior firepower and quelled the rebellion. The royal court fled Beijing. A treaty was arranged, and the Chinese paid an indemnity of about $333 million.[20]

WORLD WAR I AND AFTERMATH

Prompted by the United States, China conveyed a dispatch to the German government reprimanding it for using German submarines to sink neutral ships. The Germans were not impressed and returned an insulting communiqué to China, which declared war on Germany in 1917, although there was little it could contribute to the allied war effort.

China limped along throughout the 1920s, constantly engaged in conflicts between warlords, social unrest, and natural disasters, while the country remained backward with a primarily agrarian economy. In 1927, full-fledged civil war broke out between the Nationalists and the Communists that raged for 10 years until the two warring parties, although continuing to fight each other, found it necessary to cooperate and both fight the Japanese. Japan invaded Manchuria in 1931 and in 1937, it attacked Beijing, Shanghai, and Nanking. Within about three years, the Japanese armies were in control of most of eastern China.

WORLD WAR II

Massive amounts of aid were given by the Roosevelt administration to the beleaguered government of Chiang Kai-shek, headquartered in Chong in southwestern China. World War II soon followed on December 7, 1941, and the port cities such as Shanghai and Hong Kong soon fell to the Japanese. Nearly cut off from foreign aid, China survived World War II with great loss of life, enormous devastation, and commerce mostly at a standstill. Some materials reached southwestern China via the Burma Road, built during the war, and by "flying the hump"—a dangerous air corridor from India to China over the Himalayas.

POST-WORLD WAR II AND CHINA

World War II ended in August 1945 with the surrender of Japan, but in war-torn China, the conflict between Nationalists under Chiang Kai-shek and the Communists under Mao Tse-tung, played out in bloody civil war. The Nationalist military forces suffered heavy defeats and decamped to the island of Taiwan in 1949 to establish a government there. The Communists took over the Chinese mainland and called it the People's Republic of China.

The entire political and economic system, along with all foreign trade, was taken over by the state, which set prices and wages, controlled distribution and investments, allocated output targets for major enterprises, determined energy distribution, controlled banking policies, and—during the 1950s—collectivized farms into large communes. In the 1960s and 1970s, the Communist government undertook large-scale industrialization and by 1978, most industrial production was state owned with centrally planned agendas.

A major goal of the Communist government was to make China's economy relatively self-sufficient. Foreign trade was generally limited to obtaining only those goods that could not be made in China. Government policies kept the economy stagnant and inefficient, mainly because there were few profit incentives for firms and farmers. Competition was virtually nonexistent, and price and production controls caused widespread distortions in the economy. A brief interlude in the 1960s, called the Cultural Revolution, was orchestrated by high officials and red guards (mostly students), and carried as its main theme "self sufficiency in all things." The violent upheavals resulted in a near stoppage of international trade with China, and a major setback for the country's industrialization and growth.

China underwent economic reforms in 1979 in a move toward a market economy, privatization, decentralization, and a disposition to foreign investments. There were numerous difficulties to overcome: inefficiency of state-run banks and enterprises, corruption at every level, and rising inequality between rich and poor that promoted major discontent among the people. In addition, pollution was an ongoing threat to the environment.

During the 1980s, the consequences of reforms began to materialize. Private enterprise, previously nearly nonexistent, developed from public investment. Wages and living standards rose, poverty diminished, infant mortality decreased, and the country's role in global trade steadily increased. As restrictions on foreign trade were relaxed, more opportunities arose for individual enterprises to engage in foreign commerce. In the twenty-first century, foreign trade remains an integral part of the country's rise to prosperity.

TECHNOLOGY AND OTHER PRODUCTS

In the past several decades, China has played fast and loose with "borrowed" technology. From cars and their parts, videos, and computer software to missiles and guidance systems, China has acquired technology from the United States and from Russia and elsewhere in a manner not authorized by government officials or private companies. International copyright has been ignored. Trade in electronic instruments, in which it already leads the world, may soon result in a capacity to become foremost in automobile and aircraft parts along with shipbuilding.

Today, the country is the world's largest producer of rice and a significant contributor to the global market of wheat, corn, soybeans, peanuts, cotton cloth, tobacco, tungsten, antinomy, coal, and crude oil. Ongoing market-oriented economic reforms since

1979 have had a profound impact both on China and the world. They have led to more individual enterprise, although still within the ever-present state control.

CURRENT TRADE, MAJOR PARTNERS, AND LABOR

Imports and exports are on the rise, producing billions of dollars in surplus. Direct foreign investment in China has been a substantial impetus to trade, and China is now a major trading nation.[21]

China's largest export markets are the United States and the European Union, while most imports come from Japan, the European Union, and Taiwan. Many investors in Taiwan have shifted their labor-intensive, export-oriented firms to China to take advantage of low-cost labor. Products made by these firms are exported to the United States, whose trade deficit with China runs into many billions of dollars. China joined the World Trade Organization in 2002.

The abundance of cheap labor has made China internationally competitive in many low-cost, labor-intensive goods. For example, China imports cotton and machinery to produce items of apparel, then exports internationally. Imports also include components that are assembled in Chinese factories and then exported, such as electronic products and computers.

Recent remarkable economic growth and rising prosperity have been due to reforms such as the elimination of money-losing, subsidized, state-owned enterprises, and an overhaul of the banking system. Foreign companies find business difficult in China because of obscure and inconsistent regulations. Contracts are almost impossible to enforce, intellectual property rights are not protected. In 2009, Wayne Morrison of the Congressional Research Service wrote:

> Despite the relatively positive outlook for its economy, China faces a number of difficult challenges that, if not addressed, could undermine its future economic growth and stability. These include pervasive government corruption, an inefficient banking system, overdependence on exports and fixed investment for growth, the lack of rule of law, severe pollution, and widening income disparities.[22]

The worldwide financial crisis of 2008 hurt many companies, and the government expanded the public sector to continue growth and allowed multinational corporations to export Chinese goods, making the country a strong competitor in international markets.

The rapid growth of the Chinese economy through trade and investment, bypassing the major powers such as Japan and threatening to overtake the United States, have left some to question the wisdom of free trade. With a fifth of the global population and a labor force at least five times greater than the United States, China is on a path to dominate world trade. And with a track record of about 9 percent economic growth over the past 20 years, the country seems likely to outshine all others. The United States and other Western countries have a wide margin over China in per capita income, and this difference allows China to produce trade goods cheaper than many countries and capitalize on outsourcing that drains jobs from other trading nations. Countries in the free trade environment face a diminishing job market, but China must look toward a growing disparity between rich and poor that is accelerating in the cities and that is a major cause for unrest.

NOTES

1. *Past Worlds*, 194.
2. Curtin, 93.
3. Northrup, Vol. 2, 340.
4. Gelber, 40, 41.
5. Whitfield, 51.
6. For Eurasian upheavals in the mid-eighth century along the Silk Road, see Beckwith, 140–162.
7. Gelber, 57–58.
8. Pareti, 185–186.
9. Mackintosh-Smith, 262.
10. Mackintosh-Smith, 264.
11. Mackintosh-Smith, 264.
12. Mackintosh-Smith, 268.
13. *Past Worlds*, 264. That Chinese ships may not have been so large, see Gelber, 88.
14. Curtin, 273; Northrup, Vol. 1, 164; Gelber, 89.
15. Gelber, 89.
16. Gelber, 166–167.
17. *EWT*, Vol. 3, 755.
18. For the articles of the treaty, see Spence, 158–160. For more on these so-called unequal treaties, see Chesneaux, 105–108. See also http://www.international.ucla.edu/eas/documents/nanjing.htm.
19. See Pomeranz and Topik, 62–64 for more detail.
20. *EWT*, Vol. 1, 116.
21. International Monetary Fund, Direction of Trade Statistics, and official Chinese statistics.
22. www.congress.gov.

18

JAPAN

EARLY HISTORY

Throughout their history, the large majority of Japanese farmed the slopes and valleys of their mountainous terrain. Rice was the principle crop, grown in irrigated fields. Plowing, usually with oxen; seeding the rice plants; embedding them in the soggy soil; and weeding kept the peasants busy from sunrise until nightfall. With the rise of small states and social stratification, Japan was engaged in continuous internal warfare until the Yamato dynasty gradually spread its authority throughout much of the country between about 250 to 710 CE.

TRADE BETWEEN JAPAN AND CHINA

About 200, the first foreign ships arrived from China with pottery and bronze objects, including coins.[1] Commerce between China and Japan remained sporadic under the Chinese T'ang dynasty (618–907). Sino-Japanese contacts were made through envoys, and Chinese Buddhist monks, via Korea, assailed Japan with their religion, medicines, and incense. Japan began to imitate China in both social and technological aspects, for example, irrigation and farming, a more accurate calendar, and writing. About 710, the first Japanese capital was installed in the city of Nara, modeled on the

Chinese capital, Chang'an. It was subsequently moved to Heian (today, Kyoto).

CHINESE INFLUENCE

During the Han period in China, Japanese clothing was greatly influenced by Chinese garments. Trade between the two countries included Chinese dresses and certain styles brought to Japan that continued through the Chinese Sui and T'ang Dynasties.

Under the Chinese Song Dynasty (960–1279), and during the Japanese Heian period (794–1185), commerce was regular and encouraged by both parties. The xenophobic Japanese, however, wanted the trade to take place in China and banned Chinese merchants from Japan. Since this was not satisfactory to Japanese nobles desiring Chinese luxury goods, the Japanese government allowed a single trading ship from China to arrive once every three years. Between 988 and 1026, more ships were allowed to enter Japanese harbors, reaching up to four a year.[2]

The Heian imperial court saw the rising influence of women, and the world's first novel, *Tale of Genji Monogatari*, is thought to have been written by the noblewoman Murasaki Shikibu using the hiragana, a script developed from simplified Chinese characters.

The court set the fashions in dress and manners. Residents of the court wore special clothes to distinguish them from the ordinary people and to differentiate their rank among themselves. Under their ceremonial robes, which had a long train attached, they wore long, wide, trousers. Hats, black and lacquered, of many different shapes, and with round blinders standing out at the side of the eyes were worn, also to signify rank, as did the sash that hung down from both sides of the neck, the ends of which were just permitted to touch the ground when making a bow. Women at the court also wore special long and pleated robes, sometimes decorated with golden flowers. On occasion, they wore as many as 12 of these robes at the same time.[3] The material of choice was silk, which had long before been introduced to Japan from China.[4] Both men and women wore jewelry either imported from China or copied from Chinese sources along with cosmetics, hairpins, and other beauty aids.[5]

The garment most used by all sections of society, including the common people, was the kimono, a simple, loose robe made of silk with unique designs. It was typically worn with a sash that held it in place. Wooden clogs had been worn by everyone in Japan since ancient times, as well as footwear made of straw and fabric. Indoors, socks with thick soles were used.

In 1185, the Heian court fell into decay and was defeated in battle by another rising clan, beginning a new period of the Kamakura Emperors (1186–1336).

JAPANESE SOCIETY AND TRADE

The imperial system of government fell into disarray after the twelfth century under the pressure of the old aristocracy and gave way to shoguns (a military term referring to a governor or general of the noble class with absolute power) who ruled Japan from 1192 to 1863.[6]

The most powerful men under the shogun were the Daimyo, or warlords, who ruled over the provinces with full military and fiscal authority. They held vast hereditary lands and commanded armies of samurai warriors. The next shogun might be selected from this Daimyo class. The samurai caste held certain privileges that set them above the common people and a strict code of honor called *bushido* that tied them to the Daimyo; if the code was broken, a ritual suicide was in order.

Besides the ruling class, shogunate society consisted of peasants, among whom the highest ranking were the farmers. Those who owned land were superior to those who did not. On a social level below the farmers were artisans who worked with metal and wood, and below them those who worked with leather. The latter have been compared with the untouchables in India.[7] The lowest of the low were the merchants who made money off the labor of others.

Nonfarmers included fishermen, hunters, tanners, artisans, and peddlers. Artisans produced the tools required by the farmers such as plows, shovels, hoes, storage tubs, and cooking utensils for their kitchens. In the towns and countryside, small-scale industries, usually run by one family, produced these articles, and peddlers traveled the roads to farms, hamlets, and towns selling them. Some manor houses on large farms permanently employed personnel as plasterers, weavers, and carpenters in exchange for the fruits of a plot of land.

Japan also had long-distance traders. By the sixteenth century, commerce with Southeast Asia, Vietnam, Malaysia, and Thailand was underway, and many Japanese resided in the port cites of these countries. They exchanged copper, bronze, and silver for silk, pottery, sugar, spices, and sandalwood. This trade declined somewhat in 1685 when the shogun, concerned about so much silver and copper leaving the country, limited its export.

The period of the shogunate witnessed numerous civil wars as clans, many made up of the emperor's children, vied for power. While the emperors continued to reign, shoguns ruled from the north and eventually settled on Edo (sometimes Yedo, and today Tokyo) as their capital, where they remained until the nineteenth century. For the upper classes, there was little room for initiative. Under a military dictatorship, the feudal lords were required to live six months a year at their palaces at Edo near the shogun. Set apart from the town, they were constantly watched and when they were not in residence, their families were left behind as hostages for good behavior. Along the roads, at the inns and in taverns, were also swarms of spies and informers of the shogun.[8]

NATURAL RESOURCES

Gold, silver, and copper could be found in various places in the mountains and riverbeds, but all mining was in the hands of the government and had to be approved. As late as the eighteenth century, superstition still inhibited mining. For instance, if the shaft filled with water, it was believed that Kami, god of the soil, was angry. Silver was also abundant in the country and, like gold, it became a source of trade.[9] Both gold and silver from Nagasaki were more expensive for foreigners, but the quality was considered to be better there than anywhere else in the world.[10]

Copper, which was abundant in Japan, was sold to the Dutch; pearls were sold to the Chinese; and imported minerals included borax and quicksilver from China as well as mercury (liquidized and used for both medicine and to commit suicide). Ambergris was used by the Japanese to retain the smell of smoke from spices, but once foreigners indicated its value, it was sold to them for high prices. Cinnabar, both natural (used as medicine) or man-made (used as color) was extremely expensive.[11] After the beginning of the Song Dynasty, the Chinese used it principally in their carved lacquerware.

Tin was in short supply in Japan, while iron ore, coal, and sea salt were plentiful. Agates were known from the mountains, and pearls from oyster beds along the coasts, not originally prized by the Japanese, found a market in China.[12]

ARRIVAL OF THE PORTUGUESE

With the arrival of the Portuguese, Western influences on Japan began. In 1543, Portuguese ships reached the islands to find a people who considered them barbarians with nothing to offer; but the

Japanese soon discovered that the Portuguese harquebus and cannon were worth having. The Portuguese were not slow to note that Japan mined copious amounts of copper and silver, items of which China fell short. Soon after contact between the two countries, trade began. The Japanese court was especially pleased to learn that the Portuguese traded with China and had, in fact, Chinese goods on their ships. The Japanese and Chinese had not openly traded for some time because of China's embargo on commerce with Japan.

The Portuguese introduced new items, including firearms, wool, velvet, tobacco, clocks, and eyeglasses in exchange for silver and gold. They seized the opportunity to serve as commercial middlemen between the two Asian countries and sent carracks, their largest trading vessels, to do business with them. The Portuguese court strictly regulated who was allowed to do business with the Asian countries. It generally offered trade with Japan to the captain who bid the highest, effectively giving the Portuguese throne a share of the profit from Asia. They obtained a monopoly on direct trade between Japan and China. By 1549, Catholic missionaries, sailing with the fleet from Portugal, had become active in Japan. The Christian priests, mostly Jesuits, who accompanied the traders and infiltrated the country and by successfully proselytizing, alarmed the Japanese. Kyoto became a nest of Christians. The new religion threatened the old ways and the ruling classes especially when new Christian converts under the Jesuits burned Japanese shrines and temples. Spasmodic persecutions began in 1593 and in 1597, twenty-six Christians, some Jesuits, some Franciscans, and some Japanese converts, were crucified at Nagasaki. Within about 40 years, or by 1600, there were 150,000 converts in Japan along with 75 missionaries.[13] Christianity was banned in 1614, and an incredibly brutal persecution followed, with thousands killed and tortured. After a revolt led by native Christians erupted in 1637, foreigners were expelled two years later, and Japanese were forbidden to leave the country.

SOUTHEAST ASIA TRADE

The Japanese had other outlets for trade besides China and Europe. Between 1604 and 1635, there were 355 ships that sailed from Japan to ports in Southeast Asia, including Thailand, which became a valuable trading partner. Many Japanese merchants settled in the Thai capital and port city of Ayudhya. Japanese adventurer merchants, not unlike their European counterparts, could trade or raid as they saw fit, and the coasts of China and the South China Sea were areas in which they might do either or both until the shogun cut off foreign trade and travel in 1639.[14]

DESHIMA

The artificial island of Deshima, at the port of Nagasaki, was constructed in 1636 to house Portuguese traders and restrict them to the island. Here the so-called barbarian devils could be closely watched. When in the following year, the shogun banished the Portuguese from Japan, the Portuguese sent a delegation from Macão to Nagasaki to plead their cause for trade. The Japanese slaughtered most of the delegates and burned their ships, but allowed a few survivors to return to Macão. Portuguese missionaries still in Japan were expelled or killed. Some were crucified upside down on a beach at Nagasaki and left to wait for the tide to come in and end their sufferings.[15]

APPEARANCE OF THE DUTCH

Ships of the Dutch East India Company (VOC) appeared in Japanese waters in 1600. Five years later, Leyasu, the reigning shogun, allowed the Dutch to open trade with the Japanese. In 1609, two Dutch ships docked in Japan, thus beginning commerce between the two countries on the island of Hirado. The VOC was officially admitted to Japan by the shogun in 1611 on the condition it did not proselytize. To Edo, the Dutch brought gifts, including cheese, cloth, and wooden tables.[16]

No missionaries accompanied the Dutch, nor did they try to spread Christianity in Japan, yet the Japanese remained wary, allowing the Dutch ships to offload their cargos providing they brought mostly guns, munitions, tobacco, and spectacles.[17]

In 1641, by order of the Tokugawa shogun, all trade was relocated to Nagasaki under strict conditions whereby the Dutch were allowed to fill the void left by the Portuguese. When Dutch ships arrived in Japan, all symbols of Christianity (e.g., rosaries, crosses, religious books) were handed over to the captain for safekeeping and hidden away in the ship. The Japanese confiscated all weapons, including swords, until the ship sailed. Gunpowder had to be packed into barrels and stowed away. The Japanese, who perhaps had heard of some of the atrocities committed by the Portuguese in India, were taking no chances with these uncouth traders. The

Dutch began attacking Portuguese trade vessels in the Pacific Ocean to cripple their rivals and worked diligently to ingratiate themselves into the good graces of the Japanese. As far as the Japanese were concerned, however, the Dutch merchants were of the lowest class possible.

> Consequently to cheat the Dutch in the price of goods...swindle or deceive them, curtail the benefits and freedom of the Dutch...to find and suggest new avenues of enslavement...all are considered praiseworthy and indications of a true patriot.[18]

Dutch merchants confined at Deshima were not allowed to send letters out of the country without prior Japanese inspection, and the Dutch dead were at least for a time tossed into the sea as unworthy of being interred on Japanese soil. Later, they were buried on a mountainside, leaving no trace. The Dutch East India Company could be sued for damages by dissatisfied Japanese nobles (or even by Chinese living in Japan) but in spite of injury that others did to the company, no lawsuits were allowed to be pursued by the company.

Interpreters were, of course, required for any communications between the two parties, and according to the Dutch, the Japanese were devious, poor in the Dutch language, and as much spies as interpreters because they inspected everything and informed their superiors. Servants too performed the function of informers. Due to its lucrative trade, Japanese nobles maintained Deshima as virtually a prison for the Dutch traders. In spite of the conditions, the Dutch East India Company also found the trade profitable.

The annual market in October was a noteworthy event. The goods were stored in some 300 warehouses, the official buildings of the VOC along the four streets of Deshima, whose doors were opened to traders, and goods were displayed outside.

Spices of varying kinds were exhibited at the VOC market on the island, including cloves, pepper, cinnamon, and nutmeg. Also on display were animal skins, headgear, mirrors, musk, mercury, and amber.

Japanese traders came to Deshima at the appointed times to sell their products, including copper, camphor, porcelain, robes, tobacco, and lacquered furniture. Due to tobacco trade, the Japanese began to cultivate it in 1605. Many acquired the habit of smoking, imitating the Dutch, whose pipes became popular, as did snuff.

Other items introduced by the Dutch traders in 1645 that had great appeal to the Japanese were mechanical objects such as clocks, especially those that chimed; pocket watches; music boxes; glass bottles; and pistols. Through local trade networks, these items and others were distributed throughout the country.

TRAVEL IN SEVENTEENTH-CENTURY JAPAN

Annually, the lords of Japan were required to make an appearance at the shogun's court to pay homage and present gifts. The same obedience was expected of the representatives of the VOC at Deshima for the presents they could offer the shogun. One of those who twice made the journey accompanying his directors was Engelbert Kaempfer, an employee of the company. Numerous Japanese who acted as guides, servants, and guards escorted the company's party to the shogun's court at Edo a long way away. The Dutch merchants were forbidden to intimately converse with the Japanese people they met along the way, or to pass them any Christian relics such as crucifixes, images of saints, or anything else connected with Christianity.

Kaempfer's first journey began in 1691; the second was in the following year. Before departing, certain preparations were necessary. Presents had to be selected not only for the shogun and his councilors, but also for his officials in major cities such as Osaka that they would pass through. The trunks bearing gifts had to be carefully packed and then sealed. Nagasaki officials selected the gifts, such as precious jade objects from China, and then charged the company outrageous prices that they had determined. Sometimes, the gifts came from Europe, as was the case of two brass fire extinguishers of the latest design that were then rejected and returned to the VOC by the officials after they had them copied. The approved goods, a form of tribute trade, were sent ahead.

After the governor of Nagasaki had chosen his top ranking men—samurai, interpreters, servants, and porters—to make the trip, the meticulously prepared group struck out on horseback. The saddle was a bare wooden frame with a cushion, comfortable for the rider but hard on the horse.[19] From Nagasaki to Edo and back took about three months, including some 20 days at the court in Edo. The roads were good and well signposted from village to village. They were swept clean by villagers. Huts were provided on the routes for travelers to relieve themselves, and excrement was collected for the fields. Kaempfer noted that the villagers burned the worn-out straw shoes fastened to the horses' hoofs and those worn by the men that they had discarded along the route. The ash was mixed with excrement and placed in open barrels in the villages and alongside the roads. Destined to fertilize the fields, the mixture omitted a powerful, pervasive odor that made the journey at times unpleasant.

Inns, Rooms, and Hygiene

Most important villages and towns had post stations and inns. At the stations, it was possible to hire fresh horses and porters to replace those exhausted at that point in the journey. The prices were fixed by the lord of the district and depended on both the length of the journey and the condition of the road. Runners were on duty at the post stations day and night to relay messages from the shogun to other lords. They ran or rode in pairs in case one had an accident. All road traffic was required to immediately give way to them.

For the most part, Kaempfer found the inns comfortable and well equipped. A courtyard or pleasure garden and verandas found at the back of the inn offered a place to step outside for a breath of fresh air. Important guests could dismount from their horses and enter directly into their rooms, not having to pass through the main entrance and dirty their feet. Lower-class travelers were consigned to the area of the kitchen where smoke from fires sometimes filled the rooms and even the entire inn, as there was only occasionally a small hole for smoke to escape. The inns were partitioned with sliding doors, and the rooms, devoid of furniture, sometimes had an esteemed object for the guest to admire.

Japanese who had the means appear to have been scrupulous in maintaining both a clean body and environment. At the inns, a small toilet was located at the rear for one to squat over a hole in the floor. The bucket underneath was placed from the outside. Floors were spotless and covered with clean mats, and straw slippers were available for anyone not wanting to walk on the floor in bare feet. For important guests, the door handles were covered in clean white paper, as was anything else the visitor might have to touch. A container of water stood nearby to wash one's hands. Some inns had a steam chamber, others had only a hot water bath. People on the move bathed every day.

On the road were also inns of poor quality and food stands selling cakes and sweets or other snacks, as well as taverns stocked with beer or sake. For very little money, the poor could enjoy a cup of tea or sake at these stalls, whose owners were as poor as the clients.

Most inns, roadside teahouses, and stalls of every description had one or a contingent of prostitutes. If business was slow, an inn-keeper might send his girls to one that was crowded with guests as, in any event, he would collect the money the girls earned. "... Every public inn on the island of Nippon was at the same time a public brothel ..."[20]

Food on the Road

It was common to see small pieces of meat on bamboo sticks roasting over a fire in an open stall so that the traveler need not stop but could simply take one and hand over the money while continuing the journey. As people approached, a small cup of tea or soup might be offered with outstretched hand in the hope the traveler would take it.

Besides drinks of various kinds, there were many solid foods to nibble on. Portuguese wheat cakes about the size of an egg, boiled in a steamer and sometimes filled with black bean sauce, were common. There were jelly cakes, fried eel, small fishes, snails, mussels (fried, smoked, or boiled), young shoots of varying root plants, seaweed (boiled or fried), and seeds of many varieties. Soya sauce was a common ingredient mixed with sake, ginger, and lemon rind or other spices to cheer up the food. Some stalls had tables outside covered with biscuits of many colors and shapes that contained little sugar, and were tough and miserable to chew on. Poor travelers carried little guidebooks to locate the best and cheapest dishes. Almost all drank the tea that was served at every inn, tavern, and stall.[21]

Crime and Punishment

The system of justice, in some ways reminiscent of Europe, used torture to exact confessions from suspected criminals. A person, guilty or not, was likely to commit suicide rather than face the ordeal of torture and trial. On one occasion, smugglers traded goods with Chinese junks in the harbor and were caught. Two took their own lives, and two were decapitated. The smallest infraction could lead to a death sentence carried out at the execution grounds at Nagasaki.

In spite of the dangers of illegal trade, some people, both Japanese and Chinese, risked all to engage in it. Prostitutes of the city sometimes served as go-betweens for smugglers. Anyone under suspicion of engaging in an illegal act usually confessed immediately even if they were not involved, since a new kind of torture to elicit a confession was introduced when the naked body was dragged over a board studded with nails or needles. Dutch traders were shocked by the severe treatment of even small-time criminals. Every town had gibbets from which hung mutilated bodies.

Buildings and Houses

When the grueling daily work in the fields was finished, the peasants returned to a house that typically consisted of two small rooms with dirt and straw floors. Wealthier peasants had larger homes and wooden floorboards. The roofs were most often constructed of wooden planks, while the walls consisted of a plaster made from mud and straw. Among well-off families, plaster filled the cracks in log walls, and roofs might be made of tile.

Attached to doors of the common houses was a half sheet of paper or a painted design of a deity such as an ox head to protect the dwellers from disease. The pox was particularly prevalent. Others might have a hideous devil's head with fiery eyes and great fangs. "Jealous glances will be diverted by this spectacle, and harmful envy will not attach itself to the house."[22] Herbs also were placed above the door to ward off evil spirits and bring divine blessings. Letters of indulgence could also be bought from monasteries that were to keep evil spirits away.

Castles, Cities, Villages, and Farms

The lord of a major city or region lived in a castle or fortified site on high ground that often consisted of three rings of buildings with walls and deep moats. The rings reflected the social status of the residents. The innermost ring was occupied by the lord. The secretaries and gentlemen-in-waiting lived within the second, and soldiers and workers were in the third, which was open to the public.

Most cities lacked walls and moats and, apart from a gate, were open to the surrounding fields. Densely packed streets ran at right angles and were lined with shops. The streets had gates at both ends that could be closed if a crime was committed.[23]

Villages often straddled the highway where the inhabitants made a living selling goods and services to travelers. One village sometimes merged into another along the road. Farmhouses of the poor were wretched and small, consisting of four walls covered by rushes or straw. They had a stove on a raised floor in the back, while the doorway featured straw ropes hanging down to obscure the interior from prying eyes outside.

Notices at the entrance to cities and in villages were put up in fenced off areas to inform the public of decisions taken by the lord of the region or by the city officials. Many simply offered rewards for turning in a criminal or someone who practiced the Christian faith. Also located outside built-up areas were the execution grounds. To break any of the shogun's laws inevitably led to a death sentence.

Of impressive appearance along the roads were Buddhist temples as well as shrines to Shinto gods and their monasteries. They rose above the other buildings in majestic ornamental grandeur. The cities were replete with temples: Miyako, for example, had 3,893 temples looked after by 37,093 Buddhist priests.[24] Stone statues of various deities, some large and fearsome, were usually placed at bridges, road intersections, and monasteries.

Diet

Well-off peasants and the upper classes ate excellent rice regularly along with fish and game; most people could not afford such luxuries. The average peasant diet consisted of cheap grains such as millet, barley, or buckwheat and a few vegetables. Peasants in Kai Province, according to Nagahara (1979), raised these grains, but after they had consumed the harvested foods, they lived on ferns and plants until the next harvest. There were, however, birds and fish when they could get them.[25]

Many other foods were available. Abundant sea life surrounded the islands: fish, shellfish, seaweed, and whale meat benefited almost everyone. The whale was perhaps the most preferred animal of the sea, since every bit of it was used; even the entrails were pickled or boiled and eaten. The oil was used for lamps. Inedible parts such as fins and bones were made into kitchen utensils, while sinews were used for stringed instruments and cords.

All kinds of fish were caught and eaten, even poisonous varieties that had to be thoroughly cleaned before they could be eaten. People who wished to commit suicide often ate one of these fish before cleaning rendered its flesh innocuous. The sea bream, served at important banquets and weddings, was highly prized and considered a fish fit for the gods.

Shrimp, crabs, oysters, sea slugs, turtles, sea lizards, snails, and most everything else caught in the sea, lakes, or rivers were devoured. Some kinds of fish were of poor quality, but all were abundant and consumed only by the poor. Only the unpalatable starfish was left to its own devices.

Seafood was eaten raw, pickled, fried, boiled, and dried. Women often performed the function of divers who, armed with a spear or knife, collected rock-clinging creatures from deep underwater along with various kinds of seaweed.[26] Strangers in the country could find many foods that they were used to but some they had never seen before such as the toad fish that resembled a toad, various seaweeds and certain birds and shellfish.

DEATH AND CONTAMINATION

Death and pollution were intricately mixed in the Japanese mind. People who worked with death or the dead were considered polluted.[27] Ceremonies were often designed to reduce pollution, even to the extent of moving the court to another location when an emperor died. To die within someone's house was a great tragedy that would defile the house. If someone were near death, he or she would be removed to the outside. A dead animal could also cause a spot to be polluted and require a cleansing ceremony.

Antipathy to death and concomitant fear of its effects reflected on many people who were involved directly in it. Isolated and despised were people such as hunters, butchers, tanners, morticians, hospital workers, and so on. Even soldiers were considered to be of inferior merit during the Heian period of 794 to 1185. Such people, including criminals, often lived along riverbanks or in dry streambeds, as rivers in Japan at the time were associated with death. Especially heinous and generating great fear was the disease of leprosy, which was thought to be a punishment for crimes in an earlier life.[28] Foreign traders unaware of these superstitions might well find themselves embroiled in controversy and disgrace by associating with the wrong people or simply removing a dead animal from their premises.

LEGAL AND ILLICIT TRADE

The Japanese were quick to copy foreign trade objects and equally quick to improve them. The matchlock gun was of supreme interest to the chieftains (Daimyos) and put into production as early as 1549.

Before the Dutch East India Company closed its doors in 1799, there were numerous ways that trade goods reached the common people. Smuggling, theft, and clandestine private exchanges were common. Most smuggled goods were easy to hide such as saffron and sugar that might be brought from Deshima easily hidden in a pocket by Japanese workers on the island. Goods for officials were given as gifts by Nagasaki traders to keep on good terms.

Japan remained a nearly closed society in spite of Russian and English attempts to make contact for commercial purposes in the 1840s. Fear of Western religions and the behavior of traders in the opium trade in China were no doubt major factors in Japan's decision to spurn foreign trade. Ships from the United States also put into Japanese harbors attempting to gain entry into the country, but they were sent away.[29]

COMMODORE PERRY

A big surprise was in store for the Japanese government on May 8, 1853 when four U.S. ships under the command of Commodore Matthew Perry lowered their anchors in the Bay of Edo. The Japanese had never seen steamships, and were awed by the size and number of the guns. They ordered his small fleet to Nagasaki, the only port available to foreigners.

Perry carried a letter to the emperor of Japan from the U.S. president Millard Fillmore, however, and refused to leave Edo Bay until it was delivered. Displaying the power of his cannon in a military exercise in the bay, Perry was allowed to land and present his letter to officials of the emperor. The U.S. government was not only interested in trade with Japan, but wanted ports to recoal and supply the U.S. Pacific whaling fleet and to ascertain that U.S. seamen shipwrecked on the coast of Japan would receive humane treatment. Perry sailed away promising to return, and the following year he did so, this time with eight ships. After much debate, the Japanese realized the futility of their position, as they lacked modern arms and could not sustain a war against a Western power.

Negotiations led to the Treaty of Kanagawa in March 1854, in which the U.S. requests were met, although no trade agreements were made. These came later in 1858 with the first of the "unequal treaties" whereby foreigners were allowed to reside in Japan under their own rules, preach their own religions, and demand protection for their families and converts. The Japanese were to reduce tariffs on imports to charges set out in the treaties of 5 percent on the value of the goods, whereas European nations charged 15 to 20 percent on imports. This, of course, gave foreign traders an unfair trade advantage. These and other aspects of the treaties were one-sided, providing no protection to Japanese interests. The Japanese were humiliated, and many demanded the overthrow of the Tokugawa shogun and the installation of a new government.[30]

MEIJI RESTORATION (1868–1912)

Trade with Japan remained very limited until the Meiji Restoration in 1868, when Emperor Meiji regained power from the Tokugawa shogun and Kyoto was exchanged for Tokyo as the residence of the emperor.

The Japanese government realized the country needed to change from an agricultural nation to an industrial power if it was not to become second class in relation to the West. Western technicians were invited to Japan, and Japanese scholars were sent abroad to study. The military was modernized and enlarged. Meanwhile, negotiations opened up coal trading stations and American shipping ports in Japan. This was Japan's reintroduction to Western influence, after centuries of near isolation, which brought it out of feudalism and into a unified modern state.

By the end of the Meiji period, Japan had undergone enormous changes. It had become a modern nation with a strong centralized government, a strong military, an elected parliament, a well-educated population, had a good transportation system, and a technologically sound industrial sector. While edicts were passed in his name, the emperor took advice from those who had restored his power. During the 1870s and the 1880s, Japan strove to develop economic and social institutions in the manner of European nations.

Before World War I, Japan's economy boomed and companies such as Mitsubishi, established in 1870, produced its first automobile in 1917. Mitsui, Japan's largest general trading company, was founded in 1876.

The country played only a minor part in World War I on the side of the Western powers. Between 1912 and 1926, under the ineffectual Emperor Taisho, the parliament assumed power, and large corporations dominated politicians.

The Japanese government felt, as it had for some time, that Western discrimination against Japan was very much alive. This sentiment was not helped by the refusal to add a racial equality clause proposed by Japan to the agreement of the League of

Nations and the Exclusion Act of 1924 by the U.S. Congress, which disallowed further Japanese immigrants onto American shores.

In the course of the 1930s, the military took control of the government. In 1931, Japan occupied Manchuria, which was declared an independent region under control of the Japanese army. It abandoned the League of Nations in 1933 and four years later in 1937, the Second Sino-Japanese War began, resulting in Japanese occupation of most of the east coast of China.[31]

LACK OF RESOURCES

The Japanese lacked many things such as scrap metal for the manufacture of armaments and machinery, some of which was supplied by the United States in spite of protests in 1941 on the Seattle docks, where much of this war material was loaded. The primary ingredient that Japan needed, and lacked, however, was oil to keep the rapidly growing industry and the military machine lubricated. The developing Japanese naval and air power especially required enormous quantities of the precious petroleum.

WORLD WAR II

In 1940, Japan joined Germany and Italy as one of the Axis powers. Britain and the United States cut off sales of oil to Japan, and the country's recourse was to take over the oil fields of Indonesia, then the Dutch East Indies. To prevent American interference in its drive southward and seizure of the rich raw materials of Southeast Asia, the Japanese government attacked the U.S. Pacific fleet at station in Pearl Harbor, Hawaii.

International trade dried up throughout the western Pacific Ocean (except for Australia and New Zealand) and was greatly diminished in North and South America as ships, trucks, and planes were needed for the war effort to transport military supplies. Nations at war resorted to rationing of imported products such as sugar, palm oil, rubber, and other goods that required extensive transport.

With the surrender of Japan in August 1945, Japanese society began to undergo a transformation to a new way of life.

POST-WORLD WAR II AND JAPAN

Japanese cities and industries were in ruins, hundreds of thousands were homeless, there was great unemployment, transportation networks were destroyed, and the population was on the edge of starvation. U.S. troops occupied the country under the command of General Douglas MacArthur. Japan, under conditions in which communism could flourish, was a major worry for the United States, which was willing to rebuild the country to fend off a communist threat.

American military occupation ended in 1952 during the Korean War when Japan's economy began to increase due in large part to U.S. payments for certain goods, services, and labor, which accounted for a great percentage of Japanese export trade. By the end of the Korean Conflict in 1953, Japan was flourishing, and living standards were rapidly improving.

In the 1960s, the government's trade liberalization programs boosted the economy, as did Japan's integration into General Agreement on Tariffs and Trade (GATT), the International Monetary Fund (IMF), and The Organisation for Economic Co-operation and Development (OECD). After 1973, Japanese manufacturing moved into high technology, and the country soon became a leader in optical goods, cameras, computer chips, copying and video machines, radios, automobiles, and many other devices such as television sets and robots.

Lacking resources and raw materials with no foreign exchange to purchase them, the country had little option but to export textiles and other light industrial goods. As the country pulled itself together, exports turned to heavy industrial goods—including steel, chemicals, and glass—to bring in more foreign exchange until it could import important technologies and begin producing radios and automobiles for export. With cheap labor, it could sell its products at a profit while the United States imported many of the cheap Japanese goods. By the 1970s, Japan's economy boomed through exports, and its success became the model for other Asian countries. Inexpensive exports to Europe and the United States became the salvation of war-torn Asian countries. With a flood of exports, and money rolling in, the average standard of living in the 1990s rose to become comparable to that of the West. Depending on foreign demand for Asian products and neglecting domestic consumption led to problems, however. When U.S. consumption of Japanese products dropped, the average Japanese family's savings fell. The housing market slumped, and prices fell on the stock market as U.S. consumers bought fewer Asian goods.

Like much of the rest of the world, Japan suffered from the economic troubles of the collapse of real estate markets and banking institutions in 2008, and cheap Japanese exports have been greatly affected by competition from China and Taiwan, South Korea, and others. At present, it suffers from a declining birth rate and a lack of workers, and will have to open its borders to more unskilled immigrants or relocate industries to countries with cheaper labor costs.

NOTES

1. Hall (1970), 30.
2. Grant, 171.
3. Kaempfer, 92.
4. Benn, 103.
5. Benn, 103–106.
6. Braudel (1993), 283. For rise of states and the feudal system, see *Past Worlds*, 266–267.
7. Braudel (1993), 284.
8. Braudel (1993), 288.
9. Kaempfer, 59.
10. Kaempfer, 146.
11. Kaempfer, 62–63.
12. Kaempfer, 60–61.
13. Hall (1970), 140.
14. Curtin, 167–168.
15. Anderson (2000), 93.
16. Kaempfer, 231, 355.
17. Braudel (1993), 286.
18. Kaempfer, 199.
19. Kaempfer, 242.
20. In the words of Kaempfer, 279.
21. Kaempfer, 269.
22. Kaempfer, 261.
23. Kaempfer, 27.
24. Kaempfer, 259.
25. Nagahara (1979), 326.
26. For extensive detail on Japanese seafood eating habits, see Kaempfer, 77–83.
27. Yamamura, 347.
28. Nagahara (1979), 388–389.
29. Perez, 75.
30. See Perez, 76–77 for more details.
31. The first Sino-Japanese war was in 1894 over control of Korea.

19

PRE-COLUMBIAN TRADE TO 1500

AMERICA (FIRST PEOPLE)

Archaeological remains show that well before the end of the last Ice Age, the original inhabitants of North and South America appear to have emigrated from Asia across the Bering Strait, then a land connection, to Alaska.[1] Some of their oldest sites in America date back to over 25,000 years ago.[2] These earliest people followed a nomadic way of life, until, around 2000 BCE, some began to build villages and practice agriculture. They hunted and fished, built monuments to their gods and rulers, and engaged in trade.

Trails crisscrossed North, Central, and South America over which native people carried goods and traded with each other. Riverine exchange networks developed throughout the Late Archaic period (3000–1000 BCE). Besides nuts, berries, meat, and handicrafts, an important item of trade, obsidian, found only in certain places where volcanoes have been active, was coveted by many societies. It was traded up and down the west coast of North and South America, and in Mesoamerica.

Trails linked Indian villages throughout eastern and western North America and connected the Gulf coast and the Great Lakes. Carried along them were trade items that included figurines, clay pipes, salt, feathers, flint, seashells, pearls, animal skins, furs, leather, medicinal herbs, yaupon, tobacco, quartzite, copper, and silver.

From Alaska and across Canada from British Columbia to Labrador are many Paleo-Indian sites dating from earliest to recent times.[3]

Out of a vast array of languages spoken, trade or pidgin languages developed with vocabulary from many different native languages and a highly simplified grammar. These lingua francas greatly aided native traders from different tribes.[4] As tribes were often at war with one another, trade might occur after peace was secured along with a ritual exchange of gifts.

Eastern United States and Canada

In the forested regions of the northeast, tribes lived mostly by agriculture and hunting. The Iroquoian nation, for example, included Mohawks, Hurons, and Cherokees. Their social systems had many aspects in common, although they did not actually live together. For instance, although they worshipped different gods, religion was an equally important aspect of everyone's daily life and it was believed that everything, alive, dead, or inanimate, contained the spirit of the Creator. For all, a dread of tribal censure restrained bad behavior. Lacking a system of writing, Native Americans relied on knowledge and laws handed down orally through the generations.

Mississippian Culture

Mound builders of the Mississippian culture, appeared as the dominant group that replaced the Hopewell development about 700 CE. The tribes of this federation eventually dominated the land from Florida to Wisconsin. As agriculturalists, they grew corn and tobacco among other crops and participated in a trade diaspora that covered much of North America. Objects of long-distance trade uncovered by archaeologists involve such items as seashells from the Gulf of Mexico, colored flint from New Mexico, copper from the Great Lakes, and Carolina mica. Also discovered from their own industry or by trade were fur, feathers, lace, woven fabrics, and baskets, along with stone statues. Emphasis was placed on the ritual of death.[5] Similarities in grave mounds and contents suggest a religious and trade network from Mississippi to Minnesota and from New Mexico to the Atlantic seaboard.

Cahokia

Located near modern-day Saint Louis and the important trade routes of the Mississippi, Missouri, and Illinois Rivers, Cahokia was founded in the ninth century and became a highly developed community. By the end of the twelfth century, it contained a population of some 40,000. In the marketplace might be found marine shells, stone for making arrowheads, finished goods—such as stone hoes for cultivation, deer hides, beaver pelts, baskets, blankets—and a host of other commodities for exchange such as pipes, gorgets, cups, pots, and beads.

Archaeologists have also found evidence that ideas, often in the form of specific designs found on pottery or engraved into marine shells, were widely distributed during Mississippian times. Abstract images, hand and eye motifs, birds of prey, sun symbols, and the circle and cross are found east of the Mississippi River and west to Oklahoma.

The city of Cahokia was surrounded by a series of watchtowers, and occupied a diamond shape pattern nearly five miles across. At its height, it may have been the largest city in North America. Cahokia and the surrounding area were depopulated about 1450 for reasons unknown but due perhaps to disease, that was frequently rampant in densely populated areas.

PLAINS INDIANS

Peoples of the Great Plains of the United States and Canada obtained much of their food supply and other necessities from the great herds of bison that roamed the prairies. The nomadic tribes utilized buffalo meat, hide, and bones. Sometimes, hundreds of bison were stampeded into blind gullies or over cliffs. In the southern part of the Canadian province of Alberta, groups of animals were herded together from their natural grazing basins and then stampeded along a corridor bordered on each side by piles of stone extending about 10 miles back from a fatal cliff. Funneled along to the small but steep jump area, there was no way to go except over the ledge. Indians habitually drove many hundreds of animals over the cliff on the eastern edge of the Porcupine hills called Head-Smashed-In. The jump killed or incapacitated the bison. Next to the cliff was the Indian campsite where the animals were butchered and processed for transport. The site dates back to 3700 BCE and continued as a slaughterhouse into the nineteenth century. Often, more animals died than the people could use and were left to rot.

The Plains Indians who roamed the great grassland of the Midwest lived in teepees and produced no pottery or agriculture. They appear to have traded red stone and pipes to settled peoples, and buffalo hides and meat with the Anasazi (probably ancestors of the Hopi) and other Pueblo tribes, who exchanged vegetables in return.

SOUTHWEST PUEBLO CULTURE

The inhabitants of the Southwest congregated in centers of populations, built irrigation canals, and farmed the fields with stone tools, but they were unaware of the use of the wheel. Dogs and fowl were domesticated, and copper began to make an appearance for trinkets or jewelry. The modern city of Phoenix spreads over some 217 kilometers of ancient irrigation channels. Trade routes, along which goods such as copper, exotic fowl, and Mayan chocolate passed, extended into Mexico.

Referred to as the Pueblo people by the Spanish in the sixteenth century, they were a settled assortment of tribes in the dry and arid Southwest that includes present-day Utah, Colorado, Arizona, and New Mexico. Composed of many tribes, three primary cultures arose in the Southwest about 300 BCE: the Anasazi, who constructed dwellings in the cliffs and rocky overhangs in present-day northern Arizona, Utah, Colorado, and New Mexico; the Hohokam, who excavated irrigation canals in central Arizona; and the Mogollon, who farmed, hunted, and gathered in what is today western New Mexico and eastern Arizona. During the first millennium CE, these societies developed a high degree of sophistication, with water being their most precious resource. Houses were constructed of adobe, and residents grew corn, beans, squash, and cotton, the latter woven into blankets. They lived a life different from that of the natives of the eastern forests, the Plains Indians, and those of the Pacific coast. The ancient Pueblo culture is well known for the adobe and stone dwellings built into cliff walls such as Mesa Verde in Colorado, with large dwellings of rock cut chambers by the Anasazi Indians who resided there from the eleventh to the thirteenth centuries. The cliff palace had 200 rooms. Pueblo Indians were also well known for basket-making and pottery.

Anasazi Culture

Of the distinct civilizations that adapted to the harsh arid conditions of the Southwest, one prominent group, the Anasazi, lived in present day northeastern Arizona. This area—flat and dry—was surrounded by small areas of high plateaux, or mesas, where the soft rock layers form steep eroded canyons and overhangs along their slopes. The Anasazi used these cave-like overhangs in the side of steep mesas as shelter. They also diverted small streams of snowmelt into plots of corn, squash, and beans. Small seasonal rivers yielded natural clays and dried mud. They used dry hardened mud, along with sandstone, to construct buildings, sometimes high in the natural overhangs of the mesas and reached by ladders. A period of relatively wet conditions between 900 and 1130 allowed the Anasazi people to flourish, and their architecture and pottery became intricate and artistic. Trade in practical and luxury items was widespread over long distances. Ceramics and ornaments made up trade exchanges along with more luxurious goods such as both worked and rough turquoise exchanged in Mexico for exotic birds, shells, and metals.[6] Following this prosperous period, three centuries of drought found the Anasazi frequently engaged in warfare, probably over limited water. At any rate, they dispersed and moved away, abandoning their buildings.

Hohokam

Bordering the Anasazi, a separate tribal complex formed in southern Arizona, the Hohokam, who further developed the technology of irrigation that allowed them to live in villages with nearby watered fields. The Gila and Salt Rivers were a major source of the water. After about 200, they were well established and appear to have traded with Mayan peoples some 2,500 kilometers south—possibly through intermediaries. Jars similar to those of the Mayans have been found at their sites containing traces of cacao. With water, they could grow cotton and corn. Hohokam houses had a single room and were generally a pit dug in the dry soil and covered over with a raised roof structure of branches and brush. Villages had ball courts and competed with rubber balls imported from Central America.[7] They produced red and tan pottery, wove cloth from cotton, and made jewelry from seashells. The shells appear to have been obtained from the coasts of California.[8]

The Hohokam culture became plagued by internal unrest, and their cultural integrity started to weaken. Later, with the arrival of the Spanish who brought with them European diseases for which the Indian community had no immunity, the Hohokam faded away.

Mogollon

The land that now comprises the U.S.-Mexican border was home to the Mogollon, the least advanced of the three major Southwest groups. By around 2000 BCE, they were involved in rudimentary farming, cultivating corn, beans, and squash. By the year 300 CE, they were making ceramics, but in general they clung to their dependence on local plants and animals for their subsistence. As their ability to farm increased, they started to use terraces to maintain the soil in their mountainous area, and their houses became stronger and more stable.

Between 100 and 1450, the population increased significantly as farming expanded aided by ditch irrigation. At the same time, burial began to take place in pits dug beneath the houses, and offerings, such as pottery, were put with the bodies, especially containers with holes in them to permit the spirits inside to escape and accompany the spirit of the dead.

The strong mixing of cultures through trade was evident in the pottery where typical Mogollon ceramics in red and black on white polychrome were exchanged and copied by potters in other areas. In addition, the Anasazi style of creating black on white geometric designs suddenly began to appear in Mogollon ware.

CALIFORNIA NATIVE TRADE

Tribes in northern California received shells from Oregon that originally came from Vancouver Island. Trade trails ran from village to village, and trade was active.[9]

Made from a variety of materials including shells, bone, seeds, wood, copper, and minerals, beads have always been an important trade item. Abalone shells from present-day Southern California and Baja California were popular ornaments that moved along ancient trade routes throughout the Southwest and eastward, linking up with trails from the Gulf of Mexico. California shells have been found at sites east of the Mississippi River.

PACIFIC NORTHWEST COAST

A moderate climate and plentiful resources gave rise to numerous west coast Amerindian cultures ranging from Alaska to Oregon. Prominent among the tribes were the Tlingit and Haida peoples. There is evidence of trade with the Southwestern Indians and exchange of goods with nomadic northern plains Indians. Trade items consisted of the usual decorated pots and beads, obsidian, shells for jewelry, smoking pipes, surplus food, and colorful quartz stone from Nebraska.

Indians on the west coast fished herring and salmon, and gathered mussels, oysters, and clams, all for local food and trade.

When food was obtained along the shoreline or at sea and brought to the village, every family received a share whether or not they participated in the work. The catch of gathered mollusks was laid out on wooden cedar racks on the beach to dry or was smoked over an open fire. Mussels were steamed, skewered on sticks, and dried, and roe was sun-dried to be rehydrated later by soaking it in water overnight. Food items were often traded locally for vegetable oils, herbal medicines, and women. Gifts were sent to a neighboring tribe where a woman might be chosen as a bride even when different languages were spoken. A dugout canoe loaded with seafood and other preserved provisions, including the paddles, was offered to secure the bride.

Natives lived in longhouses, and many such sites have been unearthed along the coast of today's British Columbia. In more recent times, smallpox epidemics killed about 80 percent of the inhabitants, with the last major pandemic in 1862. Along with sudden and extensive mortality, much of the Indian lore and technology, passed down orally to each new generation, disappeared.

ARCTIC INUIT (ESKIMO) CULTURE

The Inuit seem to be a more recent people—perhaps the last wave—who crossed the Bering Strait. They used small flint tools for cutting bone, arrowheads, and harpoons. For warmth and light, blubber oil was burned in lamps with a moss wick. As hunter-gatherers, the Inuit moved by the seasons to different camps. They fed on seal, whale, duck, caribou, and fish. The ancestors of the present-day Inuit arrived in their current location about 1000 CE.[10]

An important part of Inuit life relied heavily on dogs as pack animals in summer months and in winter as sled dogs. Their keen noses also assisted in hunting, and they served as village guards at night. Contacts among different Inuit villages resulted in trade in the form of animal skins, meat, stone tools, masks, clothes, and food such as seaweed, roots, and berries. Besides warmth, products from whales and seals hunted from sealskin kayaks were used for food, clothes, and shelter.[11]

CENTRAL AMERICA

Archaeological artifacts from Central American native peoples indicate that between 1200 and 300 BCE, the basic features of civilization were formed. Cities were constructed to replace farming villages, along with temples and pyramids. In addition, a hieroglyphic system of writing was invented in some places. The major civilizations were located in the Valley of Mexico, along the southern Gulf Coast, and the Valley of Oaxaca.

One of the most prominent cultures of the early and formative years, the Olmecs, situated on the southern Gulf Coast of Mexico, shows evidence of trade with Zapotecs in Oaxaca (Monte Alban) and with the Valley of Mexico. Their trade networks seem to have been organized to obtain raw materials that included obsidian, cinnabar, jade, serpentine, basalt for monuments, and iron ore. The Olmec culture faded from view about 300 BCE.[12]

Besides local trade, the Toltecs in Mexico also traded with the Lowland Maya and other societies. It was the job of a special merchant to trade with non-Toltec peoples and in this way, they had access to pottery from Mexico and Guatemala, shells and copper from the Pacific coast, and feathers, animal skins, rubber, cacao beans, and cotton from the Gulf coast. The presence of macaw feathers and copper bells in the American Southwest suggest that the Toltec traders also reached that area. During the postclassic period, two nations struggled for control of Oaxaca—the Zapotecs, whose ancestors had held the site of Monte Alban for centuries, and the Mixtecs, who were expanding eastward and southward. Monte Alban graves have yielded gold, silver, and copper ornaments as well as animal bones carved with hieroglyphic inscriptions. The Zapotecs, the first major native culture of Oaxaca, were the second prominent civilization to materialize in Central America after the Olmec. Their cities show evidence of trade and cultural influence from other regions. Goods from the Olmecs, Teotihuacan, and the Toltecs—as well as architectural influences—have been found across the region.

Zapotec civilization went into decline shortly after Teotihuacan. Around 900, they abandoned Monte Alban and moved to their religious center of Mitla, 40 kilometers away, which they also eventually deserted. The reason may have been Mixtec occupation of their land.

MAYAN CIVILIZATION AND TRADE

The ancient Mayan civilization arose in the Guatemalan highlands and the tropical jungles to the north, reaching its apex about 800. Lacking metal tools, beasts of burden, or the wheel, they built stone cities and pyramids, and transported goods by porters. Salt for the preservation of food, as well as part of the diet, was one of the most important trade items. It was gathered along the ocean shores from beds of evaporated seawater. Chocolate beans, another significant trade commodity, were transported throughout Central America and Mexico. As mentioned, traces of cacao have been detected on shards from Mayan-style jars some 2,500 kilometers to the north among the native peoples of the Southwest United States.

The Mayans also traded obsidian chipped into sharp cutting tools such as knives and axes that could be exchanged for cotton from the lowlands. Dyes and polishing products were traded such as pyrite, hematite, and cinnabar used for colors and mirrors, travertine magnetite used for black pigment, limonite for yellow pigment, high-quality clays, macaw feathers, jaguar skins, pottery, honey, turquoise, cotton, vanilla, quetzal feathers, gold, and foodstuffs that went at least as far as the Aztec nation to the north. Granite for grinding stones, flint, and chert for arrowheads were also in demand in Mesoamerica. Locally grown food crops could be exchanged between towns or settlements, and large centers acted as redistribution points where merchants obtained the goods to barter in more remote areas.

Farmers transported their crops to market by canoe along the streams and rivers, or in baskets on their backs. Long-distance traders hired porters, as there were no horses, pack animals, or wheeled carts. Some ventured as far as Teotihuacan, introducing the much prized cocoa beans that were also traded with the Tainos in the Caribbean Islands, Cuba, and the Quechua natives in South America.[13]

Archaeologists have discovered small cobs of corn from approximately 5000 BCE; however, corn was not cultivated on any great scale until about 500 BCE, when it became a staple. By about 1200 BCE, it was known far and wide, including in western Ecuador and New Mexico. Communities began to depend more and more on agriculture as they settled down, building houses and even stockpiling surplus crops. With this came cooperative labor that gave time for leisure and such artistic endeavors as pottery.

AZTECS

In the fifteenth century, Aztecs invaded from the central highlands of Mexico and conquered the Totonacs. They soon developed a taste for the vanilla bean and forced the Totonacs to pay tribute by sending these beans to the Aztec capital, Tenochtitlan.

In the Aztec patriarchal society, women had little opportunity to participate in government and religious activities. While men worked in the fields, fought the wars, or became traders, women stayed at home with the children, cooked, and wove. Aztec girls were taught the skills necessary for marriage; they began spinning at the age of four and cooking at 12. However, housework was not women's only role. They also participated in the workforce as merchants, traders, scribes, courtesans, healers, and midwives. Ordinary women entered the marketplace as traders and could sell their handicrafts and food there.

In the Mexican highlands about 50 kilometers northeast of Mexico City was the great city of Teotihuacán. It appears to have been the first city with a population estimated at 150,000. Arising sometime in the fifth century CE or earlier, the city was abandoned for unknown reasons beginning about 750 CE. Artifacts found at the site from distant places and those found far away but originating at Teotihuacán indicate active trade with places in Northern Mexico, Mayan peoples of the Yucatan, tribes of the Guatemalan highlands, and those along the coast of the Gulf of Mexico. Trade items often consisted of ceramics and obsidian implements. Used in place of money, the chocolate bean was employed throughout Central America. It was also part of tribute paid to the Aztec emperor by conquered tribes.

INCA EMPIRE

Originally a Peruvian highland tribe, the Incas spoke the Quechua language and apparently expanded their rule among neighboring tribes about 1100. The economy—based on intensive terracing of mountain slopes and irrigation—developed urban centers, a road network, and a well-organized and efficient administration. The Incas achieved remarkable skills in architecture, weaving, pottery, and other arts. Seagoing trade was established between Peru and the Pacific coast of Mexico that mostly involved the spondylus mollusk, which was thought to be the main dish of the gods and used in ceremonial rituals.

The lower valleys of the Andes provided sweet potatoes, maize, manioc, squash, beans, chili peppers, peanuts, papaya and cotton. The hills above produced white potatoes, a cereal grain called quinoa, coca, medicine, feathers, and animal skins. The highlanders specialized in manufacture and crafts, including gold working. Gold was their favorite trade item. Cloth was also an important item of trade and for gifts as no system of money was in use. Trade in many items including gold and silver, valuable stones, exotic creatures and plants was in the hands of the government. Ordinary subjects were allowed to bargain for food or textiles and handicrafts at local markets. Goods were carried on peoples' backs or by llamas. On streams or lakes, boats or rafts were used for transport.

The empire reached its peak in the fifteenth century. The Spanish conquest put an end to the Inca Empire in 1532.

NOTES

1. Some skeletal remains unlike those of American Indians have given rise to other views of Paleo-American origins involving Pacific Ocean crossings.

2. Aston and Taylor, 158. Note that this is a controversial date.

3. For many of these sites, see Aston and Taylor, 158–160.

4. For example, words from Choctaw, Creek, Alabama, and others in the east formed a trade language.

5. *Past Worlds*, 220–221, 230–231.

6. Lister, 30–32.

7. Skinner, 312.

8. Lister, 24.

9. *Handbook of North American Indians*, Vol. 3, 881.

10. *Past Worlds*, 272–273.

11. http://www.crystalinks.com/inuit.html.

12. *Past Worlds*, 214–215.

13. www.authenticmaya.com/images/CacaoGod.jpg.

20

POST-COLUMBIAN SOUTH AND NORTH AMERICA

SOUTH AMERICA

Starting with the reign of Isabella I and Fernando, and their sponsorship of Christopher Columbus to the New World in 1492, Spanish ships carried cargos to and from the Americas and Spain. It has been reported that about every five years during the sixteenth century, Spain shipped to the New World some 40 million in *livres tournois* (a unit of French currency at the time) and returned with some 150 million in gold, silver, and other goods.[1]

The epic voyage of Columbus opened a new era of trade between Europe and the American continents that made the Spanish crown and some merchants extremely wealthy. Also for the first time, written records became available describing commerce in the Western hemisphere; before the coming of Europeans, archeological artifacts were the sole source of concrete facts about native interchange. The first regions to be explored and exploited by the Spanish were the Caribbean Islands, followed by Central and South America, where they found trade networks already in existence.

When Hernán Cortés conquered Mexico in 1519, for example, a well-developed market system near Tenochtitlán (present-day Mexico City) filled the daily needs of about 60,000 people by displaying and selling both local products and items from distant places.[2] A trade diaspora was in place throughout the Mexican highlands and coastal areas that seemingly dated back to the Olmecs. Traders from different outlying communities occupied separate living quarters in the major highland cities. When Bernal Díaz, a soldier of Cortés, entered a marketplace called Tlaltelolco, he was amazed at the number of people and products there. Each product had its own place. Luxury items such as gold, silver, feathers, and precious stones were in one section; slaves were in another, tied to long poles; and cloth and cotton were in a separate area. In another part, food was cooked, further on were skins of various animals, and there was a section for pottery. Other sections contained wood, tobacco, herbs, and so on. The merchandise was inspected by overseers who presumably reported any problems to three judges in nearby buildings.[3]

Metals

The discovery, or rediscovery, of the New World soon resulted in a bonanza of gold and silver that seemed inexhaustible. In 1545, miners discovered the enormous silver deposits of Potosí in Upper Peru (now Bolivia) that soon became the largest source of silver in the world and produced two-thirds of the silver imported into Europe.[4] The silver mines of Mexico at Zacatecas, which began operation the following year, made up the other third. Very little silver was found in Europe, and the early trade with the New World was oriented toward this precious metal.

The crown's stated goal and that of the men who crossed the Atlantic Ocean was to acquire wealth and spread Christianity.[5] Earlier, in 1492, the queen, a religious zealot, enacted the most damaging royal directive for the country's economy by expelling all nonconverted Jews, many of them men of commerce and financial expertise, from Spain. The loss of the Jews, who were experienced in trade, benefited other countries, for instance Holland, which took in many of the refugees. Spain suffered inestimable negative repercussions in the financial sectors, only relieved by the fortuitous appearance of American silver and gold.

When Mexico and Peru fell to the Spanish conquistadores, extraordinary amounts of gold and silver poured into the mother country through Sevilla, making Spain the richest country in Europe. The galleons, laden with treasure, were often attacked by French and English buccaneers and began to sail in convoys for better protection. The fleets sailed from Sevilla for ports such as Vera Cruz in Mexico and Portobello in Panama. On the return voyage, the treasure ships met at Havana to sail home together.

Spain, of course, claimed a monopoly on all goods from the Americas, and the Spanish American colonies were forbidden to trade with anyone else but the homeland. Contraband did occur on a large scale, however, to avoid the taxes imposed by the Spanish government, and smugglers even sold to foreigners. Private merchants were taxed to the extent of 20 percent, the *quinto real* or royal fifth, on precious metals.

Generally speaking, much of the wealth of the New World was dissipated in wars between Spain and other European countries as well as the Ottoman Empire.

Potosí

From 1580 until 1640, the royal crowns of Spain and Portugal were amalgamated under Felipe II, who created the largest seaborne empire in the world. Increasing its wealth by a great leap was the discovery of a mountain of silver at Potosí in Bolivia. Mercury from Spain to process the silver and shipping metal to Sevilla was big business. Here labored Spaniards, Portuguese, Indians, and slaves to extract the ore. The Potosí silver was the major supply to Spain, and from a small obscure Indian village, the mining town grew to a population of about 200,000 to become one of the largest cities in the hemisphere. Many thousands of tons of silver came out of the mines, where laborers died by the millions from accidents, disease, and mercury poisoning. In 1672, a mint was created at the site to make silver coins that, along with Mexican silver, later flooded Europe, leading to high inflation beginning in the late sixteenth century. Spanish imports of silver between 1531 and 1660 amounted to close to 17 million kilograms.[6] To the growing American communities Spain sent manufactured products, wine, livestock, and wheat.

While some of the trade from the Indies went to the ports of Málaga and Cádiz, the bulk passed through Sevilla, which served as a magnate, attracting foreign merchants and financiers, especially the Genoese, who provided capital, expertise, and banking services for the Spanish crown. They in turn received special concessions and helped Sevilla win a monopoly over Spain's colonial trade.[7]

From the start, trade with the New World and Spain was a two-way street: every year, two fleets from Spain traversed the

Atlantic with armed escorts, a voyage of about six weeks, destined for Vera Cruz in Mexico and the Isthmus of Panama.[8] The Columbian Exchange, as it was called, became an important commercial route in the sixteenth century. The system perpetuated itself inasmuch as merchants of many nationalities in Sevilla purchased the goods to be sent to the settlers in America using the silver and gold from the previous arrivals from the colonies. In time, as towns and plantations developed in America, trade items included horses, goats, pigs, and African slaves in exchange for sugar, cassava, tobacco, fruits, and vegetables.

The Joy of Tobacco

The New World plant, tobacco, was rumored to have medicinal qualities. When first discovered, the Catholic Church referred to it as Satan's herb because it was associated with smoke and with heathen American Indians. The first seeds were shipped to Portugal and Spain in the 1550s, and Europeans were curious about its rumored health benefits.

In 1565, tobacco and smoking received the greatest advertisement that any trader could hope for. A doctor in Sevilla, Nicolás Monardes, published a tract on the virtues of tobacco. This gift of heaven, he said, was beneficial for just about everything that ailed the body from shortness of breath to cancer. His list included wounds from tiger bites and poisoned arrows, kidney stones, toothache, tapeworms, bad breath, and more. Tobacco was also good for children and animals. It could cure cattle of foot-and-mouth disease among other things.[8] Throughout Europe, interest in tobacco was stimulated by the publication, which was translated into a number of languages. Portuguese and Spanish ships came laden from the New World with the wonder plant. At first, demand was based on its medicinal attributes, but English buccaneers are reputed to have introduced smoking into England where tobacco was used for pleasure. One story relates that Sir Walter Raleigh was dowsed with water when a servant saw him smoking, thinking he was on fire.[9] From the royal court, the habit of smoking descended to the common people, and tobacco shops began to proliferate in England. As the demand for tobacco grew, so did the demand for slaves on the Brazilian plantations.

Trade to American colonies stimulated many sections of the Spanish economy. In Andalucía, farmers grew more vegetables and wheat, made more oil, and produced more wine for the far-away market. More ships were needed, and shipwrights recruited workers, artisans fashioned new items to appeal to the distant settlers, bureaucracy was needed to underpin the expanding commerce requiring government officials and qualified clerks, the docks gave employment to thousands, and seamen were in demand, as were sailors for the escort ships. The spin-offs from trade were many. Even the church could send its many clerics off to the lands of the unenlightened to proselytize. The merchants of Sevilla as well as those in the Americas often became rich. As silver poured into Spain, much of it then left the country to either purchase commodities or pay debts. In the sixteenth century, the Spanish kings Carlos I and Felipe II were able to spend a good deal of money on wars and policing the empire, including the rebellious Netherlands, by borrowing from European financial houses such as the Fuggars, who then were repaid by the next shipment of silver. Felipe II spent some 3 million ducats, his entire annual income from the West Indies, just to maintain an army in Flanders to keep the Dutch insurgents in order.[10] Besides silver and gold, pearls from the Caribbean, cochineal, hides, and other New World products, Spanish traders had an enormous impact on European agriculture and diet.

Severe restrictions were placed on the colonies in the West Indies. Spanish exports were primarily wine, oil, textiles, tools, mercury (for the silver mines), manufactured components for mines and mills, and men; the colonies were not allowed to produce these goods in competition with the home country. The colonials shipped to Spain animal and vegetable products, wood, and sugar; but by far the most important items were silver and gold.

Exotic Vegetables and Fruit

When the conquest of the New World was well underway, Europe experienced an entirely distinct variety of foods exported from the new lands. On the traders' agenda were—in addition to potatoes—sweet potatoes, tomatoes (once considered dangerous to eat), corn, chili peppers (the latter suspicious), vanilla, and chocolate beans. While squash seems to be native to both North and South America, summer squash appears to have originated in the Andes Mountains. The common bean also seems to have had an American origin.

The Potato

The Aymara Indians of the Andes Mountains cultivated several hundred varieties of potatoes that made up their basic diet. Before the Spanish conquest, the lowly potato, once considered a food of divine attributes and an object of worship with its own god was unknown in the world beyond South America. The conquistadores recognized its value as a deterrent to scurvy and stocked their ships' larders with it. They soon monopolized the market, shipping the potato to Europe, where people at first were slow to accept it. It eventually became an important part of the European diet. Only after potato cultivation appeared in the Netherlands (a province of Spain at the time) and then throughout the Holy Roman Empire in the early seventeenth century was the potato recognized as a staple food.

Frederick the Great of Prussia ordered his people to plant and consume potatoes to avoid the frequent famines that occurred when other crops such as wheat failed. To overcome people's fear of the new vegetable, he threatened to amputate noses and ears of those who disobeyed, and by the mid-eighteenth century, potatoes were a basic staple of Prussian cuisine. In France also, the potato took a while to be accepted, but eventually the grand chefs of the nobility created numerous potato dishes and the common people soon wanted them. A more reliable crop than wheat in the climate of Europe, potatoes contributed to an agrarian revolution in the early seventeenth century and to a subsequent rise in the European population. Due to potato yields, farmers were able to break away from subsistence farming and turn to profitable agriculture.

Tomatoes

Like potatoes, tomatoes were native to western South America—probably coastal Peru. A member of the deadly nightshade family, they were considered poisonous for a time and were grown only for decoration. The Italian name, *pomodoro*, suggests that the first tomatoes to reach Europe were gold or yellow in color. Outside South America, Italy seems to have been first to cultivate and use the tomato, and it is still a prime ingredient in many dishes there. The fruit remained under suspicion in the United States for many years, but in 1897, Joseph Campbell, a fruit merchant, made his company very wealthy with the production of canned tomatoes and condensed tomato soup.

Vanilla

Also unknown in Europe, vanilla, which is derived from the bean of a certain orchid native to Mexico, was discovered on the Gulf coast in the early sixteenth century. The plant was first cultivated in the region of present day Vera Cruz in Mexico and relished by the Aztecs, who flavored their chocolate drink with it. They introduced it to Cortés, who in turn introduced it to Europe along with chocolate. It is now grown throughout the tropics. Today, Madagascar is the largest producer of vanilla beans, followed by Indonesia. Between them, they make up 90 percent of the world's production. Mexico held a monopoly on the bean for several centuries but now contributes only a small percentage of the product. Frustrating for traders who carried the seeds of the orchid to other regions was the fact that they would not produce beans, even in ideal climates, until it was discovered how to hand-pollinate them, doing the job that certain kinds of bees did in the place of origin.

Corn

The words "corn" and "maize" were terms used for several kinds of grains, but used here it means corn as we know it today in North America. Originally grown in Mexico, it eventually arrived in the Mississippi Valley to the north, and the Amazon Basin in the south.

Different areas developed divergent varieties; after 1492, it quickly spread to Europe, where it flourished, and later followed the trade routes to Portuguese and Spanish colonies in Asia, Africa, India, and the Philippines. By the end of the sixteenth century, it was grown in both West and East Africa, and became a widely traded international commodity. In the nineteenth century, the midwestern United States (the corn belt), produced great quantities. This nutritious crop, dried and stored or kept in powdered form, was instrumental in supporting population increases in poor areas where other plants did not do so well.[11]

Cocoa Beans and Chocolate

In 1514 on a voyage to Central America, Hernando de Oviedo y Valdez wrote letters home in which he stated that he bought a slave for 100 cocoa beans. Ten cocoa beans were enough to procure the services of a prostitute, and four would pay for a rabbit.

The word "chocolate" comes from the Mayan *xocoatl*.[12] The first shipment of beans intended for the market arrived in Spain in 1585. Chocolate found its way to the French Court at Versailles and soon spread throughout France and later Europe, perhaps helped along by its reputed aphrodisiac properties.

A Frenchman opened London's first chocolate shop in 1657, and chocolate houses became trendy meeting places where elite London society savored their new luxury. A chocolate factory opened its doors in the American colonies in 1765.

By the nineteenth century, increased production lowered the price of cocoa beans, and chocolate became a common, inexpensive beverage. It appeared in a solid form about 1830 in England and by 1849, Cadburys exhibited its first chocolates. U.S. military emergency rations still include chocolate due to its high energy content.[13]

While chocolate is consumed by millions, the cost is very high for some working in the industry. Thousands of African children are still used to produce the product. In the Côte d'Ivoire, for instance, these children with no education, no medical care, often separated from their families, with no prospects of a better life, are bonded to their employers. Too often parents with too many children to support simply sell them to traffickers or force them to work as soon as they are able.

Guano

The rocky islands off the coast of Peru, devoid of predators, were the nesting places of several types of sea birds including cormorants, pelicans, and gulls. Over millennia, droppings from these hundreds of thousands of birds built up deposits, up to 150 feet deep, of what is called guano, a superb fertilizer. The local native people used it to nourish their crops over many centuries. Europeans found this source of fertilizer rich in nitrogen and phosphate, and having seen its effects on local farms, introduced it to Europe in 1840. English farmers found that using it doubled and even tripled their crop yields.

The island sources were difficult to mine, as the guano was solidified in the dry atmosphere and had to be cut into manageable chunks with pickaxes and shovels. Slaves, convicts, and indentured servants performed the hard and dangerous work, and suffered lung and intestinal problems from inhaling the dust. They worked as many as 20 hours a day cutting trenches some 30 meters deep and transporting the blocks of guano by wheelbarrow to a chute down the steep slopes that led directly into a ship's hold. With little rest, poor food, and unhealthy conditions, workers died in large numbers. U.S. farmers, eager to obtain this amazing fertilizer, found prices high, and the government tried to negotiate a free-trade deal with Peru, but to no avail. The United States passed the Guano Act in 1856 that allowed its citizens to take possession of any guano island not already under another government's lawful jurisdiction. U.S. entrepreneurs claimed approximately 94 rocks and islands, of which 66 were recognized by the United States government. These were returned to Peru when the development of artificial fertilizers lessened the demand for guano. At the height of its guano trade between 1840 and 1880, Peru exported around a million tons and made an enormous profit.

Smugglers and Merchants

If the colonists in the Americas and elsewhere fell short of supplies from Spain, there were numerous smugglers—English, French, and Portuguese—who were ready to step in, bribe local officials, and trade their illegal goods. The *Casa de Contratación*, or House of Trade in Sevilla, created in 1503, kept strict records of ships, cargos, and crews. A Dominican friar, Tomás de Mercado (1524–1575), recorded:

> The merchants of Sevilla traded with all of Christendom and even in Barbary. They shipped wool, oil, and wine to Flanders in exchange for all kinds of haberdashery, tapestries, and books. To Florence went cochineal and hides, and back came gold, brocades, and silk. At Cape Verde they traded in black people that required large capital, but yielded large returns. To the Indies they shipped great cargos of all kinds of merchandise and return with gold, silver, cochineal, and hides in vast quantities.[14]

Goods shipped on warships that accompanied the cargo vessels were not inspected and taxed, and officers could make a good deal of money through illicit trade. For the crown, taxes gathered from commerce were offset by the need after about 1535 to defend the Indies from interloping foreigners and their piratical practices, by building forts, stocking them with soldiers and artillery, initiating coastal patrols, and building more warships to protect the Atlantic crossing of the treasure ships.

An Unexpected Import

As traders and explorers came into contact with native peoples, they spread European diseases not known in America, and for which the indigenous inhabitants had no immunity. In 1520, for example, after the arrival of Cortés with 600 Spaniards, one infected with small-pox, the disease spread rapidly throughout the Aztec nation and beyond. An Indian population of approximately 20 million in Mexico when the Spanish arrived fell to about 1.5 million by the early seventeenth century, much of the decrease due to the lethal microbe.[15]

The Catalan Economy

Excluded from commerce with the West Indies and America, the kingdom of Cataluña (under the crown of Castilla) in northeastern Spain, with the major cities of Barcelona and Valencia, turned its attention to the east and was allotted a monopoly over the markets of Spanish possessions in the Mediterranean that included southern Italy and Sicily. Catalan trade also encompassed North Africa and Northern Europe. Exclusion from the rich American trade was due to the Castilian claim that the commerce in the New World was their undertaking alone, as they had discovered it and Castilla paid most of the royal taxes. The merchants of Sevilla, including the Genoese in southern Spain, also applied pressure on the crown to keep others out.

The Anglo-Spanish War (1585–1604)

Although war was never officially declared, England and Spain fought intermittent battles mostly on the high seas for nearly 20 years. The animosity between the nations became palpable in 1585 when England sent military aid to the Netherland Protestants to support the Dutch resistance against the Spanish who occupied the country. There were religious reasons the Spanish under Catholic Felipe II hated the English under Protestant Queen Elizabeth, but perhaps more important than religion, English privateers, sanctioned by the English throne, affected Spanish commerce and royal revenue by raiding towns on the Spanish main and capturing their treasure ships in the Caribbean and on the open Atlantic Ocean.

Pacific Crossings[16]

The Philippine Islands were known in Europe since the time of Magellan on the first voyage around the world in 1521. Beginning in 1565, a Spanish galleon made an annual voyage to Manila from Acapulco (Mexico) and back. For the Spanish, the city of Manila became the hub between Asia and their American trade. From the East, the ships brought high-value products such as silks, porcelain, spices, and quicksilver. According to one traveler, Chinese quicksilver fetched a 300 percent profit.[17] Other goods were cotton, indigo, jade, ivory, and lacquerware. From the West went silver, gold, and coin from the Mexican mines.

For captains and sailors, the voyage across the Pacific Ocean was long and dangerous. New routes had to be found, and the ships often sailed near or beyond 30 degrees north latitude in search of favorable winds. Scurvy was rampant on such voyages, and seamen died by the score. From Acapulco, goods were carted overland to Vera Cruz and transshipped to Havana, where they joined the treasure fleets on their way to Spain. For gold and silver shipments from Peru, the Isthmus of Panama served as the staging area. Goods were carried overland through the steaming jungle from the Pacific to the town of Nombre de Dios, which was founded in 1510 on the Caribbean side, and sent on their way to Spain.

Seventeenth-Century Imperial Decline

About 1625, colonial exports to Spain of American treasure began a rapid decline, falling off from a previous high of approximately 7 million pesos annually to 500,000 in the years between 1556 and 1660. Reasons for the decline were several: Spanish colonies that once depended on Spain for needed manufactured and finished goods began to develop their own production of food and tools as they became more independent. Investors turned more and more to the colonies rather than the mother country to invest their capital, rich silver mines in Mexico and Peru were playing out, and competition from other nations that ignored the Spanish monopoly increased dramatically. Fraudulent practices, diminished commerce, higher taxes to pay for defense and insurance—all these factors and more were relevant in a declining empire.[18]

Eighteenth and Nineteenth Centuries

By the eighteenth century, the Dutch had an enormous merchant fleet that far surpassed all other European nations. The struggles for international trade were carried out in the East and West Indies, North and South America, and western Africa. The Dutch lost their maritime supremacy in the eighteenth century to the British and French. Planting colonies in the West Indies, British and French colonists sent home tobacco, cotton, coffee, sugar, and indigo—all items that could not be grown in most of Europe. The British swallowed up Barbados, Jamaica, and Bermuda; the French grabbed Saint Domingue, Martinique, and Guadalupe. The Dutch kept a few islands such as Curaçao in the West Indies. The Spanish retained Cuba and Hispaniola (now the Dominican Republic). European nations found the Caribbean Islands a stepping stone for further inroads into Central and South America.[19]

Early in the nineteenth century, most of the Spanish colonies declared their independence and shook off the control of Spain. By the end of the nineteenth century, Cuba and the Philippines were also lost.

NORTH AMERICA

In the early sixteenth century, European fishermen (French, Spanish, Portuguese, and Basque) began putting out their lines on the Grand Banks off Newfoundland and the Gulf of Saint Lawrence for the abundant cod that was found there. Dried or salted, the cod was carried back and sold in Europe for good profit. The fishermen spent the summer months in the region, since preparing fish for the journey home required several weeks on shore where native peoples congregated, anxious to obtain knives and axes, copper kettles, blankets, trinkets, and beads. The Indians had little to offer in return except fresh meat and fur pelts. Grand Banks fishermen soon found that furs could be sold in Europe for high prices and big financial gain.

When English and French colonists arrived in New England and Canada, they found a land heavily forested and thriving with animals and Indians. Skillful hunters, the native people bartered pelts and meat with the colonists for European articles of all kinds, including woolen blankets, colored cloth, guns, and whiskey. The

Native Americans bringing beaver pelts to white traders. (North Wind Picture Archives.)

pelts were shipped to Europe and made into fur clothing that had come into fashion among the elite with an ever-growing demand.

Colonial expansion into the hinterland and the European desire for fur, supplied by native peoples, brought European trappers into the market who, striking out on their own, could dispense with the native middlemen and go into business for themselves. Further exploration inland opened an entirely new world for trade in furs, a trade that generated skirmishes and outright open warfare between Indian tribes protecting what they considered their land and between French, English, and American colonists competing for the best hunting grounds. Felt hats that Europeans favored in the sixteenth century stimulated trade and caused a great demand for beaver pelts.[20]

Hudson Bay Company

By 1670, the English Hudson Bay Company had been chartered and claimed all lands that drained into the Hudson Bay as their privileged trading area. It established trading posts on the shores of the bay where Indians brought and exchanged their furs. Two or three ships were sent out annually to bring back pelts, mostly beaver that were sold in England at auction or sometimes by private arrangement. The trade was interrupted in 1689 when war broke out between New France (Canada) and New England, and their respective Indian allies, which lasted some nine years. Each proclaimed authority over the Great Lakes region, where the Iroquois Indians controlled the regional fur trade and each raided the other's settlements.

Indians placed high value on garments, scarves, and blankets supplied by the Hudson Bay Company. Rice and molasses were also supplied to Indians, who took a particular liking to eating the two mixed together. Tobacco might be traded by the head or by the leaf. Guns were a major trade item not only for hunting but also for war with neighbors. Those traded to the Indians by the Hudson Bay Company were generally old, inaccurate, dangerous, and inclined to explode when fired.

North West Company and American Fur Company

In 1779, in competition with the Hudson Bay Company, the North West Company, a joint-stock venture, the first in Canada, was formed in Montreal and refused to recognize the former's trading rights around the Hudson Bay. Mostly Scotsmen formed the company, and confrontations between the two were unleashed. The North West Company came to operate 117 trading posts, and the rivalry sometimes reached dangerous levels.

In 1801, a wealthy fur trader for the North West Company, Alexander Mackenzie, broke away and joined the XY Company. Intense competition for furs increased. Whiskey and rum became an important part of any exchange. The fervent competition brought the XY and the North West together against the Hudson Bay Company.

Meanwhile, a direct land route across the continent was explored by the Lewis and Clarke expedition (1804–1806) in which one of the objectives was to find a suitable course to the Pacific Ocean over which trade could be conducted with the Far East. By around 1800, the Pacific coast had already been mapped by explorers such as Captain Cook and Captain Vancouver.

To add to the competition for furs, the American Fur Company—established in 1810 in New York City by the American merchant John Astor—entered the fray. In 1812, he built a trading fort near that of the North West Company in Spokane, Washington. Both were in a race for the Columbia River fur resources.

Increased use of liquor and trading with the Indians during drinking sessions became common. Resources in furs declined as areas were overexploited, sending trappers off to explore new territories and causing Indians who had become dependent on the European fur trade to move into new areas, which often caused conflict and wars with the indigenous people living there.[21]

The Seven Years' War (1756–1763)

The immediate issue at stake in the Seven Years' War fought in America was the upper Ohio Valley. Was it French or English? Who had the right to trade there? The larger issue was who would control the nucleus of North America. English settlers were many in the region, but French traders predominated and were in alliance with Indian tribes. The governor-general of New France, some years before in 1749, had ordered the area cleared of all the English and their activities restricted to the area east of the Appalachians. Successful at first, the French were ultimately defeated. The Treaty of Paris in 1763 deprived France of territory east of the Mississippi River, allotting it to England. Furs from the Ohio Valley now went to London brokers and fashion houses instead of to Paris.

American Revolution

Many colonists were angry about the high-handed British Stamp Act of 1765 that taxed the colonies to pay for garrisoned English troops in America. There were a number of reasons the American colonies rebelled against the British Crown, not least among them was the state of affairs concerning commerce. The colonies were told to adhere to British policies on foreign trade that were passed by the British parliament. The Navigation Act, for example, required that trade within the British Empire be carried out on British ships owned and mainly crewed by British subjects. Certain products for the colonists had to be shipped via England regardless of their origin and destination. Parliament then altered the rules by the Tea Act in 1773, which allowed the British East India Company to ship tea directly to America and on which the colonists paid a tax. The colonists rebelled and threw the tea into Boston harbor—an incident that precipitated the American Revolution.

Trade War (1812–1815)

At war with Napoleonic France, England tried to prevent American trade with its enemy across the channel. As a neutral country, the United States had the right under international law to trade where it pleased. Protests were made, but nothing came of it. The number of U.S. merchant vessels had greatly increased during the first decade of the nineteenth century, and England may have also feared that its merchant marine would be surpassed and control of the seas would wind up in American hands. The war disrupted trade not only on the high seas, but all across the North American continent as the British in Canada were thought to have armed Indian tribes in the forlorn hope that the natives, by forming a confederation, would stop U.S. expansion westward. After this, the United States forbade any foreign traders to operate in U.S. territory. The North West Company withdrew.

In 1821, the North West and the Hudson Bay Companies merged under the latter's name. A major factor in the decision to merge was the high transportation costs of shipping through the Great Lakes. In addition, the Hudson Bay Company's charter had stronger legal backing to the right of land by discovery than the claims of the North West Company. After this time, most trade goods were shipped through Hudson Bay for the interior posts. A border war continued between the Hudson Bay and the American Fur Companies. It did not end until 1833, when the American Fur Company abandoned its posts along the border in exchange for an annual cash payment from the Hudson Bay Company.

At its Fort Langley trading post, which as early as 1829 purchased salmon from Indians on the Fraser River and pickled them in barrels, the Hudson Bay Company conducted the first commercial fishery operations by white men in British Columbia. This trade increased, and by about 1835, from 3,000 to 4,000 barrels of salted salmon were being exported, mainly to the Hawaiian Islands and Asia. The salmon business became common with the development of a West Coast canning industry in the 1860s. The fish and furs reached the East Coast by large three- and four-masted, square rigged clipper ships that began to be built in the mid-nineteenth century for ocean sailing. From coast to coast of the United States, the route, which required a voyage of about three months, went around the dangerous Cape Horn.

Around 1850, the popularity of the beaver hat in England and Europe began to fade as silk started to take its place, and demand for furs greatly slackened. Also by this time, pelts were harder to find, as were Indians from the decimated tribes who were expert trappers. Numerous white traders and trappers went out of business and took up other occupations such as mining, lumber, railroad construction, or as small storeowners. Some became scouts and pathfinders for settlers moving west.

Many of the men who ranged the mountains, forests, and prairies of the vast territories in the West in search of wealth or adventure did not fit in a conventional life among their contemporaries. Those who did not work for a company were often at home among Indian tribes and married the local women. They often worked alone hunting the beaver and setting their traps. They endured sweltering or freezing temperatures, swarms of mosquitoes, dangerous animals, constant movement from camp to camp, hazardous rivers and portages, sometimes bad food, hunting game, and often eating what they could find such as berries and fruits, including pemmican made from dried buffalo meat. They slept under the stars or under canoes; if they fell ill, there was little recourse except to hope for the best. In the twilight of the forest, hunting could easily end in tragedy when unfriendly Indians ambushed a party. Besides what food he could carry, the trapper had to have a rifle and ammunition, a knife, a small tent, blankets, warm clothes, and maybe a mule to carry supplies and trade goods.

Pacific Maritime Trade and the Russian-American Company

In the nineteenth century, Alaska, British Columbia, and the Pacific Northwest became a vast new region of fur trade based primarily on the sea otter. The new maritime trade encompassed connections with Japan and China, and furs from this area were bartered in China for silk and porcelain that were sold in the United States or sent on to Europe. First pioneered by Russian traders from Kamchatka, the Aleutian Islands were exploited, the Aleut people were enslaved, and were forced to hunt and supply otter furs, the harvesting of which continued along the coasts of Alaska, a territory that was Russian until it was purchased by the United States in 1867. With native workers, the Russians, headquartered at Sitka, hunted sea otters as far south as San Francisco.[22]

U.S. and British traders penetrated the maritime commerce in the 1780s, especially along the coast of today's British Columbia. Around the beginning of the nineteenth century, trade thrived for two decades until the annihilation of the sea otter. The northwest coast witnessed ferocious competition between British and American ships. In the 1820s the Hudson Bay Company intruded in the northwest trade and by about 1840 had driven most U.S. traders out of business. The English and the Russian-American Company continued in the trade that linked China, the Hawaiian Islands, the Pacific Northwest, England, and New England.

West coast Indian communities benefited from the business but suffered from increased warfare over trading rights and depopulation from epidemic diseases. The Hawaiian people felt the results of the trade, both positive and negative, and on the other side of the American continent, New Englanders reaped great profits that could then be invested in manufacturing enterprises.

For better communication among the various and disparate peoples of the northwest, a pidgin language called Chinook Jargon developed with vocabulary from Indian and European sources. This language was used chiefly for trading purposes.

PACIFIC NORTHWEST INDIANS

With the appearance of the Russian-American and Hudson Bay Companies, the fur-bearing animals went into decline. The Russians stripped the Aleutian Islands one by one of fur-bearing animals such as the sea otter as they progressed eastward toward Alaska. In Canada, the impact of English and French fur traders was equally devastating to furry animals, and trade fell off to almost nothing, as did the presence of the once bountiful otters, whose furs became so scarce that the price for them skyrocketed. A Fort Simpson trader bargained for days with the Indians, offering an astronomical seven blankets for each fur, but the Indians demanded eight blankets and a gun. Such a price was unheard of. The Indians, however, gave in and bartered their 12 sea otter furs for seven blankets each.

While Indian folklore has come down to us in which the native peoples were solicitous of animal lives, considering them almost sacred and taking only what was needed for the "people's" survival, the facts speak otherwise. In the case of the beaver, the spring hunt was a great event, eagerly sought by Indian tribes. The females were easily killed after whelping and the cubs, useless for fur, were slaughtered or left to die. Hudson Bay officials attempted to persuade Indians not to pursue the spring hunt in order to preserve the young, but to no avail. Both the company and the Indians became distressed when beaver nearly disappeared from the scene. Not until 1907 was beaver hunting outlawed, and the few remaining began a comeback.

Sable, in high demand, also lost ground to the point of extinction, and its relative, the martin, became the choice animal of fur trade. Bears also ranked high on the list in England, where their coats made up the hats of the busbies. Mink rated low at the time, and one squirrel skin was traded for one tobacco leaf.[23] Slaves were sometimes an item for barter, as Indian tribes often captured men and women from an enemy tribe and traded them to their home people.

The small village of Port Simpson in northern British Columbia[24], perhaps not unlike many villages of the northern west coast, was isolated and self-sufficient. In 1834, a Hudson Bay trading post was established there with the idea of usurping the U.S. fur trade in the region. The natives lived mostly on fish, especially salmon, but they also hunted. A delicacy was fish eggs—cooked, dried, or fresh; those dried in seaweed were best of all, as the whole parcel was eaten. Christian missionaries and their families followed the founding of the Hudson Bay post and, while mostly Indian, the village had a minority community of whites.

Accustomed to taking what they needed for survival, the Indians found the Hudson Bay settlement a source of many items that they could use in one way or another and continuously made off with objects they desired, much to the frustration of the white population. Potato patches were particularly vulnerable to theft.

Neighboring Indians arrived at the fort with fresh and dried venison to trade for tobacco, cotton, and bullets. A Hudson Bay ship supplied the white settlement from time to time with needed items, and sometimes dissension among the tribes cut off the trade and caused hunger to beset the residents of the company.

Whiskey and Guns

Unused to the effects of alcohol, native peoples throughout the United States and Canada began to acquire a taste for it. Brought to the Indians by European fur trappers, it became a desired trade item. Instead of a blanket for a beaver pelt, a little bad whiskey or rum served the same purpose.

Both the Hudson Bay Company and the Russian-American Company suffered from Boston traders whose ships dashed up the west coast loaded with cheap rum, guns, ammunition, and tobacco. They grabbed up all available furs, many to be sold in China at inflated prices, leaving behind intoxicated Indians to be dealt with by the companies, which saw their profits decimated. When laws were passed outlawing the selling of spirits to Indians, the trade continued unabated in hidden coves and out-of-the-way places.

The on-and-off troubles with Indians may be illustrated by the small shooting war in 1937 engaged in by Fort Simpson, a ship's cannons, and a local Indian tribe. Several days later the Indians, having gathered up grape shot and cannon balls, sold them back to the fort, which dispensed four gallons of whiskey for their trouble!

Indian Women

In some of the North American matrilineal cultures, for example, the Iroquois, women had political power. Among the Cherokee, as in most tribes, they had equality and respect. Male and female occupations differed but were of equal value. Girls learned from their mothers' knowledge of plants the use of herbs for illness and the preservation of food, and many other matters for survival. Influence in tribal councils was also accorded to women in some cultures.

Sometimes, rivalry between women of the same tribe reached extremes. On July 16, 1838, according to the Hudson Bay journal, two women of the same tribe, the Kygarnie, each considered themselves "women of consequence" and both proposed killing their slaves to show who could best afford the loss. Officials of the company talked them out of it, and instead they both tore up blankets, one 10, the other seven, and gave away a gun. Both parties were satisfied and came to good terms.

Tribal Clashes

Trade was not only disrupted by tribal wars that might simmer for months, but more unexpected and dangerous were hit-and-run raids as, for instance, when the Indians from the southern Queen Charlotte Islands, across the narrow stretch of water from Port Simpson, ambushed a party of Fox Indians at their fishing ground, killed 10 warriors, and made off with the women and children. Such deadly offensives always called for vengeance in the form of retribution or retaliation. How much fighting can be blamed on whiskey and rum is a moot question.

Southern United States

European colonies in the southern sections of the United States began growing by the beginning of the eighteenth century, and soon large plantations owned by wealthy colonists began to appear. Most people lived on small farms with agriculture the main compo-nent of their livelihood, but those who could afford it developed the land into great estates for cotton and tobacco, cash crops that were easily exported to England. Imports from England often consisted of tea and manufactured goods; from Africa came slaves; and sugar came from the Caribbean plantations. The southern towns, of which Charleston was the most important for trade, maintained independent commercial ties with England.

Triangular Trade

A system of trade in the shape of a triangle developed in which colonists in America shipped cotton, tobacco and rum among other items to England and Europe while the English and Europeans shipped horses, guns and powder, alcohol, and products such as pots, pans and knives to the western coast of Africa. From there, black slaves were sent to the Americas and the Caribbean to work the plantations. Caribbean sugar was shipped to New England for making molasses and rum. This trade generated a good deal of wealth for the plantation owners, especially as their slave laborers worked for only enough food to keep them alive.

American Civil War and Trade (1860–1886)

During the U.S. Civil War, the Lincoln administration promoted trade with southerners for several reasons, although the policies were controversial. The Confederate government received critical supplies in exchange for southern staple products, and some people believed this prolonged the war. A *New York Herald* article published July 21, 1865 claimed that prominent men in the North, some conspiring with Treasury Department officials, were involved in wartime trade with the South. A merchant who could cheaply send cotton to New York or provisions to the South stood to make a handsome profit. New York resident Charles Gould, who had declined to participate in such a venture, described the potential profits from trading cotton. For an initial $100, a trader could buy a 400-pound bale of cotton in the South. The bale would be worth $500 in the New York market.

NOTES

1. Braudel (1985), 176.
2. Curtin, 85.
3. Diaz, 215–217.
4. Lynch, 242.
5. Pierson, 53.
6. See Payne, 274, for a breakdown in years.
7. Paine, 375.
8. Gately, 40–41.
9. Noted in Gately, 44.
10. Elliot (1989), 23
11. *EWT*, Vol. 1, 235.
12. Wild (1995), 9.
13. Wild (1995), 44.
14. Quoted in Lynch, 192, and paraphrased here.
15. Diamond, 210.
16. McAlister, 371–372.
17. Braudel (1985), 406.
18. Payne, 296–297.
19. For more detail see Woloch, 125.
20. King, 207.
21. *EWT*, 389–340.
22. Pomeranz and Topik, 120.
23. Meilleur, 108–110.
24. Meilleur, passim.

21

MODERN TRADE: GLOBALIZATION

A costly trade war between Japan and Russia (1904–1905) began the century. In need of a warm water Pacific port for maritime trade and naval facilities, the Russian government leased Port Arthur (now Dalian) from the Chinese in 1898 and wasted no time in occupying and fortifying the strategic site. It began constructing a rail line from Harbin to the port while it also transacted business with Korea to acquire forested land and mineral mines. The Japanese took a dim view of Russian competition in the Far East, and the two rival countries with imperial ambitions came face to face. To maintain a dominant position in Korea and Manchuria, the Japanese were prepared to come to blows. They had already fought a successful war with China over these two countries (1894–1895) and intended to hold on to their gains, insisting the Russians leave Manchuria. Before the Trans-Siberian railroad was completed, over which Russia could transport supplies and soldiers, the Japanese made a surprise attack in February 1904, driving the Russians out of Korea. They pushed them back to North Manchuria, winning a major victory by overrunning the critical Russian stronghold at Port Arthur. The war ended with the Treaty of Portsmouth (New Hampshire) in September 1905, brokered to some extent by Theodore Roosevelt, confirming Japanese hegemony in Korea and South Manchuria, including Port Arthur.

COMPETITION IN THE WEST

Even before the beginning of the century, England and Germany entered into a race for naval supremacy. It became more intense by 1906 with the launching of the H.M.S. *Dreadnought*, which outclassed all previous battleships in firepower and size. Command of the sea and thus command of world trade were on the minds of politicians of both countries, but Britain, with a powerful navy and merchant marine, was well ahead of all other countries at the time.

Great Britain was also challenged by the growing industrial might of Germany, that dominated trade in the steel and chemical industries. Germany's growing industry worried the British.

SCRAMBLE FOR ALLIANCES

In 1882, Germany, the Austro-Hungarian Empire, and Italy formed the Triple Alliance and France, somewhat isolated, formed a military pact with Russia in 1894. The British government signed treaties with France in 1904 and Russia in 1907, including military pacts that became known as the Triple Entente. The two formidable and opposing European blocs each feared one would dominate the other, and increasing the tension was Germany's rapidly growing army. Further from home, they also quarreled over possession of lands and islands in the South Pacific and territory in Africa.

WORLD WAR I

Trade competition was one of the causes of World War I. For the most part, seafaring commerce was in England's hands and was carried on abundantly with India, Australia, New Zealand, South Africa, Latin America, and Canada. Germany, only unified in 1871, was fast catching up to become a major broker in commercial competition, as well as aspiring to its own colonies and empire. Germany's desire to become a commercial world power was mostly to the detriment of England, which it surpassed in industrial strength at the turn of twentieth century. A naval race began between the two powers. The English had little to worry about but nevertheless feared German industrial growth.

The flashpoint came on June 28, 1914, with the assassination in Serbia of Franz Ferdinand, heir to the Austro-Hungarian Empire, and his wife, by Gavilo Princip, a Bosnian Serb, in a plot to gain independence from the Austro-Hungarians.

The bloody conflict opened with the Austro-Hungarian attack on Serbia followed by the German invasion of Belgium and France. England came to Belgium's aid, and more nations were drawn into the fray as it spread to become a global conflict.

Trade and Neutral Countries

Master of the sea lanes, England continued to trade with its colonies and dominions for purchases of war materials the Allied powers needed. England and France relied on the United States for loans. While hundreds of thousands of men on both sides were sent to their deaths by fatuous generals to gain a few kilometers of ground, those nations not engaged in fighting reaped enormous profits selling arms to the warring countries. It has been said that the banking firm of J. P. Morgan loaned over $2 billion to England and France, and that the president of Bethlehem Steel, Charles Schwab, obtained contracts for the production of millions of rounds of ammunition as well as 10 submarines for England. In 1916, J. P. Morgan earned $61 million in profits from the war.[1]

Just as Napoleon had to contend with a continental blockade from the English, Germany, too, suffered from this kind of military strategy during World War I. The Allied powers used their navies to block the Central powers from importing and exporting goods in order to deprive them of war materials and food, the latter to demoralize the civilian population. Germany retaliated effectively at first, with underwater mines, submarines, and disguised raider ships to keep supplies from flowing to Britain and France.

On the eastern front, the poorly equipped Russians, having cast off the rule of the tsar, opted out of the war in 1917 after heavy losses and the beginning of the Russian Revolution. This same year, the United States entered World War I.

End of World War I

With the defeat of Germany and its partners along with the breakup of the Austro-Hungarian, German, Ottoman, and Russian Empires, a new world dawned in Europe. Representatives of the victorious nations gathered at Versailles near Paris to determine the punishments to be meted out to Germany—blamed for the war—and to reshape the map of Europe as well as the overseas possessions of the Central powers. In the Treaty of Versailles, new states were carved out of the chaos, for example, Czechoslovakia,

Estonia, Finland, Latvia, Lithuania, Poland, and Yugoslavia. France remained torn apart, with nearly a generation of men lost in battle. An estimated 40 million casualties resulted from the four years of conflict, most in Europe.

Bitter feelings on the part of the Allies prompted the continued use of the blockade, even after the armistice, in spite of U.S. and Herbert Hoover's attempts to have it lifted as thousands of Germans and Austrians were starving to death. Hoover wrote in his memoirs concerning a meeting in London upon his arrival there:

> This morning's session was at once an enlightenment in national intrigue, selfishness, nationalism, heartlessness, rivalry and suspicion, which seemed to ooze from every pore [of those attending]— but with polished politeness...[2]

To rebuild the economy of Germany and relieve the worst starvation since the seventeenth-century Thirty Years' War was of little concern to the Allies, even though the victims were mostly women and children. The Allies were too frightened by Germany's industrial and commercial potential and forgot about Article XXVI of the Armistice Agreement that promised food for the German people. None was sent.[3] The French, with a prodigious hatred of Germany, had only one thing in mind—to extract every penny from Germany for the costs of the war to France.

The Germans were willing to pay for food with gold, but the Allied Blockade Committee turned the offer down, and the British navy prevented any ships from arriving at German shores. An entry from the notes of Vance C. McCormick, head of the U.S. War Trade Board, on February 28, 1919, noted that the French and British were anxious to maintain the blockade in order to deprive Germany of trading for raw materials that could be used to compete with them in world markets in the form of manufactured goods.[4]

The bankrupt country was in despair and had no prospects of credit from any quarter. Only when it became clear that Germany was ripe for communism was the blockade relaxed. Food began coming into Germany, but a partial blockade continued that, among other things, prohibited German fishing boats in the North Sea, which was patrolled by the British navy, presumably on behalf of the British fishing industry. All restrictions on Germany involving the blockade were finally removed on June 30, 1919.

WEIMAR REPUBLIC

After the war, the new Germany was in perpetual crisis. The Weimar Republic came into existence in 1919, but to pay its debts, it needed to export manufactured goods. Allied governments, backed by trade unions, prevented this. Confiscating German merchant ships and rolling stock as well as imposing high tariffs on their products, the Allies effectively cut off any economic progress. Germany was to pay for the war but was denied the means to do it. The country was allowed to pay in kind, such as 38 million tons of coal annually for 10 years, great amounts of timber, and so on, and German labor might be used to rebuild devastated areas, but none of this helped the German economy. Apart from the reparations payments, the Allies occupied the Rhineland at German expense.[5]

Deterioration of the German currency began at once as the government printed more and more money to pay the debts. The paper currency fell from 60 to 310 marks to the dollar, and Germany's debt by May 1921 came to 750 billion marks. By November 15, 1923, it came to 4,200,000,000,000.0—a meaningless figure. A chief white-collar worker for a rubber factory reported he was paid twice a day his salary of 200 billion a month and was then, along with other employees, given 30 minutes off to make haste to the stores for purchases before further inflation reduced his money to half its value.[6]

The dozen new states created out of the old empires by the Treaty of Versailles soon erected trade barriers in the form of tariffs to protect their homegrown industries and agricultural products. The United States increased tariffs but encouraged its farmers to grow surpluses to feed not only Americans, but also hungry war-ravaged Europeans. Farmers invested in more land to meet the demand, but when prices dropped in 1922 due to the growing self-sufficiency of European farmers, many U.S. farmers were unable to pay their mortgages, and agricultural trade went into a slump. Manufacturing business, on the other hand, continued to grow throughout the 1920s until the stock market crash and the Great Depression at the end of 1929, which reverberated in the economies around the world.

Unable to pay the large sums demanded by France for war reparations, and with inflation out of control, the Weimar Republic collapsed, bringing Adolf Hitler to power in 1933. He refused to make any further payments to the Allies and began building up the country's military forces, setting the stage for World War II. The U.S. Congress adhered to the policy of isolation from world problems and voted to remain outside the League of Nations. Most statesmen present at the Versailles conference did not take free trade seriously as advocated by some, for example, Woodrow Wilson and John Maynard Keynes, and the results, 21 years later, led to an even more devastating and widespread world war.

THE GREAT DEPRESSION

The financial capital of the world in 1929 was Wall Street with large banks, investment companies, and the New York Stock Exchange. In that year, stock prices were booming as investors poured in their money. The world appeared full of promise, and many people were busy making money—at least on paper.

On October 24, a day now known as Black Tuesday, the Stock Exchange opened as usual but within the hour, there was a big rush to sell stocks. Investors panicked, and sell orders snowballed and came so fast that the ticker tape could not keep up. The following week saw further descent of prices, and sellers could not find buyers. Billions of dollars on paper vanished. Within a few months, unemployment rose, wages and prices fell, and industrial output slowed. By 1932, factory production had fallen by 50 percent, thousands of businesses shut their doors, banks closed, and millions of people lost their savings. Unemployment rose from about 3 percent at the beginning of the crash to 25 percent in 1933. Stock traders lost some $74 billion. International trade all but dried up.

During the course of World War I, Europe had acquired huge debts, most of which were owed to the United States. However, the U.S. government hindered European economic recovery and repayment of the loans by imposing tariffs on European imports to protect local industries. Other countries also set up protectionist tariffs. The increased trade barriers aggravated the crisis. The Great Depression caused global economic devastation but impacted the United States and Germany the most. In 1931, the Weimar Republic tried to implement a customs union with Austria that other countries were free to join. Once again, fearful of German power, France vetoed the proposal at the League of Nations. Many turned to the National Socialist Party, the Nazis, that promised a revived Germany. By 1932, the Nazis had become the largest party in the German parliament. Shortly thereafter, Adolf Hitler overturned the Weimar Republic and concentrated all power in his own hands. The Great Depression lasted until 1939; meanwhile, other events took center stage in Europe.

NAZI GERMANY AND TRADE

Hemmed in by nations suspicious of German ambitions and ideology, such as Poland, England, and France, and having lost her colonies as a result of the Treaty of Versailles, Germany had little access to vital resources such as rubber, oil, and most nonferrous metal, and had little credit available. Germany had economic reasons for aggressive action and seeking resources and vital manpower to fuel the nation's economy, and military conquest was a solution.[7]

In the 1930s, German politicians and financiers had to choose between free market trade and a reduction in state spending on the military, and full or partial autarky. Hitler chose autarkic policies and major spending on the buildup of the armed forces. His four-year plan was to have the nation ready for war within that time. To achieve this, he selected Hermann Göring to carry out the mandate. Göring reduced imports and set controls on wages and prices. Workers who objected were sent to concentration camps and used as slave labor in the new synthetic rubber and steel factories. Full self-sufficiency was, however, impossible as some raw materials were not found in Germany and had to be imported. The Nazi regime chose to trade only with countries sympathetic to it and under its influence. Foreign policy was designed to force Southern European and Balkan countries that could supply needed raw materials to become dependent on Germany, which supplied them with manufactured goods. These countries—including Hungary, Rumania, and Bulgaria—conducted at least half of their foreign trade with Germany, and some South American nations were willing to extend credit to the Nazi regime and buy manufactured products from it.[8] Hitler's primary goal was Germany's self-sufficiency, and a land grab in Czechoslovakia and Poland to the east—with their raw materials and food production—would help fulfill that goal. No doubt he was looking beyond, to the conquest of Russia. German armament factories, short on supplies, were the reason to annex Austria and Czechoslovakia, as Hitler told his military leaders in November 1937.[9]

SPANISH CIVIL WAR (1936–1939)

In July 1936, backed by the Catholic Church, General Francisco Franco initiated the Spanish Civil War with a view to overthrowing the democratic Republic of Spain that had been in power since 1931. England offered no help to the Republicans, sheltered right-wing refugees in Gibraltar, and soon convinced France to stay out of Spain's war. England had vested interests in Spain and was afraid of losing them if, as seemed possible, the leftist Spanish government were to fall into communist hands. Germany and Italy sent considerable aid to Franco and in desperation the prime minister, José Giral, appealed to the Soviet Union for guns and munitions. In the meantime, a Nonintervention Committee was formed in London that included representatives from Great Britain, France, Germany, Italy, the Soviet Union, and Portugal. The committee and everyone else knew that Germany and Italy (although they denied it) were sending military aid to the Nationalists under Franco, while Portugal was sending troops. The deceitful committee was a total farce and in spite of abundant and concrete evidence, it refused to call Hitler and Mussolini liars and investigate the intervention. Instead, it passed another resolution that no evidence could be submitted unless it came from one of the members. Stalin was unsure of his position. Prestige demanded that he aid the Republic, but a leftist leaning state in Spain might cause England and France to side with Hitler's Germany. He acted, however, when the Republic was willing to transfer all the gold in its treasury to the Soviet Union to pay for arms. The gold-for-guns deal was secretly delivered in October when Russian cargo ships arrived in Spanish ports with armaments in exchange for 510 tons of Spanish gold.[10] The Republic was not only deceived, deluded, and cheated by the dissembling, hypocritical, Nonintervention Committee, perhaps the most absurd organization of the century, but it was also swindled out of its gold by Stalin, who sent obsolete, worn out guns, many of which belonged in a museum, and so little ammunition that the weapons were next to useless.[11] Franco won the war in 1939, and Russia kept the gold.

OUTBREAK OF WORLD WAR II

The outbreak of World War II on September 3, 1939, the subsequent fall of France in June 1940, and with England next on the list of Nazi aggression, all failed to alert Americans to the dangers ahead. The U.S. Congress, opposed to direct intervention in the European war, maintained a strict neutrality while the Roosevelt administration endeavored to aid England in its fight for survival through a Lend-Lease arrangement. By 1941, Britain was desperate for American assistance.

Neutral countries found it expedient to trade with Nazi Germany during World War II, which benefited the Germans who required products from foreign governments. For neutrals to do business with both sides in war was common. The gold and money looted from banks of the nations that were overrun by German armies, as well as confiscated property of Jews, helped pay for raw materials, fuel, and spare parts to keep industry and the army functioning, as well as food to feed the population. Countries most involved in German commerce during the war were Sweden, Portugal, Spain, Turkey, and Argentina. Swiss banks looked after German financial affairs as well as the gold Germany robbed from nations and individuals.

These so-called neutral countries handled half a billion dollars in assets for the German government and its citizens during the war, and dealt in prodigious amounts of looted gold that in today's dollars amounted to about $7 billion. The Swiss Central Bank, the largest buyer of Nazi gold, was either unconcerned or unaware that much of the metal was stolen from victims of the Holocaust. Germany also traded coal for Swiss steel and other items, while the Swiss railroads fully cooperated with Germany in moving products to and from Italy through the Saint Gotthard tunnel. There was little choice for the Swiss. The alternative would have been occupation.

The dictatorships of Antonio Salazar in Portugal and Francisco Franco in Spain were German trading allies. That Franco's government was strongly pro-Nazi and perhaps fearful of Hitler is clear from the fact that Franco sent a division of Spanish troops to the Russian front to assist the Nazis as well as supplied refueling stations for German submarines. Portugal and Spain provided most of Germany's tungsten; Turkey furnished Germany's chromite, used to harden steel to make armor; and Argentina did business in needed food. The Allied blockade of Germany prevented Argentina from exporting large amounts of goods to Germany, which previously had been a major trading partner, but small quantities of platinum, palladium, drugs, and other chemicals were smuggled to the Nazis. Argentina also maintained commercial ties with the Allies. Its exports during the war, such as beef to the United States and England, were much more considerable than pre-war tallies.

Portugal and Spain

Antonio Salazar in Portugal incorporated tenets of fascism into his government and was viewed in a favorable light by Hitler and

Mussolini, as well as by Spain's General Franco. Sympathetic to the Nazis, Salazar exported to Germany clothing, foodstuffs (especially sardines), and many tons of tungsten, which was vital to Hitler's war machine. Some of the German payments in exchange for these goods were in gold that first passed through Switzerland. The Bank of Portugal's gold reserves nearly quintupled between 1939 and 1944, German espionage agents were permitted to operate in Portugal, and, like Switzerland, the country was swarming with spies during the war.

Despite his connections to the Axis, Salazar also cooperated with the Allies, at times leasing bases in the Azores to the British and permitting refugees who escaped the Nazis to travel through Portugal on their way to other destinations. Much of the gold, mostly looted from Belgian banks, was returned after the war at the insistence of the United States.

General Franco's sympathy with Hitler's National Socialism almost led him to the brink of an alliance with the Third Reich, but like Salazar, he refrained from becoming too close a partner. He kept Spain out of the war while pursuing a policy of collaboration, providing valuable raw materials to the Third Reich. By the end of the Spanish Civil War, Franco had incurred large debts to the Germans that he helped repay by signing a treaty with Germany in December 1939 in which he agreed to reserve for the Reich the lion's share of Spain's exports, namely iron ore, zinc, lead, mercury, tungsten, and wool. Trade relations between the two nations continued until the end of the war, but Spain's contribution to the German war effort became more circumspect after the U.S. invasion of North Africa in the autumn of 1942.

The United States and Britain imposed an oil embargo against Spain in 1940 to force Franco to expel German spies from the country, tone down the pro-Axis propaganda in the Spanish press, and halt exports to Germany of raw materials, especially tungsten. The Allies wanted Franco neutral and were wary that he might reexport the petroleum products to Germany. Concerned about its railroads, buses, fishing boats, military, and industries, as Spain had little other access to oil, Franco pretended to accede to Allied demands for neutrality, and oil again flowed into the country. When a Spanish division was sent to aid the German army on the Russian front in 1941, a second partial embargo was imposed that cut oil supplies to Spain by one third; but this was not totally successful. Franco delayed withdrawing his troops from the eastern front until October 1943, when victory seemed dim for the Axis powers. Still, disingenuously, the Spanish dictator allowed German planes to land and refuel in Spain, while Allied aircraft and crews were impounded. Highly censured, the Spanish press remained pro-Axis, and the Spanish government turned a blind eye to the continued exports to Germany. In January 1944, a third total embargo on oil was initiated against Spain, but the British were far from enthusiastic and worried that demands on Franco might make trouble for Britain's imports of potash and iron ore from Spain. Mindful of their investments on the Iberian Peninsula, as well postwar trade transactions, the British objected to the embargo, which caused a temporary breach between Roosevelt and Churchill.

Lend-Lease and Imperial Preferences

The Roosevelt policy of Lend-Lease aimed to alleviate trade payments from a financially strapped England but required provisions of an unspecified benefit that the president of the United States would consider satisfactory. England was thus spared financial repayments, but the United States demanded certain foreign policy considerations, one of which was the abolishment of the Imperial Trade Preferences between the dominions of the British Empire, and a more liberal and uniformly fair international trade policy to be put in place.

In 1932 at a meeting in Ottawa, the dominions of Canada, Australia, India, New Zealand, South Africa, some smaller states, and England agreed to lower tariffs among themselves for each other's benefit. Duties were to be higher elsewhere, a matter that elicited the anger of other world countries that saw this as discrimination. The U.S. secretary of state, Cordell Hull, believed that freer trade would ensure economic and political conditions more favorable to peace. Conservatives in the British government, who were in favor of colonial trade preferences, threatened to bring down Winston Churchill's government if concessions were made to the United States on this issue. The matter was settled when the General Agreement on Tariffs and Trade (GATT) came into effect in 1947.

Trade and Neutrality: The Case of Sweden

During World War II, the Swedish economy was integrated into the Nazis' New Order. Sweden remained neutral during World War II but was Germany's largest trading partner, supplying iron ore, foodstuffs, wood, manufactured goods, especially ball bearings required for cars, aircraft, tanks, and a host of other equipment for the Nazi war effort. This policy was a matter of survival. Unlike the sympathetic dictatorships of Spain and Portugal that willingly supplied the Nazis, Sweden was a democracy, and it was either do business, or the Nazis would take what they wanted by force. The Swedish government was only too aware that cooperation with Germany was necessary to preserve its precarious neutrality. In matters of finance, the Swedes cooperated with Germany by providing credit. This pragmatic approach to trade relations with Germany satisfied the Nazis. Germany supplied Sweden with some food and fuel at high prices while demanding Swedish exports at lower than market prices. Despite Sweden's geographical position in the zone of German influence, cut off by German-occupied Norway and pro-German Finland, it still managed to clandestinely export some material to the Allies by running the German naval blockade and by secret flights. However, until 1944 Germany called the tune on the Swedish economy. After the war, the Swedish central bank returned a vast quantity of gold that was stolen from Belgium and Holland and received from the Nazis in payment for goods.

Trade with Sweden was sometimes conducted via other nations such as neutral Argentina in matters of food, and by the United States, a belligerent in the war after 1941, which supplied oil and gasoline—items Germany could no longer provide as the war went on. Swedish ball bearings, as essential to the Allies as they were to Germany, found their way to England and the United States.

War in the Pacific

In search of primary resources, Japan annexed Korea (after driving the Russians out) in 1910 and invaded Manchuria in 1931. By 1937, Japanese armies moved into China. By 1940, Japan controlled eastern China and had established a puppet court in Nanking. The U.S. demand that Japan abandon Manchuria and China as the price for mutual trade infuriated the Japanese high command. In July 1941, with Japanese incursions into French Indo-China just after the fall of France, the United States ceased oil exports to Japan, which left Japan hard pressed to keep its industries running and its navy afloat. War seemed inevitable. The Japanese prime minister, Konoe Fumimaro, attempted to negotiate with the United States to avoid it, but when the militant General Tojo Hideki replaced Konoe in October 1941, the decision to wage war against the United States was reached. On December 7, 1941, Japan launched attacks on Pearl Harbor, the Philippines, Hong Kong, and Malaya. The Japanese considered the Western nations (United States, England, France, and Holland, which all had vested interest there) to have usurped their natural spheres of economic interest.[12] The Japanese, who desired to expand and to create an empire that provided them with needed products such as iron ore, oil, and rubber, felt thwarted and hemmed in by foreign powers.

These rash attacks were designed to prevent U.S. naval interference in the South Pacific, as well as to establish a fortified perimeter throughout the region in order to discourage the United States from future military action, and to extract the resources that Japan lacked from a conquered China, along with the oil, rubber, and other products from the English, Dutch, and French possessions in Southeast Asia. Within about four months, Japan controlled Southeast Asia, reaching one of its major objectives.

POST–WORLD WAR II TRADE

When Germany and Japan were defeated in 1945, mistakes of the past that had led to two world wars were obvious to foreign policymakers who, in the process of creating a new and peaceful world, undertook to rectify old problems. The U.S. government eschewed tariffs as a way to avoid hostilities. One aspect of this, the Marshall Plan, was a temporary, four-year economic expedient begun in 1948 to aid the countries ruined by war and to promote free trade among European nations in the hope of rapid economic recovery. There was, as is often the case, a powerful political motive. A strong and prosperous Europe would be in a better position to withstand communist aggression.

In 1948, the United States persuaded the European nations to establish a permanent Organization for European Economic Cooperation (OEEC), and by 1952, production levels exceeded those of prewar years, and trade barriers gradually disappeared, ending the earlier and prevailing approach of chauvinistic autarky. By 1955, the OEEC consisted of most European countries with more members joining, including the United States, Canada, and later Japan, Finland, Australia, and New Zealand. The OEEC soon totaled 30 member nations. On the agenda, along with promoting economic growth of member states and underdeveloped countries, was to boost world trade on a fair and nondiscriminatory basis. Not unlike Europe, Japan underwent a dramatic recovery after the war, especially once the United States opened its markets to Japanese products, many of them copied from the United States and Europe but cheaper in price.

Communist Countries

There seems to have been no overall and systematic communist approach to trade. Each country that fell under communist rule was considered individually. Unlike capitalist countries where most trade is conducted by private enterprise (setting aside military hardware such as fighter planes, rockets, guidance systems, and so forth), foreign trade in communist states was highly centralized and under the control of government monopolies. State planning commissions decided what exports and imports should be, and set quotas. Tariffs, under the circumstances, were irrelevant. Foreign trade was also seen as risky, since communist leaders thought their countries might come to depend on it for certain items and foreign ideas were dangerous. Trade between communist states often went smoothly enough and could be used as a tool to keep wayward satellite states in line. Trade with the Western capitalist nations was often beset with political problems.

Trade Organizations

On July 22, 1944, a conference was held at Bretton Woods in New Hampshire to establish a new international economic order. Trade as a means of recovery from World War II and in competition with communist states was a major factor of the conference. The talks led to the establishment of the International Monetary Fund (IMF) and the World Bank.

Three years later (in 1947), dignitaries of 22 nations convened in Geneva, Switzerland, and signed the General Agreement on Tariffs and Trade (GATT), taking into account some 50,000 items.[13] Subsequent meetings of GATT were concerned with reductions in tariffs throughout world markets that, it was hoped, would reduce tension in trade and lead to more peaceful international coexistence.

U.S. import tariffs fell from about 30 percent in 1945 to about 5 percent.[14] GATT was established to fix trading ground rules and try to avoid a recurrence of the disastrous protectionism of the 1930s. But in spite of these efforts, most nations resisted lower tariffs on agricultural products.

Trade rounds by GATT countries, called at various times, discussed and examined trade questions and issues. The Kennedy round from May 1964 to June 1967 drew the United States out of its protectionist policies with large reductions in tariffs between the United States and European countries.

World Trade Organization (WTO)

The Uruguay round of GATT talks, begun in 1986, was less concerned with tariffs and instead paid more attention to trade in services and intellectual property. The conference saw the expiration of GATT and its replacement in 1995 by the World Trade Organization (WTO), with headquarters in Geneva. The new organization soon had 153 member countries, but in general, farmers were against it. At its meetings in Qatar in 2001, the WTO strove to cut through barriers to trade and make globalization more global, especially by reducing or eliminating subsidies in agriculture. Little agreement was reached, and the subsidies remained a contentious issue. One of the primary purposes of the WTO was to generate trade policies and set up a forum for mediating disputes. Another priority was to assist developing countries with their commercial business.

European Economic Community (EEC) and North American Free Trade Association (NAFTA)

To stimulate economic integration and growth, the nations of Europe joined together in a single market, generally known as the Common Market. Combined, it is a major world trading power, with its output of goods and services surpassing that of the United States. While most trade is internal among the European nations, world imports and exports amount to one-fifth of global trade. The largest trading partner is the United States, with China close behind. The United States, Mexico, and Canada adhere to the North American Free Trade Agreement (NAFTA), but this agreement has been plagued with difficulties.

Rise of China and India

From a cautious nation in international commerce, China has opened its doors to global trade in the past few decades. Imports and exports with the United States, Canada, and the Common Market are now in the hundreds of billions of dollars, and as a powerful economic entity, it is rapidly catching up to the United States. Becoming well entrenched in Africa, mainly due to Africa's oil resources, Chinese trade has grown to levels never seen before.

In exchange, China gives African nations large aid and loans, below market rates, with no strings attached (whereas the West might insist on more liberal and more democratic governments). Africans, however, have protested over poor and dangerous working environments—for example, in the Chinese-owned mines— and are unhappy with Chinese textiles inundating local markets. To counter anti-Chinese sentiment, China needed only to threaten to stop investment. India, too, has taken great strides in imports and exports, and interchange with China, its largest trading partner, amounts to many billions of dollars. Indian trade with the United States and the European Union amounts to only a fraction of that with China. Western nations are uneasy about China's abundant and cheap labor, and consequently very large export surpluses, and India's cheaper costs for electronic proficiency that lead to much outsourcing of work to the subcontinent.

Economic Globalization (Free Trade)

Free trade, a form of economic globalization, refers to worldwide distribution of goods and services free of quotas, subsidies, import and export duties, or tariffs. The concept is not new. Trade, free of restrictions, was practiced to some extent by various empires such as the Roman, Portuguese, Mongol, and British. Since the world is far from uniform in the distribution of its wealth, and there are both poor and rich countries with high standards of living and with poverty-stricken populations, globalization is beset with problems. With globalization of trade came angst for some workers that it might cost them their jobs as competition from low-wage workers in other countries could produce products more cheaply, and commercial agents would look to them for their sources of supply. Another concern of those who profess antiglobalization views is that outsourcing of jobs to countries where labor is less expensive deprives the workers in more developed countries of work. If free trade is available, then a company can simply hire workers in a foreign country to do the work for less money with no tariff penalties when the product enters the outsourcing country. If, for example, a U.S. author writes a book for a U.S. publisher, that publisher may send the manuscript to India for editing and printing, significantly cutting the cost of producing the book in the United States, where wages are higher; however, a U.S. printing house may be out of a job as a result. In the current age of electronic communication, the cost to send such work overseas is minimal. Technology has simplified beyond imagination the worldwide flow of money, goods, and ideas. The basic economic point of view, however, is that while some businesses or even corporations in some countries may suffer from free trade, the world as a whole is better off and the net gains of all the people benefiting through free trade outweighs the loss of those to whom it was detrimental. Increased taxes can be used to make up transfer payments (social security, welfare, subsidies, and other forms of financial aid) to compensate the losers. Theoretically free trade should benefit everyone, but in an imperfect economic world, the paltry sum of transfers, and often unfair tax systems, leaves some segments of the population, generally, the most vulnerable, worse off. If, for example, Saudi Arabia lowered the price of oil, the effect on other oil-producing but poor countries, could send the price of their petroleum down along with the wages of workers in the industry without adequate compensation by transfers.

An Iniquitous Side of Trade

The wealthy Fanjul family, which fled Castro's Cuba in 1958 and owns the Flo-Sun Company, is one of the richest families, owning 160,000 acres of prime sugar cane land in Florida and much more in the Dominican Republic. The company has been accused of abuses and underpayment of workers by the U.S. Labor Department, and it has been fined for toxic runoff into the Everglades. The U.S. Department of Agriculture, on the other hand, pays the company handsomely, twice the world price for sugar, as general support for agricultural products. The U.S. taxpayers are hit to the tune of $8 billion annually. Quotas keep foreign crops out of the United States and raise store prices, costing consumers billions more for sugar. The Army Corps of Engineers spent some $52 million a year maintaining dry sugar cane fields for the company. Federal money to the Fanjuls pours in as the family continues to give generously to political campaigns.[15]

Trade Embargos

Despite efforts to encourage and enact fair and free trade among nations for a more unified and peaceful world, trade has also been used as an economic weapon to force conformity to certain demands generally concerning political ideological differences. When one nation finds fault with another, it may impose an embargo on trade, insisting on higher tariffs on all imported goods from the target country, selective embargos on certain goods, or a total embargo on all trade. Such actions usually precipitate retaliatory measures.

A total embargo may be backed by military power when countries are at war, preventing third parties from trading with one belligerent or the other. An embargo may be ineffective, producing slight consequences for the target nation except, perhaps, to arouse the citizens to condemn the country responsible for it. A case in point is Cuba, where U.S. sanctions on U.S. imports and exports have stretched over a span of more than half a century, with little result in changing Cuba's dictatorial communist political structure.. Embargos sometimes lead to war, as was the case at the advent of World War II in the Pacific when Japan was desperate for oil due to a U.S. embargo on it. Even UN sanctions on rogue countries, especially in their quest for arms, have too often been thwarted by others willing to ignore UN mandates.

An historical study will show that oftentimes not only the target nation suffers from the effects of an embargo, but the economic harm may also have negative repercussions for the nation imposing the sanctions. When the United States imposed an embargo in 1807 on agricultural products to punish Great Britain, the English simply turned to South American suppliers. This deprived U.S. traders of a market, the U.S. economy declined, and the act was repealed soon after.

It is not easy to tell if sanctions work. The military dictators of Myanmar, for instance, have recently modified their repressive stance to allow some democratic reforms to enter into their political agenda, but it is unclear how much they were influenced by the sanctions implemented by western countries that impacted the discontented populace.

Trade has been instrumental and vastly influential worldwide. Disputes, military conflicts, exploitation and enslavement of millions of people, and the rise and fall of civilizations have all played their part. Nonetheless, trade, as an agent for sharing of resources, ideas, and cultural interchange, has benefited a number of people, greatly enriching some and aiding others to attain a better life in an unequal world. The hope is, of course, that global contacts will leave a level playing field for all participants.

NOTES

1. *EWT*, 984.
2. Quoted by Lochner, 32

3. Lochner, 55.

4. See Bane and Lutz.

5. Craig, 437.

6. Craig, 450–451.

7. See Keegan, 104 for another view.

8. Craig, 608.

9. Ferguson, 369.

10. Howson, 121.

11. Howson, 126.

12. Perez, 131.

13. Bernstein, 357.

14. See chart, Bernstein, 359.

15. For more on this subject, see Bernstein, 363–364. See also *Eye on Miami*, January 4, 2012.

BIBLIOGRAPHY

Abbott, Elizabeth. *Sugar: A Bittersweet History.* Toronto: Penguin Group Canada (2008).

Abulafia, David. *The Great Sea: A Human History of the Mediterranean.* London: Penguin Group (2011).

Aldrete, Gregory S. *Daily Life in the Roman City.* Westport, CT: Greenwood Press (2004).

Anderson, James M. *Spain: 1001 Sights.* Calgary: University of Calgary Press and London: Robert Hale (1991).

Anderson, James M. *The History of Portugal.* Westport, CT: Greenwood Press (2000).

Anderson, Siwan. "Caste as an Impediment to Trade." *American Economic Journal: Applied Economics 3* (January 2011), 239–263.

Aston, Mick and Tim Taylor. *The Atlas of Archaeology.* New York: DK Publishing Inc. (1998).

Aubet, Maria Eugenia. *The Phoenicians and the West: Politics, Colonies, and Trade,* 2nd ed. Cambridge: University Press (2001).

Bahn, Paul G. ed., *Archaeology.* San Francisco: City Press (2002).

Beckwith, Christopher I. *Empires of the Silk Road.* Princeton, NJ: Princeton University Press (2009).

Benin, Charles. *Daily Life in Traditional China: The Tang Dynasty.* Westport, CT: Greenwood Press (2002).

Bernstein, William J. *A Splendid Exchange: How Trade Shaped the World.* New York: Atlantic Monthly Press (2008).

Boardman, John. *The Greeks Overseas*. London: Thames and Hudson (1980).

Borschberg, Peter, ed. *Iberians in the Singapore-Melaka Area (16th to 18th Century)*. Wiesbaden: Harrassowitz Verlag (2004).

Bown, Stephen. *Scurvy: How a Surgeon, a Mariner, and a Gentleman Solved the Greatest Medical Mystery of the Age of Sail*. Toronto: T. Allen (2003).

Bown, Stephen. *Merchant Kings: When Companies Ruled the World, 1600–1900*. Vancouver: Douglas & McIntyre (2009).

Boxer, Charles R. *The Portuguese Seaborne Empire, 1415–1825*. London: Hutchinson & Co. (1969).

Braudel, Fernand. *Structures of Everyday Life*, Vol. 1. Siân Reynolds, transl. New York: Harper & Row (1979).

Braudel, Fernand. *The Wheels of Commerce*, Vol. 2. Siân Reynolds, transl. London: Fontana Paperbacks (1985).

Braudel, Fernand. *A History of Civilizations*. Richard Mayne, transl. New York: Penguin (1993).

Brøndsted, J. *The Vikings*. English edition, Kalle Skov, transl. Harmondsworth: Penguin (1965).

Cantor, Norman F. *The Civilization of the Middle Ages*. New York: HarperCollins (1993), pp. 230–232.

Caubet, Annie and Patrick Pouyssegur. *The Ancient Near East: The Origins of Civilization*. Peter Snowdon, transl. Paris: Bayard Press (1998).

Ceram, C. W. *The Secret of the Hittites*. New York: Schocken (1955).

Chadwick, John. *The Decipherment of Linear B*. Cambridge: University Press (1958).

Chadwick, Nora. *The Celts*. Harmondsworth: Pelican (1981).

Chaiklin, Martha. *Cultural Commerce and Dutch Commercial Culture: The Influence of European Material Culture on Japan, 1700–1850*. Leiden University: Research School (2003).

Chaudhuri, K. N. *Trade and Civilisation in the Indian Ocean: An Economic History from the Rise of Islam to 1750*. Cambridge: University Press (1985).

Chesneaux, Jean, Françoise Le Barbier, and Marie-Claire Bergère. *China from the 1911 Revolution to Liberation*. Paul Auster and Lydia Davis, Anne Destenay, transl. New York: Pantheon Books (1977).

Confer, Clarissa. *Daily Life in Pre-Columbian Native America*. Westport, CT: Greenwood Press (2008).

Conlin, Joseph. *The American Past, Part II*. New York: Harcourt, Brace, Jovanovich (1984).

Constable, Olivia Remie. *Trade and Traders in Muslim Spain*. Cambridge: University Press (1994).

Craig, Gordon A. *Germany, 1866–1945*. Oxford: University Press (1978).

Crampton, R. J. *A Concise History of Bulgaria*. Cambridge: University Press (1997).

Crosby, Alfred W. *Ecological Imperialism: The Biological Expansion of Europe, 900–1900*. Cambridge: University Press (1986).

Culican, William. *The First Merchant Ventures: The Ancient Levant in History and Commerce*. London: Thames & Hudson (1966).

Curtin, Philip D. *Cross-Cultural Trade in World History*. Cambridge: University Press (1984).

Davids, K. *Coffee*. San Romon, CA: Ortho Information Services (1976).

Diamond, Jared. *Guns, Germs, and Steel*. New York: W. W. Norton & Co. (1999).

Díaz del Castillo, Bernal. *The Discovery and Conquest of Mexico, 1517–1521*. A. P. Maudslay, transl. New York: Farrar, Straus and Cudahy (1956).

Diffie, B. W. and G. Winius. *Foundations of the Portuguese Empire, 1415–1850*. Minneapolis: University of Minnesota Press (1977).

Dottin, Georges. *The Civilization of the Celts*. Geneva: Editions Minerva, S.A. (1970).

Edey, Maitland. *The Sea Traders*. New York: Time Life Books (1974).

Elliott, J. H. *Europe Divided, 1559–1598*. London: Fontana Press (1968).

Elliott, J. H. *Spain and its World, 1000–1700*. New Haven, CT: Yale University Press (1989).

Encyclopedia of World Trade from Ancient Times to the Present (EWT). Cynthia Clark Northrup, ed. Armonk, Vols. 1–4, NY: M. E. Sharpe (2005).

Ferguson, Niall. *The War of the World*. New York: Penguin (2006).

Findlay, Ronald and Kevin H. O'Rourke. *Power and Plenty: Trade, War, and the World Economy in the Second Millennium*. Princeton, NJ: Princeton University Press (2007).

Fournier, Lucien. *L'alimentation des équipages dan la Marine*. La Rochelle, France: La Découvrance (2007).

Franck, Irene M. and David M. Brownstone. *Trade and Travel Routes from Gibraltar to the Ganges*. New York: Facts on File (1990).

Francois, Patrick. *Social Capital and Economic Development*. London and New York: Routledge (2002).

Franklin, John Hope. *From Slavery to Freedom*. New York: Alfred A. Knopf, Inc. (1967).

Fremont-Barnes, Gregory. *The Wars of the Barbary Pirates*. Botley, Oxford: Osprey Publishing (2006).

Gabriel, Judith. "Among the Norse Tribes: The Remarkable Account of Ibn Fadlan." *Saudi Aramco World 50*, no. 6 (November/December 1999), 36–42.

Garland, Robert. *Daily Life of the Ancient Greeks*, 2nd ed. Westport, CT: Greenwood Press (2009).

Gately, Iain. *Tobacco*. London: Simon & Schuster (2001).

Gelber, Harry G. *The Dragon and the Foreign Devils*. London: Bloomsbury (2007).

Gibb, H.A.R. and cf. Beckingham eds. *The Travels of Ibn Battutah Princeton, NJ, AD 1325–1354*. Society (1994).

Goitein, S. D. *Letters of Medieval Jewish Traders*. Princeton, NJ: University Press (1973).

Goode, Walter. *Dictionary of Trade Policy Terms*. Cambridge: University Press (World Trade Organization) (2007).

Gordon, Stewart. *When Asia Was the World*. Philadelphia: Da Capo Press (2008).

Grant, Nicolas. "Chinese-Japanese Trade" in *Encyclopedia of World Trade*, C. Northrup, ed. Armouk, New York: Sharpe Inc. (2005).

Greenfield, Amy Butler. *A Perfect Red*. New York: Harper Perennial (2006).

Greif, Avner. "Reputation and Coalitions in Medieval Trade: Evidence on the Maghribi Traders." *Journal of Economic History 49*, no. 4 (December 1989), 857–882.

Greif, Avner. "Institutions and International Trade: Lessons from the Commercial Revolution." *American Economic Review 82*, no. 2 (May 1992), 128–133.

Greif, Avner. "Contract Enforceability and Economic Institutions in Early Trade: The Maghribi Taders' Coalition." *American Economic Review 83*, no. 3, 525–548 (1952), reprinted 1990.

Guerny, O.R. *The Hittites*. Harmondsworth: Penguin Archaeology (1952), reprinted 1990.

Hakluyt, Richard. *Voyages and Discoveries*, Jack Beeching, ed. London: Penguin Books (1972).

Hall, John. *Japan from Prehistory to Modern Times*. New York: Delacorte Press (1970).

Hall, Richard. *Empires of the Monsoon*. London: HarperCollins (1996).

Hallam, Elizabeth, ed. *Chronicles of the Crusades*. Godalming, Surrey: Bramley Books (1996).

Handbook of North American Indians, Vol. 3: Environment, Origins, and Population. Douglas H. Ubelaker, ed. Washington, DC: Smithsonian Institution (2007).

Harden, Donald. *The Phoenicians*, 2nd ed. New York: Frederick A. Praeger (1963).

Harris, Joseph E. *Africans and their History*. Harmondsworth: Penguin (1972).

Herman, Arthur. *How the Scots Invented the Modern World*. New York: Three Rivers Press (2001).

Herman, Arthur. *To Rule the Waves: How the British Navy Shaped the World*. New York: HarperCollins (2004).

Hermann, Paul. *Conquest by Man*. Michael Bullock, transl. New York: Harper & Brothers (1954).

Hitti, Philip. *History of Syria*. London: Macmillan Company (1951).

Hourani, George F. *Arab Seafaring*. Princeton, NJ: Princeton University Press (1951).

Howson, Gerald. *Arms for Spain*. New York: St. Martin's Press (1998).

Hunt, Edwin S. and James M. Murray. *A History of Business in Medieval Europe, 1200–1550*. Cambridge: University Press (1999).

Ibn Khaldûn. *The Muqaddimah: An Introduction to History.* Franz Rosenthal, transl. Princeton, NJ: Princeton University Press (2005).

Jackson, Joe. *The Thief at the End of the World: Rubber, Power, and the Seeds of Empire.* New York: Penguin Group (2008).

Jacobs, Els M. *In Pursuit of Pepper and Tea: The Story of the Dutch East India Company.* Zutphen, Netherlands: Walburg Pers (1991).

Jensen, Hans. *Sign, Symbol and Script.* London: George Allen and Unwin Ltd. (1970).

Kaempfer, Engelbert. *Kaempfer's Japan.* Beatrice M. Bodart-Bailey transl. Honolulu: University of Hawaii Press (1999).

Keay, S. J. *Romans in Spain.* Berkeley: University of California Press (1988).

Keegan, John. *The Second World War.* New York: Penguin Books (1987).

King, J. C. H. *First Peoples First Contacts.* Cambridge, MA: Harvard University Press (1999).

Klein, Ernest. *A Comprehensive Etymological Dictionary of the English Language.* Amsterdam: Elsevier (1971).

Kranz, Rachel. *Trade and Travel Routes across Africa and Arabia* (adapted from *To the Ends of the Earth* by Irene Franck and David Brownstone). New York: Facts on File (1991).

Kurlansky, Mark. *Cod.* New York: Penguin Books (1998).

Lamb, Harriet. *Fighting the Banana Wars.* London: Rider Press (2008).

Landes, David S. *The Wealth and Poverty of Nations.* London: W. W. Norton (1999).

Larousse. *World Mythology.* Patricia Beardsworth transl. London & New York: Hamlyn Publishing Group (1965).

Leiner, Frederick C. *The End of Barbary Terror.* Oxford: University Press (2006).

Levinson, Marc. *The Box: How the Shipping Container Made the World Smaller and the World Economy Bigger.* Princeton, NJ: Princeton University Press (2006).

Lewis, Jon E., ed. *The Mammoth Book of Pirates.* London: Robinson (2006).

Lewis, Raphaela. *Everyday Life in Ottoman Turkey.* New York: Dorset Press (1971).

Lindsay, James E. *Daily Life in the Medieval Islamic World.* Westport, CT: Greenwood Press (2005).

Lister, Robert H. and Florence C. Lister. *Those Who Came Before.* Tucson, AZ: Western National Parks Association (1993).

Livermore, H. V. *A History of Portugal.* Cambridge: University Press (1947).

Livermore, H. V. *A New History of Portugal.* Cambridge: University Press (1966).

Lochner, Louis P. *Herbert Hoover and Germany.* New York: Macmillan Company (1960).

Lockwood, W. B. *A Panorama of Indo-European Languages.* London: Hutchinson University Library (1972).

Lunde, Paul and Alexandra Porter. *Trade and Travel in the Red Sea Region.* Oxford: Archaeopress (2004).

Lynch, John. *Spain, 1516–1598*. Oxford: Blackwell (1991).

Mackintosh-Smith, Tim, ed. *The Travels of Ibn Battutah*. London: Pan Macmillan (2002).

Macnamara, Ellen. *Everyday Life of the Etruscans*. New York: G. P. Putnams' Sons (1973).

Masselman, George. *The Money Trees, The Spice Trade*. London: World's Work Ltd. (1967).

Mather, James. *Pashas Traders and Travellers in the Islamic World*. New Haven, CT and London: Yale University Press (2009).

McAlister, Lyle N. *Spain & Portugal in the New World, 1492–1700*, Vol. 3. Minneapolis: University of Minnesota Press (1984).

Meilleur, Helen. *A Pour of Rain*. Victoria, BC: Sono Nis Press (1980).

Millton, Giles. *Nathaniel's Nutmeg*. London: Hodder & Stoughton (1999).

Nagahara, Keiji. "The Medieval Origins of the Eta-Hinin." *Journal of Japanese Studies 5*, no. 2 (Summer 1979), 393–394.

Nagahara, Keiji. Kozo Yamamura, ed., "The Medieval Peasant," in *Cambridge History of Japan: Vol. 3. Medieval Japan*. Cambridge: University Press (1990).

Natkiel, Richard and Antony Preston. *Atlas of Maritime History*. London: Bison Books (1986).

Newton, Arthur Percival. *Travel and Travellers of the Middle Ages*. New York: Alfred A. Knopf (1930).

Palmer, L. R. *The Latin Language*. London: Faber and Faber Ltd. (1954).

Pareti, Luigi, Palo Brezzi, and Luciano Petech. *The Ancient World*. New York: Harper & Row (1965).

Parry, J. H. *The Establishment of the European Hegemony, 1415–1715*. New York: Harper & Row (1966).

Past Worlds. The Times Atlas of Archaeology. London: Times Books, Ltd. (1996).

Payne, Stanley G. *A History of Spain and Portugal*, Vol. 1. Madison, WI: University of Wisconsin Press (1973).

The Penguin Encyclopedia of Ancient Civilizations. Arthur Cotterell, ed. New York: Penguin Books (1980).

Perez, Louis G. *The History of Japan*. Westport, CT: Greenwood Press (2009).

Piggott, Stuart. *Ancient Europe from the beginnings of Agriculture to Classical Antiquity*. New York: Aldine Publishing (1979).

Pires, Tomé. *Suma Oriental, 1512–1515*. London: Hakluyt Society (1944).

Polomé, Edgar C. *The Indo-Europeans in the Fourth and Third Millennia*. Ann Arbor, MI: Karoma Inc. (1982).

Pomeranz, Kenneth and Steven Topik. *The World That Trade Created, 1400 to the Present*. New York: M. E. Sharpe, Inc. (2006).

Powell, T. G. E. *The Celts*. London: Thames and Hudson, Ltd. (1958).

Preece, Rod. *Animals and Nature*. Vancouver, Canada: University of British Columbia Press (1999).

Presley, Lucinda Hanks. "Mughal Empire" in *Encyclopedia of World Trade*, C. Northrup, ed. pp. 678–684. Armouk, NY: Sharpe, Inc. (2005).

Previté-Orton, C. W. *The Shorter Cambridge Medieval History. I.* Cambridge: University Press (1978).

Reid, Anthony. *Southeast Asia in the Age of Commerce, 1450–1680.* New Haven, CT and London: Yale University Press (1993).

Reynolds, Paul. *Trade in the Western Mediterranean, AD 400–700: The Ceramic Evidence.* Oxford: BAR International Series 604 (1995).

Rice, Tamara Talbot. *Everyday Life in Byzantium.* New York: Dorset Press (1967).

Roth, Norman, ed. *Medieval Jewish History: An Encyclopedia.* London & New York: Routledge (2002).

Rowling, Marjorie. *Everyday Life of Medieval Travellers.* New York: Dorset Press (1971).

Russell-Wood, A. J. R. *The Portuguese Empire, 1415–1808.* Baltimore, MD: The Johns Hopkins University Press (1992).

Sadler, Nigel. *The Slave Trade.* Botley, Oxford: Shire Publications (2009).

Saggs, H. W. F. *Civilizations before Greece and Rome.* New Haven, CT: Yale University Press (1989).

Saggs, H. W. F. *Everyday Life in Babylonia & Assyria.* New York: G. P. Putnam's Sons (1965).

Saraiva, José Hermano. *História de Portugal.* Mem Martins, Portugal: Publicações Europa-America (1993).

Saumitra, Jha. "Trade, Institutions and Religious Tolerance: Evidence from India." *Stanford Research Paper Series* (2008).

Schoff, Wilfred H., transl. *The Periplus of the Erythraean Sea: Travel and Trade in the Indian Ocean by a Merchant of the First Century.* New York: Longmans, Green, and Co. (1912).

Sherman, Dennis. *Western Civilization: Sources, Images, and Interpretations,* Vol. I. New York: McGraw-Hill (2003).

Shillington, Kevin. *History of Africa,* rev. ed. Oxford: Macmillan Publishers Ltd. (2005).

Shinnie, Peter. *Meroë: Civilization of the Sudan.* Westport, CT: Praeger (1967).

Smith, Frederick H. *Caribbean Rum: A Social and Economic History.* Gainesville: University Press of Florida (2006).

Spence, Jonathan D. *The Memory Palace of Matteo Ricci.* New York: Penguin Viking Books (1984).

Spence, Jonathan D. *The Search for Modern China.* New York: W. W. Norton (1990).

Thomas, Hugh. *The Slave Trade: The Story of the Atlantic Slave Trade, 1440–1870.* New York: Simon and Schuster (1997).

Time-Life Books. *The Rise of Cities.* Alexandria, VA: Time Life (n.d.).

Todd, Malcolm. *The Early Germans.* Oxford: Blackwell (1992).

Trump, D. H. *The Prehistory of the Mediterranean.* London: Allen Lane (Penguin) (1980).

Van Doren Stern, Philip. *Prehistoric Europe from Stone Age Man to the Early Greeks.* New York: Norton & Company (1969).

Varley, H. Paul. *Japanese Culture*, 3rd ed. Honolulu: University of Hawaii Press (1984).

Walker, D. S. *The Mediterranean Lands*. London: Methuen & Co. Ltd. (1962).

Wallbank, T. Walter, et al. *Civilization Past and Present*. Glenview, IL: Scott, Foresman and Company (1962).

Waugh, Teresa, transl. *The Travels of Marco Polo*. London: Sidgwick & Jackson (1984).

Whitfield, Susan. *Life along the Silk Road*. Berkeley and Los Angeles: University of California Press (1999).

Wilcox, R. Turner. *The Mode in Costume*. New York: Charles Scribner's Sons (1958).

Wild, Antony. *The East India Company Book of Chocolate*. London: Harper Collins Publishers (1995).

Wild, Antony. *Black Gold*. London: Harper Perennial (2004).

Williamson, James A. *A Short History of British Expansion: The Old Colonial Empire*. London: Macmillan & Co. (1968).

Woloch, Isser. *Eighteenth-Century Europe: Tradition and Progress, 1715–1789*. New York and London: W. W. Norton & Company (1982).

Wright, Clifford A. *A Mediterranean Feast*. New York: William Morrow (1999).

Wright, Ronald. *Stolen Continents*. Toronto: Penguin Canada (1992).

Wright, Ronald. *What Is America?* Toronto: Alfred A. Knopf (2008).

Yamamura, Kozo, ed. *The Cambridge History of Japan, Vol. 3: Medieval Japan*. Cambridge: University Press (1990).

Yon, Marguerite. "Ougarit, Ville Royale de L'Age du Bronze." *La Recherche* (March 1995), 262–269.

INDEX

About the Author

Dr. JAMES M. ANDERSON obtained his doctorate from the University of Washington, Seattle and taught historical linguistics at Georgetown University in Washington, DC, University of Barcelona (Spain), University of Valladolid (Spain), University of Deusto (Spain), and University of Alberta, Canada. He holds the position of Professor Emeritus from the University of Calgary, where he also taught decipherment. He has spent many years researching and writing in Europe as the recipient of multiple Canada Council, Fulbright, and Social Sciences and Humanities Research Council of Canada (SSHRC) grants. He has written numerous articles as well as some 16 books, including *Daily Life during the French Revolution, Daily Life during the Spanish Inquisition, The Spanish Civil War, Daily Life during the Reformation,* and *The History of Portugal.*